Cicero, *Against Verres*, 2.1.53–86:

Latin Text with Introduction, Study Questions, Commentary and English Translation

Ingo Gildenhard

OpenBook
Publishers

Open Book Publishers CIC Ltd.,
40 Devonshire Road, Cambridge, CB1 2BL, United Kingdom
http://www.openbookpublishers.com

As with all Open Book Publishers titles, digital material and resources associated with this volume are available from our website:

http://www.openbookpublishers.com/product.php/96/7

ISBN Hardback: 978-1-906924-54-6
ISBN Paperback: 978-1-906924-53-9
ISBN Digital (pdf): 978-1-906924-55-3
ISBN e-book (epub): 978-1-906924-63-8
ISBN e-book (mobi): 978-1-906924-64-5

Cover Image: Statue of Cicero at the Palace of Justice in Brussels, photo: Stuart Bell.
Typesetting by www.bookgenie.in

All paper used by Open Book Publishers is SFI (Sustainable Forestry Initiative), PEFC (Programme for the Endorsement of Forest Certification Schemes) and Forest Stewardship Council (FSC) certified.

Printed in the United Kingdom and United States by
Lightning Source for Open Book Publishers

CICERO, AGAINST VERRES,
2.1.53–86

Contents

Acknowledgements

I am very grateful to the friends and colleagues who provided comments and feedback during my work on this volume, notably Benjamin Biesinger, Wolfgang Havener, Ted Kaizer, Myles Lavan, who also generously shared forthcoming work of his own, Mathew Owen, and Rik Van Wijlick. Closer to home, I would like to acknowledge the help of Norbert Gildenhard who read through an early draft, offering comments and corrections page by page, and Paola Ceccarelli who volunteered to design the map. I had hoped to include a reprint of Catherine Steel's superb analysis of the Lampsacus episode ('Being Economical with the Truth: What Really Happened at Lampsacus?', in J. Powell and J. Paterson (eds.), *Cicero the Advocate*, Oxford: Oxford University Press, 233–51) in this volume; unfortunately, problems to do with copyright interfered, but I am nevertheless very grateful for her personal agreement and support. Alessandra Tosi and Corin Throsby at Open Book Publishers have simply been wonderful in accommodating this rather unusual project as well as its urgent time frame. I also benefited much from the speedy endorsement and feedback offered by the two anonymous referees. As previous work, this volume profited considerably from the library resources of the Philologische Seminar of Tübingen University, and I am once again extremely grateful to Professor Maennlein-Robert for offering hospitality. My most significant debt is to three PhD students in the Department of Classics & Ancient History at Durham University. Zara Chadha, Louise Hodgson, and Lauren Knifton generously volunteered to read through the penultimate draft, provided invaluable annotations, and agreed to join in a series of workshops ('having fun with Cicero') devoted to discussing issues to do with the volume large and small. Their eagle eyes spotted more embarrassing mistakes than I care to remember; and their good sense and sensibility vastly improved the final product. Their critical engagement with the commentary and ability to improve upon my own reading of Cicero exemplify my notion of this volume's ideal reader. It is thus a particular pleasure to dedicate this book to them and their spirit of intellectual camaraderie.

Preface

This little volume has its origins in a coincidence. I had just finished writing *Creative Eloquence: The Construction of Reality in Cicero's Speeches* (Oxford, 2011), which involved some close analysis of Cicero's orations against Verres, when I was asked to give a lecture on how best to teach a new set-text that the Examination Board of Oxford, Cambridge, and the Royal Society of Arts (OCR) has specified for their A-Level Latin examination for the years 2012–2014. The passage in question, *in Verrem* 2.1.53–69, consists of some paragraphs on Verres' looting of artworks from Greek cities in Asia Minor during his legateship under Dolabella (§§ 53–62) and of about a third of the infamous episode at Lampsacus. Paragraphs 63–69 contain an account of what happened when Verres visited the Greek city. According to Cicero, he tried to abduct and rape the daughter of the local notable Philodamus, which resulted in the death of one of his lictors and brought the inhabitants of the town to the brink of rioting. Paragraphs 70–86 deal with the aftermath of the sordid affair, including the trial and public execution of Philodamus and his son in what Cicero portrays as a blatant miscarriage of justice designed to cover up Verres' crimes.

Part of the brief was to talk about the resources available for teaching the text. These turned out to be rather less spectacular than the chosen passage. There is, of course, T. N. Mitchell's superb Aris & Phillips edition with translation and commentary of *Verrines* II.1 (London, 1986), which remains an invaluable port of call for anyone working on, or teaching, (portions of) the speech. Yet one of the main purposes of the edition is to render the oration accessible to students without Latin, and thus the commentary, which is keyed to the translation, focuses on historical context rather than details of language and style (even though Mitchell's explication of the rhetorical texture is uniformly excellent). And other than that, one pretty much draws a blank, at least in terms of commentaries. I therefore decided to write up my own set of notes, drawing on the work done for *Creative Eloquence*. Feedback from the Latin teachers to whom I had the chance to circulate a draft version in June was sufficiently encouraging to explore the possibility of making the material more generally available, not least since it seemed an excellent opportunity to link research and outreach.

For the commentary, it seemed inadvisable to follow OCR in their (understandable) decision to chop the Lampsacus episode in half. Hence the present volume includes *Ver.* 2.1.53–86 rather than just §§ 53–69. And while I have to agree with one of the anonymous referees that a full-scale linguistic commentary on the entire speech would have been very desirable, exigencies of timing militated against including more. For one thing, extending the coverage from the 33 paragraphs now covered to the full 158 that comprise the oration would have rendered the exercise useless for the current generation of Latin A-level students. There is only so much one can do in the course of a summer. At the same time, A-level students are not the only constituency I had in mind when designing this volume. The portion of Cicero explicated here would also seem to lend itself for study in other settings, such as Latin summer schools, undergraduate reading courses in American or British universities, or postgraduate Latin courses at MA-level. I have therefore added content meant to widen the appeal, even though not all of it will seem immediately relevant to all users. The edition now tries to cater to students as well as their teachers, to dedicated students of Latin as well as to language learners (such as ancient historians at postgraduate level) who study Latin perhaps not so much for its own sake but as a research tool.

All users, however, should be able to relate to the primary mission of the commentary: it is to render Cicero's text intelligible and resonant with meaning and thereby to enhance appreciation and enjoyment of the chosen passage as a fascinating historical document and a superb specimen of rhetorical artistry. The commentary offers help in three areas in particular. First, while a basic grasp of Latin grammar and syntax is presupposed, the notes explicate more unusual grammatical phenomena as well as difficult syntax and sentence construction. Secondly, the commentary pays careful attention to the craftsmanship of Cicero's text, not least in showing how his rhetorical design interacts with, and reinforces, his arguments and themes. And thirdly, the edition tries to situate Cicero's prose within wider contextual and historical frames, such as the courtroom setting and Rome's system of imperial exploitation. The principle that informs the commentary is simple: the more one sees in his text, the more enjoyable, indeed exciting, reading

Cicero becomes. And he merits re-reading: it took some time, for instance, for the penny to drop that the eight connectives Cicero uses in the massive sentence in § 82 produce a pleasing symmetrical pattern.[1] The example is a good illustration of the care Cicero took over the most insignificant detail, easily overlooked: his verbal craftsmanship is simply extraordinary, and I am sure the text under discussion hides many more delights than I managed to spot: I encourage every student to ponder, discover, and enjoy.

In an attempt to render this edition as useful as possible to as many different end-users as possible, I have included the following features:

(a) *Introduction*: excellent accounts of the wider historical background and the legal circumstances of Cicero's prosecution of Verres exist in abundance (and are cited in the introduction). It nevertheless seemed useful to include a rudimentary survey of some basic facts and figures, and brief indications of key issues and themes to help orient those who are new to Cicero and his speeches. The introduction therefore provides brief biographical sketches of Cicero and Verres, offers information on the trial, situates the passage under consideration within the *Verrines* as a whole, discusses some important aspects of Cicero's oratory and relates the text in question to developments in late republican history and culture. In all, it is meant to provide quick and easy access to some basic contextual information, with references to works of secondary literature for those who wish to pursue a specific aspect further.

(b) *The Latin text*: the Latin text of Cicero's *Verrines* is available online in various formats. The text printed here is taken from The Latin Library (www.thelatinlibrary.com/cicero/verres.2.1.shtml), with some minor changes and corrections, mainly of a typographical nature. I have consulted the apparatus of the standard critical edition (W. Peterson's *Oxford Classical Text*), but discuss variants only occasionally. Even these rare instances might be considered too much for an edition such as this, which is primarily addressed to students still in the process of learning the language. But even at this stage, an occasional reminder that any classical text we nowadays read is not an autograph, but the result of transmission and editorial constitution, seemed appropriate. From the point of view of transmission, at any rate, the chosen passage

---

1. *atque, et, et, et, -que, -que, -que, atque*. See further below, p. 159.

is fairly unproblematic. It is worth mentioning, too, that the text of Cicero's *Verrines* is freely available on the website of the Perseus Project (http://www.perseus.tufts.edu/), which offers the *Oxford Classical Text* edition with critical apparatus and hyperlinks of each word to the *Lewis & Short Latin Dictionary*. I imagine that many students will want to read the text online in this format, perhaps with the commentary opened in a separate window (or in hardcopy on the desk).

(c) *Study questions for grammar and syntax, style and theme*: each paragraph of the Latin text is followed by some study questions designed to draw attention to features in the passage that are either difficult or interesting (or both). They are meant as gateways into the passage. The distinction between 'grammar and syntax' and 'style and theme' is of course somewhat artificial, but seemed nevertheless worth making for didactic reasons, even though some of the questions deliberately try to blur the boundary. Answers to the questions can usually be found embedded in the commentary (though they are not explicitly marked up as such).

(d) *Help with grammar and syntax*: I assume that users of this edition, who are still in the process of acquiring facility with the technical terminology of Latin grammar and syntax, will have access to a Latin grammar, such as James Morwood's excellent *Latin Grammar* (Oxford 1999), which is a model of concision and clarity and is as accessible as it is affordable.[2] It includes a Glossary of Grammatical Terms on pages ix–xv, and I have tried to abide by his terminology. I am aware that different systems of grammatical nomenclature exist, but, despite the suggestion of one of the referees, felt that multiple labelling of phenomena (such as 'ethic dative' or the 'polite dative' or – the way I learned it – the *dativus ethicus*) would add a lot of clutter for fairly limited returns. I have therefore only supplied alternative terminology occasionally, when it seemed especially appropriate for one reason or another.

(e) *Technical terms for figures of speech*: figures of speech (*anaphora, *chiasmus, *pleonasm, etc.) are prefaced by a star (*) in the commentary

---

2. A note of caution: not every grammatical and syntactical feature in the set passage finds explication in Morwood. When it comes to the use of the subjunctive in relative clauses, for example, he covers the two most frequent types, i.e. expression of purpose (under Purpose clauses, p. 97) and the generic or consecutive use (under Result Clauses, pp. 100–1), but has nothing on the – admittedly less frequent – use of the subjunctive in a relative clause to convey a causal or concessive sense.

and briefly glossed in the List of Rhetorical Terms on p. 169. Apart
from enabling students to acquire familiarity and ease with a range of
rhetorical figures, the star-system is also designed to draw attention
to recurrent features of Cicero's style and could be used to raise
questions to do with aesthetic value. Readers may wish to ponder,
for instance, whether Cicero's use of *alliteration in the passage is
'excessive', a sign of his youthful exuberance, to be scaled back in his
more mature writing.[3] Enhanced awareness of figures of speech is a
significant side benefit of studying Latin and of a classical education
more generally; but the identification of rhetorical features can easily
turn into a mechanical exercise (along the lines of 'give me three
tricola and a climax, please'). To draw attention to the risk of turning
the hunt for rhetorical figures into an end in itself and to highlight
the powerful presence of classicizing rhetoric in the western cultural
tradition, I have chosen to illustrate the terms in the glossary
with examples drawn from Shakespeare, especially the staging
of the Pyramus-and-Thisbe episode from Ovid, *Metamorphoses* 4,
towards the end of *A Midsummer Night's Dream*. The passage is
arguably the greatest spoof of rhetorical ornamentation ever written,
full of frivolous fun with figures and forms, not least excessive
*alliteration and a brilliant *reductio ad absurdum* of classical rhetoric.
A 'compare-and-contrast' exercise on the (effective) use of figures in
Cicero and Shakespeare should produce interesting results.

(f) *References to secondary literature*: in the introduction and throughout
the commentary I have included, in footnotes, a very selective – but,
I hope, judicious – sample of some of the best scholarly literature
available on the various themes mentioned in or raised by the passage
from Cicero considered here. The reasons behind this practice, which
is unusual for a commentary keyed to language learners, are various.
Some issues may capture the imagination of readers who want to
pursue them further. The references offer teachers the opportunity
to introduce extra material or perspectives according to personal
preference, perhaps via student reports. And some of the language
students may come from sub-disciplines of classics such as ancient
history where greater knowledge of the background gathered by
following up on some of the secondary literature will enhance the

---

3. Cf. Hofman, J. B., Szantyr, A. (1965), *Lateinische Syntax und Stilistik*, vol. 2, Munich, 701.

inherent interest of the Latin text. Even for those users who do not feel the need or desire to chase up any of the items mentioned, the presence of references may be of benefit: it serves as a useful reminder that a mountain of scholarship exists, has accumulated over centuries and is growing on a daily basis. This mountain does not obstruct our view of the ancient world, but enables it, even if the view from the top and more gradually from any of the lower foothills is constantly changing. While most of the references are to secondary literature in English, I have not shied away from titles in various European languages, partly to acknowledge intellectual debts and partly to underscore the point that classics is, and has always been, an international enterprise. Any such material, however, has been confined to the footnotes. I cite all items in full on the spot (sacrificing economy and elegance in presentation to convenience of use) with four exceptions: recurrent references to Gildenhard (2011), Mitchell (1986), Morwood (1999), and Steel (2004) are presented in the Harvard system of author's name + year of publication. Full details are included in the List of Abbreviations on page 167.

(g) *Translation*: I have decided to include my own translation of the passage. It is solely meant as an aid to understanding the original and stays as close to the Latin as possible. As such, it has no literary value. Put differently, memorizing *this* version for the exam won't earn students any style-points.

(h) *Map*: the edition includes a map of the geographical names mentioned in the commentary. The hard copy is a snapshot of a map designed with the help of Google Earth. The (interactive) 3D version of the map is available under 'Extra Resources' on the book's website at Open Book Publishers.

(i) *Appendix: issues for further discussion*: finally, I have included an appendix that flags up some 'big themes' and open-ended questions raised by the text. They lend themselves for debate and group discussion and should help to relate the detailed work on the passage to wider frames of reference.

For any one reader the edition may include information that may appear either too basic or too advanced. Less may perhaps have been more, but in the end I decided to trust in the ability of all users to screen out data deemed superfluous. Selective reading for pertinent information is, in any case, an increasingly important transferable skill.

Introduction

In 70 BC, when Gnaeus Pompeius and Marcus Licinius Crassus shared the consulship for the first time, Rome's rising star in oratory, Marcus Tullius Cicero, successfully prosecuted Gaius Verres on the charge of misconduct, especially extortion, during his term as governor of Sicily (73–71 BC). Cicero won the case against major resistance. Verres' pockets were sufficiently deep for an extensive campaign of bribery. In Quintus Caecilius Metellus Pius Scipio Nasica, Lucius Cornelius Sisenna, and Quintus Hortensius Hortalus, the consul designate for 69 and a formidable public speaker, Verres managed to recruit a group of defence advocates brimming with nobility and talent. Not the least of their skills was the ability to think up procedural shenanigans to derail or at least delay the trial until the following year. These included the nomination of Verres' former quaestor Quintus Caecilius Niger as a rival prosecutor, which meant that Cicero had to argue for the right to bring Verres to justice in a preliminary hearing (he obviously won). Other powerful supporters chipped in by embarking upon strategic intimidation of the Sicilian witnesses. None of this mattered: at the actual trial, Cicero triumphed resoundingly by out-witting, out-preparing, and out-talking the opposition. His stunning success helped to eclipse Hortensius' reputation as Rome's leading orator and establish Cicero as the 'king of the courts', a moniker previously owned by his rival.

After the conclusion of the proceedings, Cicero published the set of speeches he had given in the context of prosecuting Verres as well as those he had prepared for delivery – 'prepared for delivery' because the case came to a premature end before the speeches could be delivered. Soon after the first hearing (*actio prima*), Verres withdrew into voluntary exile; he was found guilty *in absentia* without the need for a second hearing (*actio secunda*). The so-called *Verrine Orations* thus comprise the *Divinatio in Caecilium* ('Preliminary hearing against Caecilius'), which won him the right to act as prosecutor of Verres; the decisive speech he gave during the first hearing (*in Verrem* 1); and the material Cicero prepared for the second hearing, repackaged into five undelivered orations (*in Verrem* 2.1–5).[4] The dissemination of this corpus of speeches constituted an unprecedented enterprise, 'the largest single publication of [his] entire career, if not the biggest such undertaking in the first century B.C.'[5] Cicero's rationale for publishing the speeches against Verres in written form was most likely complex and will have involved his desire to consolidate his standing as an orator and the wish to broadcast the enormous amount of work he had put into the trial.

The orations are brilliant models of eloquence (as well as spin) by arguably the supreme prose stylist ever to write in Latin. The *Verrines* are full of magnificent passages that illustrate Cicero at his best: as a superb raconteur who generates a gripping story out of precious few facts; as a heavy-hitting cross-examiner who lays into his adversaries with a remorseless flurry of rhetorical questions; as a master in the projection or portrayal of character (so-called *ethos* or *ethopoiea*) and the manipulation of emotions (so-called *pathos*); and, not least, as a creative individual gifted with an impish imagination who knows how to entertain. The passage under discussion here is no exception. It covers a series of lurid incidents from an early stage of Verres' career, which, so Cicero argues, all originated in the defendant's insatiable lust for two primary sources of pleasure: art and sex. First, we get a detailed account of the shameless looting of artistic treasures Verres committed as legate in the Greek East in the late 80s BC. This is followed by an account of the infamous episode at Lampsacus, which revolves around an unsuccessful attempt to abduct and rape a local woman that resulted in the death of a Roman official, provincials pushed to the brink of rioting, and judicial murder. Cicero's version of what happened at Lampsacus is the centrepiece of the first oration he prepared for the second hearing (i.e. *in Verrem* 2.1) and affords a privileged glimpse of the sordid underbelly of Roman imperialism – whatever degree of truth we are willing to grant to his spin on the events.

---

4. I follow the practice of the *Oxford Latin Dictionary* in referring to the speeches, but reference systems vary. Some cite the five speeches designed for the second *actio* as 2*Ver.* 1, 2*Ver.* 2 etc. or use a Roman numeral (*Ver.* II.1, II.2 etc.).

5. Settle, J. N. (1962), *The publication of Cicero's orations*, Diss. North Carolina, 83, cited by Frazel, T. D. (2004), 'The Composition and Circulation of Cicero's *In Verrem*', *Classical Quarterly* n.s. 54, 128–42 (133). See also Gurd, S. (2010), 'Verres and the Scene of Rewriting', *Phoenix* 64, 80–101.

This introduction contains some background material designed to aid in the understanding of the rhetorical and historical dimension of the chosen passage. Section 1 provides a minimum of biographical information on Cicero and Verres. Section 2 takes a look at the circumstances of the trial and situates the chosen passage within the corpus as a whole. Section 3 outlines the main modes of persuasion in (ancient) rhetoric and briefly indicates how Cicero applies them in our passage. Section 4 explores some pertinent issues in late republican history. And Section 5 offers a short introduction to the type of law court in which Verres stood trial. Each section is supposed to give easy access to pertinent contextual information, with a sprinkling of references to works of secondary literature for those who wish to pursue a specific aspect further.

1. The Protagonists: Cicero and Verres

The *Oxford Classical Dictionary* (3rd revised edition, edited by S. Hornblower and A. Spawforth, Oxford, 2003) offers good overviews of the lives and careers of Marcus Tullius Cicero and Gaius Verres.[6] About the former we know more than about any other person from antiquity, mainly from his own writings; about the latter we know very little beyond what Cicero tells us in the *Verrines*.

Given the lack of independent evidence, one of the greatest challenges in dealing with Cicero's orations against Verres is doing Verres justice. This may sound perverse, but Cicero was an absolute genius when it came to the 'tactical' (mis-)representation of evidence. Indeed, his talent for spin was only topped by his ability to assassinate someone's character. Helped by the fact that ancient Rome had no slander or libel laws, he verbally tarred and feathered his adversaries with imaginative gusto.[7] While Cicero took care that his recourse to personal abuse always aided the aims of his argument, he must have made up many of what we would consider slanderous or libellous details that he hurled at his opponents, blurring the boundary

---

6. Beware, though: looking for Cicero in the *OCD* under 'Cicero' will prove futile. He is entered under his *nomen gentile* 'Tullius, Marcus Cicero' See Morwood (1999) 149 for a brief introduction to Roman names.

7. On Cicero and invective, see the papers in Booth, J. (ed.) (2007), *Cicero on the Attack: Invective and Subversion in the Orations and Beyond*, Swansea. For the problem of plausibility in abuse, see Craig, C. (2004), 'Audience Expectations, Invective, and Proof', in J. Powell and J. Paterson (eds.), *Cicero the Advocate*, Oxford, 187–213. More general studies include Corbeill, A. (1996), *Controlling Laughter: Political Humor in the Late Roman Republic*, Princeton and Edwards, C. (1993), *The Politics of Immorality in Ancient Rome*, Cambridge. Both monographs are excellent pieces of scholarship as well as highly entertaining reads.

between fact and fiction, hard data and rhetorical invention. It is therefore
unwise to take anything he says about the character of any of his seemingly
sociopathic villains at face value – including Verres. In the context of the
Verrines, the opportunity of inventing his facts was particularly available
when Cicero covered the early stages of Verres' career, which he did in *in
Verrem* 2.1.

This is not to say that Verres was a particularly delightful human being.
The son of a first-generation senator, he did well for himself in the turbulent
years of the civil war between Marius and Sulla and afterwards as a minor
magistrate in the (wild) East during the period that saw Rome's protracted
struggle with King Mithradates of Pontus, not least by showing a fine
sense of judgement when best to doublecross his superiors. His service as
quaestor under the consul Gnaeus Papirius Carbo came to an abrupt and
disgraceful end when he scarpered with the public money entrusted to
him (some half million sesterces) to Carbo's enemy Sulla.[8] And a couple of
years later he repaid the support he had enjoyed as legate under Gnaeus
Dolabella in Cilicia by acting as prime witness in the extortion trial that
Dolabella faced upon his return to Rome.[9] Complaints about his abuse
of power dogged his governorship in Sicily throughout his term in office,
even necessitating the (futile) intervention of a consul in 72 BC. But Cicero
put an end to Verres' crimes and his career: after the trial, Verres remained
in exile until his death in 43 BC.

If Verres advanced his career by means of his strategic treachery, Cicero,
the son of a knight (*eques*) and hence a so-called 'new man' (*homo novus*),
that is, someone without senatorial ancestors in the family, invested in a
superb education as a means of getting ahead.[10] He was under no illusion:
battlefield success was the privileged pathway to glory at Rome and Cicero
did his best to accumulate military accolades when the occasion presented
itself – as it did during his stint as pro-consul in Cilicia in 51, the same
province in which Verres served as legate thirty years previously. On the
basis of some minor military victories, he unsuccessfully petitioned his

---

8. See below § 77.
9. See again below § 77.
10. Wiseman, T. P. (1971), *New Men in the Roman Senate*, Oxford; Gildenhard, I. (2011),
    Creative Eloquence: The Construction of Reality in Cicero's Speeches, Oxford, 50–58, which
    includes a discussion of how Cicero positions himself vis-à-vis the established ruling
    elite in the *Verrines*. A good account of educational practices in the late Roman republic
    can be found in Corbeill, A. (2002), 'Rhetorical Education in Cicero's Youth', in J. M. May
    (ed.), *Brill's Companion to Cicero: Oratory and Rhetoric*, Leiden, Boston, Cologne, 23–48.

senatorial peers for the right to celebrate a triumph. In the main, however, Cicero built his career, and even more so his legacy, on supreme ability in the realms of language, literature, and thought. He was the best orator Rome produced, authored a large number of rhetorical and philosophical works, and also distinguished himself as a poet (though few of his verses have survived). In the law courts, he saw his role mainly as an advocate for the oppressed. Even in the case against Verres, where he acted as prosecutor, he stressed that he entered into the fray as an advocate of the Sicilians.

Overall, the careers of Cicero and Verres share a series of coincidental parallels that are fun to ponder. In the years before their showdown in 70 BC, each of the two men spent time in the Greek East and in Sicily. Some years after his consulship in 63 BC, Cicero suffered the same fate as Verres: voluntary exile. And several ancient authors comment on the remarkable irony that Cicero and Verres died in the same year, proscribed by the same man – the former for his tongue, the latter for his art collection.[11] A bare skeleton of their respective careers in the form of a table would look something like this:

Year	Verres	Cicero
c.115 BC	born	
106		born
90–88		Military Service
84	Service as quaestor under the consul Cn. Papirius Carbo	
83	Continuing service probably as pro-quaestor; desertion to Sulla	
81		First surviving public speech (*pro Quinctio*)
80	Service as *legatus*, then also as pro-quaestor under Cn. Dolabella, proconsul in Cilicia	

(continued)

11. See Pliny the Elder, *Natural History* 34.6; Seneca the Elder, *Suasoriae* 6.24 (citing a brilliant passage from Asinius Pollio's history, in which the Caesarian contrasts the 'brave death' of Verres with the pitiable death of Cicero, in the context of an ingeniously malicious appraisal of Cicero's character overall); and Lactantius, *Divine Institutes* 2.4.37.

(continued)

Year	Verres	Cicero
79–77		Rhetorical and philosophical studies in Rhodes and Athens
78	Trial and conviction of Dolabella for extortion; Verres acting as main witness for the prosecution	
75		Quaestor in Sicily
74	Urban Praetor	
73–71	Governance of Sicily as pro-praetor	
70	Trial and voluntary exile	Prosecution of Verres
69		Aedile
66		Praetor
63		Consul
58		Pushed into exile on account of the execution of the Catilinarians (till 57)
51		Pro-consul in Cilicia
43	Proscription by Mark Antony; death	Proscription by Mark Antony; death

2. The Trial of Verres and Cicero's Set of Speeches against Verres

2.1 The run-up[12]

When the Sicilians turned to Rome for help against the plundering and extortion perpetrated by Verres, Cicero was a natural point of contact: he

---

12. For issues of chronology, see Marinone, N. (1950), *Quaestiones Verrinae*, Turin; and (1977), *Cronologia Ciceroniana*, Rome, 65–7. Many more detailed accounts of the circumstances of the trial exist than the bare-bone coverage provided here. Two of the best are Berry, D. H. (2006), *Cicero. Political Speeches: A New Translation*, Oxford, 3–12, and Lintott, A. (2008), 'Cicero and the Citadel of the Allies', in *Cicero as Evidence: A Historian's Companion*, Oxford, 81–100.

had been quaestor in Sicily only a few years earlier, knew the province well, had close ties with various leading locals, and saw himself as their patron.[13] He agreed to act as the Sicilians' legal representative, in what shaped up as a case for one of Rome's 'standing courts', the so-called *quaestio de repetundis*.[14] Because Roman officials enjoyed immunity from prosecution during their time in office, the trial could not start before Verres' period as pro-magistrate finished at the end of 71 BC. His return to the status of *privatus* ('an individual not holding public office') set in motion the following procedural steps:

postulatio (c. 10 January 70): in early January of 70, Cicero applied to the praetor presiding over the extortion court, Manlius Acilius Glabrio, for permission to prosecute Verres (*postulatio*).

divinatio (c. 20 January 70): no doubt at the instigation of Verres or his advocate Hortensius Verres' quaestor Q. Caecilius Niger also applied for the leave to prosecute; such rival requests entailed the need for a so-called *divinatio*, which consisted of a hearing before a jury presided over by the praetor at which the rival parties staked their claims. Cicero triumphed with the (surviving) speech *Divinatio in Caecilium*, in which he showed that his adversary was just not up to the task.

nominis delatio and *nominis receptio* (c. 20 January 70 or soon thereafter): after his victory over Caecilius, Cicero submitted a formal charge (*nominis delatio*), which was accepted by the praetor (*nominis receptio*).

inquisitio: to prepare his case, Cicero asked for, and was granted, 110 days, during which he travelled to Sicily to secure witnesses and documentation. Time was precious: he was aware of the fact that the defence wanted to delay the trial until the following year. At various places in the *Verrines*, he boasts about the speed with which he marshalled evidence. Thus he calls the period he requested for gathering evidence 'astonishingly brief' (*Ver.* 1.6: *dies perexigua*). About sixty of the 110 days he had available, he spent on a trip to Sicily, priding himself on 'the speed of his return' (*Ver.* 2.1.16: *celeritas reditionis*).

2.2 The trial

After the selection of the jury in the second half of July, the trial began on 5 August. As already mentioned, Verres and his supporters tried to prolong

---

13. Brunt, P. A. (1980), 'Patronage and Politics in the *Verrines*', *Chiron* 10, 273–89.
14. See below Section 5: The Roman extortion court.

the trial until the following year. In 69, Hortensius, one of his advocates, and Q. Caecilius Metellus Creticus, one of his main friends and supporters, would have been consuls, and M. Caecilius Metellus (a brother of the aforementioned Metellus) would have presided over the extortion court as praetor. In a society that placed a premium on esteem for magistrates, this would have meant a powerful boost to Verres' cause. Likewise, there was the prospect of a more favourable jury (that is, one more liable to corruption) since several of the chosen jury members were due to leave Rome in 69 BC to take up offices, ruling them out of jury duty.[15] At one point, when it looked as if the ploy were to succeed, a third brother, L. Caecilius Metellus, who had taken over the governorship of Sicily from Verres as pro-praetor, tried to intimidate the Sicilians against giving testimony against Verres, boasting somewhat prematurely that Verres' acquittal was certain and that it was in the Sicilians' own interest not to cause difficulties. As a countermove and to accelerate proceedings, Cicero broke with conventions in his opening speech: instead of a lengthy disquisition setting out all of the charges (*oratio perpetua*), followed by a prolonged hearing of supporting witnesses, he quickly and summarily sketched out each of the charges and produced a limited number of supporting witnesses.

Verres' advocate Hortensius did not expect this deviation from standard procedure and faced a difficult challenge. As M. Alexander points out, he was 'put in the invidious position of having to reply to charges that had not been fully argued, and while [he] probably had a good idea of the arguments which Cicero would be making at the second hearing, he would not have wanted to give credence to them by stating them himself, and then trying to refute them.'[16] In the *Orator*, a rhetorical treatise he wrote in 46 BC, Cicero seems to imply that Hortensius never gave a formal speech in reply and only cross-examined some witnesses during the first hearing (*Orat.* 129).[17] With the *actio prima* completed on 13 August, the court adjourned for the Votive Games that began on 16 August (*comperendinatio*). It never reconvened: Verres considered the case that Cicero presented against him during the first hearing so compelling that he went into voluntary exile. The *actio secunda*, for

---

15. For details, see Marshall, A. J. (1967), 'Verres and Judicial Corruption', *Classical Quarterly* 17, 408–13; McDermott, W. C. (1977), 'The Verrine Jury', *Rheinisches Museum* 120, 64–75.

16. Alexander, M. (1976), 'Hortensius' Speech in Defense of Verres', *Phoenix* 30, 46–53 (52).

17. The speech of Hortensius that Quintilian read (*Institutio Oratoria* 10.1.23) might have been 'a mere literary composition' or the one he 'delivered at the *litis aestimatio*, after Verres' condemnation in absence': Brunt, P. A. (1980), 'Patronage and Politics in the *Verrines*', *Chiron* 10, 273–89 (280 n. 44).

which Cicero had prepared a massive amount of material adding up to five full speeches, never took place.

2.3 The corpus of speeches[18]

In the aftermath of the trial, Cicero not only published the *Divinatio in Caecilium* and the speech he gave during the *actio prima* (commonly labelled *in Verrem* 1), but also the five speeches he had prepared for the *actio secunda* (*in Verrem* 2.1–5). In outline, we have the following corpus:

> *Divinatio in Caecilium* [delivered January 70 BC]
> *in Verrem* 1 [delivered August 70 BC, during the *actio prima*]
> *in Verrem* 2 [planned for the *actio secunda*, but never delivered]
> > *in Verrem* 2.1: Verres' youth and public career prior to his governorship of Sicily
> > *in Verrem* 2.2: Sicily - abuse of judicial power
> > *in Verrem* 2.3: Sicily - extortion of taxes
> > *in Verrem* 2.4: Sicily - robbery of artworks
> > *in Verrem* 2.5: Sicily - Verres as magistrate with *imperium*, responsible for public safety and endowed with the power to punish

Cicero only decided to publish a selection of his speeches.[19] The fact that he circulated all the speeches to do with the trial of Verres indicates his high opinion of the set and his belief in their value as documents of self-promotion. Scholars have debated, more or less inconclusively, whether and, if so, to what degree Cicero revised speeches after delivery before circulating them in written form. No clear consensus has emerged, not least since his practice will most likely have differed from case to case, ranging from almost instant release with only minor adjustments to significant revision and publication several years after the original delivery.[20] The speeches that Cicero prepared for the second hearing belong to those that he anyway never gave, so here

---

18. For an excellent account of the corpus and its context, see Vasaly, A. (2002), 'Cicero's Early Speeches', in J. M. May (ed.), *Brill's Companion to Cicero: Oratory and Rhetoric*, Leiden, Boston, Cologne, 71–111 (87–103).

19. For those speeches that he decided not to disseminate in written form, see Crawford, J. W. (1984), *M. Tullius Cicero: The Lost and Unpublished Orations*, Göttingen.

20. Excellent recent discussions include Berry, D. H. (2004), 'The Publication of Cicero's *Pro Roscio Amerino*', *Mnemosyne* 57, 80–87, Gurd, S. (2007), 'Cicero and Editorial Revision', *Classical Antiquity* 26, 49–80, and Lintott, A. (2008), *Cicero as Evidence: A Historian's Commentary*, Oxford, 15–9.

the question is moot. Still, it bears stressing that in the form we have them they are indistinguishable from the written versions of those speeches he actually delivered. In all of his published orations, Cicero maintains the illusion that the text is the record of a performance. (Devices that sustain this illusion include direct addresses to the audience, in particular the defendant, members of the jury, or opposing advocates, orders to the clerk to read out documents, and the use of deictic pronouns such as *iste* that suggest the presence of the person thus referred to.) It would have been Cicero's practice in any case to work up extensive written notes for a speech before its oral delivery – which of course does not mean that he read from a script in court – and he most likely had his contribution to the *actio secunda* more or less ready to go by the time the trial began.[21]

The first speech intended for the second hearing (*Ver.* 2.1), from which our passage comes, contains an exhaustive discussion of Verres' career *before* he took on the governorship of Sicily. In outline the speech breaks down into the following sections:

1–23: Preface
24–31: Explanation why Cicero didn't indict in detail during the *actio prima*
32–34: Blueprint of the *actio secunda*[22]
34–40: Verres' quaestorship
41–102: Verres' stint as legate and pro-quaestor of Dolabella in Cilicia
    41–61: Verres' thefts of artworks
    62–86a: The Lampsacus episode
    86b–90: The theft at Miletus
    90–102: Verres' crimes as a guardian and pro-quaestor
103–58: Verres' urban praetorship
    103–27: Abuses of his judicial powers
    128–54: Misconduct as a supervisor of the maintenance of public buildings
    155–58: His jury-tampering in other trials

---

21. See Frazel, T. (2004), 'The Composition and Circulation of Cicero's *In Verrem*', *Classical Quarterly* n.s. 54, 128–42.

22. Cicero uses *praeteritio* to pass over Verres' (singularly depraved) youth, limiting his coverage of Verres' crimes to the four periods in which he acted as a magistrate of the Roman people: his quaestorship, his legateship in Asia Minor, his urban praetorship, and his governorship of Sicily (§ 34). *Ver.* 2.1 deals with the first three parts of this fourfold division (*quadripertita distributio*), *Ver.* 2.2–5 with the fourth.

The Lampsacus episode stands out as the centrepiece of the oration – a sustained and largely self-contained unit, in which Cicero explores Verres' past in particular depth and detail. Yet while it is the centre of *Ver.* 2.1, in the trial as a whole this particular oration (and hence the Lampsacus episode as well) is a bit of a sideshow. If one only reads an excerpt from this speech, it is easy to forget that Verres was not – nor had ever been – on trial for any of his actions as legate. Cicero here reconsiders events that happened about a decade earlier, in an effort to portray Verres as evil through and through. True, consistency of character was an important argument in Roman law courts – anyone who could be shown to have a criminal record was considered more likely to have perpetrated the crime for which he was on trial, whereas an unblemished past could be marshalled in support of a plea of innocence. Thus Cicero does his best to depict Verres as a heinous and hardened criminal, with a particular penchant for debauchery from his early youth. But in the larger scheme of things, *Ver.* 2.1 is primarily a warm-up to his account of Verres' governorship of Sicily, to which he devoted the four subsequent speeches.[23]

3. Modes of persuasion[24]

Public speaking is designed to persuade an audience of a specific point of view. If the setting is a court of law, the prosecutor tries to convince those who judge the case of the guilt of the defendant, whereas the advocate aims to achieve a verdict of innocence. But how *does* one succeed in causing another person to consent to one's own point of view and to act accordingly? Is it the rational force of the better argument? Or is it the authority of the speaker, deriving, perhaps, from (superior) age, position, or prestige? What audiences find persuasive differs from culture to culture and, within a given culture, from one setting to another. Ancient rhetorical theory identified three main modes of persuasion: a speaker could prove his points or render

---

23. See Steel (2004) 251 for some comments on how Cicero employs the Lampsacus episode to prefigure events in Sicily.
24. From among the large number of books on ancient rhetoric available, I recommend Habinek, T. (2005), *Ancient Rhetoric and Oratory*, Malden, Mass., as both stimulating and concise. It includes a bibliographical essay on further reading (111–20). See also Kennedy, G. (1994), *A New History of Classical Rhetoric*, Princeton; and, for the afterlife of ancient rhetoric, Kennedy, G. (1980), *Classical Rhetoric and its Christian and Secular Tradition from Ancient to Modern Times*, Chapel Hill. The most important handbook on invention and style in classical and classicizing rhetoric is Lausberg, H. (1998), *Handbook of Literary Rhetoric*, Leiden.

(Aristotle)

his arguments plausible by means of *logos* (that is, reasoning, analysis and argument), *ethos* (that is, the characters of the individuals involved in the trial, especially that of the defendant and the speaker), or *pathos* (that is, strong emotions roused by the speaker in his audience).[25] The chosen passage showcases Cicero's resourceful handling of all three modes.

3.1 Reasoning and argument

In his handling of the affair at Lampsacus, Cicero opts for a two-pronged approach to prove Verres' guilt: to begin with, he simply presupposes that the sequence of events has as its unifying factor Verres' inability to keep his lecherous instincts under control. In his account of what happened at Lampsacus and the aftermath (the trial and execution of Philodamus and his son) Verres is presented as the mastermind behind the scene, first by plotting sexual assault, then by trying to cover up his guilt. By showing the defendant in action (as it were), Cicero thus makes narration (or a narrative) do the work of argumentation.[26] Only after he has established his version of the event as a compelling point of reference does he switch into a more explicitly argumentative mode. In §§ 78–85, he explores and rebuts potential lines of defence Verres might have adopted to cast doubt on Cicero's interpretation and give an alternative explanation of what happened. According to Cicero, Verres' counter-arguments do not amount to much and crumble under scrutiny. When all is said and done, so Cicero claims repeatedly, Verres is unable to explain why what occurred did occur. And this, so Cicero asserts, means that his own version of the events, for which he has two reliable witnesses, must represent the truth. After reading the passage, are you convinced that Cicero has proved Verres' guilt?

3.2 Ethopoiea

Cicero takes great care to provide vivid portrayals of the characters he deals with in his speeches.[27] The *Verrines* are no exceptions. The greatest effort

---

25. The classic treatment of *ethos* and *pathos* in ancient rhetoric is Wisse, J. (1989), *Ethos and Pathos from Aristotle to Cicero*, Amsterdam.

26. One may wish to distinguish the act of narration or the result thereof, i.e. a story or narrative, from the technical term *narratio*, which is used of that part of a forensic speech in which the speaker sets out the facts of the case: see Levene, D. S. (2004), 'Reading Cicero's Narratives', in J. Powell and J. Paterson (eds.), *Cicero the Advocate*, Oxford, 117–46 (117).

27. On ethopoiea: Gildenhard (2011) 20–22 with much further bibliography.

goes of course into his characterization of Verres. But Cicero also gives us insidious character appraisals of Gnaeus Dolabella, the governor of Cilicia and Verres' superior in command, and Gaius Nero, the governor of Asia, that is, the province in which Lampsacus was located. The traits Cicero emphasizes in the former are his murderous villainy and conspicuous stupidity, whereas the latter comes into Cicero's rhetorical crosshairs for his yellow-bellied cowardice. Cicero also spends some time on Verres' worthless entourage, notably Rubrius. And even individuals or groups that only make a cameo appearance in his text have a distinct (if often one-sided) identity and personality profile that enables the audience to relate to them. Examples of minor characters include envoys (*legati*) from Asia and Achaia (§ 59), Ianitor, Verres' host in Lampsacus (§§ 63–4), the Roman citizens who were in Lampsacus for business reasons (§ 69), the Roman creditors of the Greeks (§ 73), one of whom acts as accuser of Philodamus (§ 74), and the *praefecti* and *tribuni militares* of Dolabella (§ 73). Cicero also knows how to underscore the reliability of his two prime witnesses: P. Tettius and C. Varro, who both served on the staff of Nero (§ 71).

When it comes to the depiction of character, Cicero likes to paint in black and white. Whereas Verres and his ilk appear as villains and perverts, he lavishes praise upon the inhabitants of Lampsacus and in particular Philodamus and his son. Cicero portrays Verres and Dolabella in such a way as to remove them from civilized society: they come across as beasts ruled either by their passions or even worse instincts such as delight in cruelty; the Lampsacenes, in contrast, represent a peace-loving community that cherishes private and public values dear to the Romans as well, such as devotion to family members, unselfish courage, and commitment to civic life. One rewarding exercise in responding to Cicero's ethopoiea is to colour in shades of grey – that is, to interrogate his categorical condemnations as well as his unqualified embraces, in an effort to arrive at a more realistic picture of his personnel.[28]

In this context, it is also worth noting how Cicero constantly engages the audience: he appeals to them as persons endowed with a special disposition and committed to certain values, but does not hesitate to let them know how disastrous it would be if they did not decide the case at hand in his favour. In particular, it would put the judges at the same level as the defendant. A keynote of the speech (2.1: *Neminem vestrum ignorare arbitror, iudices...*) is that Cicero's audience is in the know: Verres'

---

28. For Cicero's tendency to split his personnel into the good and the bad and to characterize accordingly see Gildenhard (2011) 74–98 ('The good, the bad, and the in-between').

shenanigans, trickery, and attempts at deception cannot fool them.[29] But since his guilt is so glaring and well-established, a verdict of innocent would reveal the judges inevitably as corrupt and unfit for their role.

3.3 Pathos

Cicero's report of Verres' looting of artworks and his narrative of the Lampsacus affair are both fraught with pathos, meant to generate indignation, if not downright outrage, at Verres' conduct. In addition, the portion of text under consideration here includes two paragraphs that are especially designed to appeal to the emotions. In § 59, Cicero recalls one of the rare occasions in which Verres adorned the city of Rome with his plundered treasures for public viewing. 'By chance' (*casu*), a great number of embassies from the towns Verres had ravaged happened to be in Rome at the time, and Cicero describes heart-wrenching scenes of Greek ambassadors setting eyes on long lost treasures, often statues of gods and goddesses of profound religious value and significance, breaking down on the spot, in public, in worship and tears. And in § 76, Cicero describes the public execution of Philodamus and his son in the city of Laodicea as a tragic spectacle, matching the bestial cruelty (*crudelitas*) of the Roman officials Verres and Dolabella against the *humanitas* (humanity) and the family-values of the condemned. The sight, so Cicero, even moved the presiding Roman magistrate Nero to tears – precisely the sort of response he wishes to generate in his present audience as well, grounded in sympathy and compassion for Verres' victims and righteous anger at his abuse of power and violation of Roman values.

4. Rome and the Mediterranean in the Late Republic

Ver. 2.1.53–86 can serve as an excellent point of departure for branching out into Roman history and culture, especially the imperial culture of the late republic and themes to do with the imperial expansion of Rome across the Mediterranean world, in particular the Greek East. In turn, a basic grasp of historical facts and figures will aid in understanding our passage.

---

29. The judges are addressed in the second person plural or as *iudices* throughout our passage: 53: *scitis, audistis*; 57: *cognoscite*; 58: *iudices*; 60: *iudices*; 62: *existimatis?*; 63: *iudices*; 71: *potestis dubitare ... ?*; 72: *audite, quaeso, iudices et ... miseremini ... et ostendite...!*; 76: *putatis?*; 81: *parcetis?*; 82: *Nolite ... cogere, ... nisi vos vindicatis!*; 86: *accipite nunc!*

4.1 Rome's military conquest of Greece and Asia Minor[30]

While Rome stood in contact with the wider, Greek-dominated world of the Mediterranean from early on (witness the legend of Aeneas arriving in Italy after the destruction of Troy, as preliminary step towards the foundation of the city), it had no military presence in the Greek East until the end of the third century BC. Yet after the so-called 'First Illyrian War' (229 BC) matters proceeded quickly. In 167 BC, the Greek historian Polybius considered Rome's conquest of Greece (and the known world more generally) an accomplished fact. That assessment, though, may have been somewhat premature as further military adventures and significant territorial gains continued to happen afterwards. The driving forces and motivations behind Rome's imperial expansion have been the subject of much controversial debate.[31] But whatever the intent, by the time of the *Verrines*, the rise of Rome from a town on the Tiber to the centre of an empire that spanned the entire Mediterranean world was by and large complete. Landmark events in Rome's conquest of the Greek East include the following (those in bold Cicero mentions in § 55):

229: First Illyrian War

197: T. Quinctius Flamininus defeats Philip V, King of Macedonia, at Cynoscephalai

190: L. Cornelius Scipio Asiaticus defeats Antiochus III, King of Syria

168: L. Aemilius Paulus defeats Perseus, King of Macedonia

146: L. Mummius destroys Corinth; establishment of the province of Macedonia

133: Attalus III, King of Pergamum, bequeathes his kingdom to Rome upon his death

129: Establishment of the province of Asia

c. 100: Establishment of the province of Cilicia

---

30. For a highly readable and very stimulating account of how Rome became involved with the Greek world that includes all the important facts and figures with a hard look at scholarly orthodoxies, see Gruen, E. S. (2004), 'Rome and the Greek World', in H. I. Flower (ed.), *The Cambridge Companion to the Roman Republic*, Cambridge, 242–67.

31. For a range of views on how and why Rome conquered the Greek East (from deliberate policy to mainly reactive to Greek concerns and invitations) see Harris, W. (1979), *War and Imperialism in Republican Rome*, Oxford; Gruen, E. S. (1984), *The Hellenistic World and the Coming of Rome*, Berkeley; and Morstein Kallet-Marx, R. (1995), *Hegemony to Empire. The Development of the Roman Imperium in the East from 148 to 62 B.C.*, Berkeley.

88–84: First War between Rome and Mithradates VI, King of Pontus
83–81: Second War between Rome and Mithradates VI, King of Pontus
73–63: Third War between Rome and Mithradates VI, King of Pontus[32]

The Romans organized conquered territories into so-called *provinciae* (provinces). Sicily was the first, established in 241 BC, in the wake of the First Punic War. For each province, a *lex provinciae* defined the rights and obligations that the otherwise by and large self-governing civic communities (*civitates*) within a province had towards Rome. All provinces were required to submit tribute to Rome, which was collected by the so-called *publicani* ('tax-farmers').[33] The nature of the Roman presence varied greatly across the provinces. And in each province, the Romans interacted with a complex patchwork of communities as well as – when the province was located at the border of Rome's imperial sway – with neighbouring kings and peoples. Diplomatic activity within and across provinces was fairly intense. In fact, what brought Verres to Lampsacus was an embassy to two kingdoms bordering on the Roman province of Asia, a journey Verres undertook, so Cicero insinuates spitefully but not necessarily correctly, entirely for personal profit. Verres' legateship in the Greek East fell into a period marked by much unrest across the entire region. The Second War between Rome and Mithradates VI, King of Pontus, had just come to an end, and the civic communities were groaning under the punitive sanctions imposed upon them by Sulla for the lack of support they had shown to Rome in the recent struggle.[34]

---

32. For a spectacular biography of a spectacular subject, see Mayor, A. (2009), *The Poison King: The Life and Legend of Mithradates, Rome's Deadliest Enemy*, Princeton.

33. The classic treatment is Badian, E. (1972), *Publicans and Sinners. Private Enterprise in the Service of the Roman Republic*, Oxford.

34. For Rome's imperial presence and diplomatic interaction with civic communities within the provinces and beyond see e.g. Badian, E. (1958), *Foreign Clientelae: 264–70 BC*, Oxford; Gruen, E. (1984), *The Hellenistic World and the Coming of Rome*, Berkeley; Williams, C. (2008), 'Friends of the Roman People. Some Remarks on the Language of *amicitia*', in A. Coşkun (ed.), *Freundschaft und Gefolgschaft in den auswärtigen Beziehungen der Römer (2. Jahrhundert v. Chr. – 1. Jahrhundert n. Chr.)*, Frankfurt a. M., 29–44; Edmondson, J. (1993), '*Instrumenta Imperii*: Law and Imperialism in Republican Rome', in B. Halpern and D. W. Hobson (eds.), *Law, Politics and Society in the Ancient Mediterranean World*, Sheffield, 156–92; and Kaizer, T. and Facella, M. (2010), 'Introduction', in *idem* (eds.), *Kingdoms and Principalities in the Roman Near East*, Stuttgart, 15–42.

4.2 Roman provincial administration[35]

As fans of the 1980s British sitcom *Yes Minister* by Antony Jay and Jonathan Lynn will know, the personnel of modern democratic nation-states involved in government consists in part of publicly elected politicians, who are voted into (and out of) office from time to time, and the bureaucratic functionaries of the civil service, whose positions are permanent, i.e. unaffected by the mood-swings of the electorate, and who can therefore ensure a certain degree of institutional continuity from one legislative period to the next. In contrast to many modern institutions where the administrative staff is permanently employed and remains in post, regardless of which official is elected, governance and administration in republican Rome were non-bureaucratic, with a high level of personal involvement by the appointed magistrate in all affairs.

After their year as magistrates, consuls and praetors were customarily appointed as governors of provinces, assuming the title of pro-consul ('acting consul') or pro-praetor ('acting praetor') during their time in office (usually one year, but often prolonged). Assignments were usually done by lot, but could also be 'arranged' by those who were entitled to take up a provincial governorship in any given year. Roman magistrates and pro-magistrates relied on an extensive staff (called *apparitores*) in the execution of their office. Some of the more high ranking staff was elected, but the pro-magistrate had by and large a free hand in selecting whom he wanted to take along in what capacity. The staff included fairly high-ranking Romans with ambitions of entering the *cursus honorum*, that is, a political career involving magistracies and military commands. Staff of provincial governors also included such functionaries as lictors, messengers (*viatores*), heralds (*praecones*), and scribes (*scribae*).

In the course of the section considered here, Cicero mentions a wide range of Roman personnel involved in provincial administration. We encounter:

(i)   *Pro-magistrates responsible for the administration of a province*: Nero (Asia), and Dolabella (Cilicia).

(ii)   Their staff or subordinates, some of whom with official or semi-official designations: thus Verres was a legate of

---

35. A vast subject. For excellent and accessible treatments see Richardson, J. (1984), *Roman provincial administration, 227 BC to AD 117*, Princeton; and Lintott, A. (1993), *Imperium Romanum. Politics and Administration*, London and New York, 70–96 and 206–12.

Dolabella; and Cicero's two witnesses Tettius and Varro were part of Nero's staff in Asia: the former as a so-called *accensus*, the latter as a military tribune.[36]

(iii) *Lower functionaries and friends*: during the diplomatic mission that brought him to Lampsacus, Verres was most likely accompanied by two lictors; one of them, Cornelius, died at Philodamus' dinner party.[37] In addition, he brought along personal friends from his social networks, thereby helping young acquaintances to become familiar with Rome's imperial opportunities, in what was the ancient equivalent of modern 'work experience'. Cicero makes much of the worthless villains that formed Verres' *cohors* (entourage) and points out one Rubrius as being particularly gifted in aiding his master's criminal desires. The conduct of both magistrates and members of their *cohors* in the provinces often left much to be desired. To be a Roman abroad in a position of power constituted a test of character that many failed to meet.[38]

In addition to provincial governors and their staff, Cicero also mentions Romans who had come to Asia independently to pursue business interests. In § 69, he reports that Roman citizens in Lampsacus on business successfully intervened when the local mob was trying to burn down the house in which Verres stayed. Conversely, he makes a damning reference to Roman money-lenders active in the region and their unscrupulous greed (§ 74).

5. The Roman Extortion Court
(*quaestio de repetundis*)

Verres stood trial in the so-called *quaestio de repetundis*. *quaestio* (from *quaero* + *tio*) refers, in its most basic sense, to 'the act of searching' and then came to mean 'judicial investigation, inquiry' and, more specifically,

---

36. See below § 71.
37. Lictors carried the *fasces*, a bundle of wooden sticks that symbolized the power of the office both *domi* and *militiae* (in the latter sphere, the *fasces* contained an axe). Their number indicated the importance of the magistracy: consuls had twelve, praetors six. Towards the end of the republican period, legates who travelled in the company of pro-magistrates were also given lictors, especially when they represented their superior in military command or jurisdiction.
38. Braund, D. C. (1998), '*Cohors*. The Governor and his Entourage in the Self-Image of the Roman Republic', in R. Laurence and J. Berry (eds.), *Cultural Identity in the Roman Empire*, London, 10–24.

'a commission appointed to try certain cases of serious public crimes' (*Oxford Latin Dictionary* s. v. 4). Such commissions could be either *ad hoc* or permanent ('standing'). The first such permanent criminal court or tribunal (*quaestio perpetua*) was the *quaestio de repetundis*, which was set up in 149 BC to deal with acts of embezzlement by Roman magistrates. The gerundive phrase *de repetundis* means, literally, 'about matters that need to be recovered', so the *quaestio de repetundis* was a standing criminal court that heard cases of corruption or misconduct in office and concerned itself especially with the recovery of extorted money. Many, but by no means all, cases that came before the *quaestio de repetundis* involved the exploitation of provincial subjects by Roman magistrates. While it may go too far to see this institution, in which members of Rome's ruling elite sat in judgement over their peers, as a means by which Rome's imperial republic maintained for itself the myth of beneficial imperialism, in practice the court can be considered 'the chief countervailing force against the all-powerful Roman magistrate and his companions in the military field and provincial government.'[39]

In the course of its history, arrangements of who could act as prosecutor and who manned the juries underwent several changes. One such reform coincided with Cicero's prosecution of Verres, who was the last person judged in a *quaestio de repetundis* under the system put in place by Sulla: 'The year 70 was momentous. The full power of the tribunes was restored. The senatorial monopoly of criminal jurisdiction was terminated.'[40] Cicero obliquely links the case at hand to this imminent judicial reform, thereby putting his individual stamp on a watershed-year in Roman history. Throughout the *Verrines* (though not in the passage under consideration here) Cicero plays on a sense of constitutional crisis.[41] It was part of a larger strategy 'to make Verres' guilt matter', not least for purposes of self-promotion.[42]

---

39. Lintott, A. (2008), *Cicero as Evidence: A Historian's Companion*, Oxford, p. 81 and 83.
40. Brunt, P. A. (1980), 'Patronage and Politics in the *Verrines*', *Chiron* 10, 273–89 (284).
41. Cf. though § 58 and the note on **iudiciorum ... dominos ... cupiditatum ... servos**. For details, see Vasaly, A. (2009), 'Cicero, Domestic Politics, and the First Action of the *Verrines*', *Classical Antiquity* 28, 101–37.
42. Vasaly, A. (1993), *Representations: Images of the World in Ciceronian Oratory*, Berkeley, Los Angeles, Oxford, p. 110.

Latin Text and Study Questions

[53] Aspendum vetus oppidum et nobile in Pamphylia scitis esse, plenissimum signorum optimorum. Non dicam illinc hoc signum ablatum esse et illud. hoc dico, nullum te Aspendi signum, Verres, reliquisse, omnia ex fanis, ex locis publicis, palam, spectantibus omnibus, plaustris evecta exportataque esse. Atque etiam illum Aspendium citharistam, de quo saepe audistis id quod est Graecis hominibus in proverbio, quem omnia 'intus canere' dicebant, sustulit et in intimis suis aedibus posuit, ut etiam illum ipsum suo artificio superasse videatur.

Grammar and Syntax:

- Identify the three superlatives in the paragraph.
- What case is *Aspendi*?
- What case is *Verres*?
- Explain the syntax of *quem omnia 'intus canere' dicebant*.

Style and Theme:

- How does geopolitical space feature in this paragraph? Answer this question with reference to **(i)** place names and other geographical indicators; and **(ii)** the phrases *ex locis publicis* and *in intimis suis aedibus*.
- What is the technical term of the stylistic device that links *intus* and *intimis* in the phrases <u>intus</u> *canere* and *in* <u>intimis</u> *suis aedibus*?
- Describe the 'dramaturgy' of the paragraph: whom does Cicero address when, and to what effect? How would you describe his interaction with the senators sitting in judgement?

[54] Pergae fanum antiquissimum et sanctissimum Dianae scimus esse: id quoque a te nudatum ac spoliatum esse, ex ipsa Diana quod habebat auri detractum atque ablatum esse dico. Quae, malum, est ista tanta audacia atque amentia! Quas enim sociorum atque amicorum urbis adisti legationis iure et nomine, si in eas vi cum exercitu imperioque invasisses, tamen, opinor, quae signa atque ornamenta ex iis urbibus sustulisses, haec non in tuam domum neque in suburbana amicorum, sed Romam in publicum deportasses.

Grammar and Syntax:

- Explain the syntax of *auri*.
- What is the subject accusative of the second part of the indirect statement (*ex ipsa Diana … ablatum esse*) introduced by *dico*?
- What are the antecedents of the relative clauses introduced by *Quas* and *quae*?

Style and Theme:

- Compare the degree of Cicero's rhetorical aggressiveness in this and the preceding paragraph.
- Explore how Cicero continues and develops his 'rhetoric of space' from the previous paragraph.
- Discuss the theme of 'violence' in the paragraph: what forms of physical force does Cicero distinguish and on what grounds?
- What is the name of the stylistic device that underwrites the word order of *non in tuam domum neque in suburbana amicorum*?

[55]   Quid ego de M. Marcello loquar, qui Syracusas, urbem ornatissimam, cepit? quid de L. Scipione, qui bellum in Asia gessit Antiochumque, regem potentissimum, vicit? quid de Flaminino, qui regem Philippum et Macedoniam subegit? quid de L. Paulo, qui regem Persen vi ac virtute superavit? quid de L. Mummio, qui urbem pulcherrimam atque ornatissimam, Corinthum, plenissimam rerum omnium, sustulit, urbisque Achaiae Boeotiaeque multas sub imperium populi Romani dicionemque subiunxit? Quorum domus, cum honore ac virtute florerent, signis et tabulis pictis erant vacuae; at vero urbem totam templaque deorum omnisque Italiae partis illorum donis ac monumentis exornatas videmus.

Grammar and Syntax:

- *Quorum domus*…: explain the syntax of *quorum*.
- Explain the case and function of *signis et tabulis pictis*.

Style and Theme:

- *Quid ego de ... loquar?* What is the technical term for this rhetorical device?
- Explore how Cicero employs ellipsis in his catalogue of rhetorical questions.
- Identify chiastic patterns within Cicero's list of historical precedents.
- Map the history and geography of imperial conquest and expansion built into Cicero's list of generals and battles.
- Discuss the argumentative force of the *exempla* that Cicero adduces: what are they designed to illustrate?
- Explore the thematic correlation of the two phrases *vi ac virtute* and *honore ac virtute*.

[56] Vereor ne haec forte cuipiam nimis antiqua et iam obsoleta videantur; ita enim tum aequabiliter omnes erant eius modi ut haec laus eximiae virtutis et innocentiae non solum hominum, verum etiam temporum illorum esse videatur. P. Servilius, vir clarissimus, maximis rebus gestis, adest de te sententiam laturus: Olympum vi, copiis, consilio, virtute cepit, urbem antiquam et omnibus rebus auctam et ornatam. Recens exemplum fortissimi viri profero; nam postea Servilius imperator populi Romani Olympum urbem hostium cepit quam tu in isdem illis locis legatus quaestorius oppida pacata sociorum atque amicorum diripienda ac vexanda curasti.

Grammar and Syntax:

- Explain the case and function of *hominum* and *temporum illorum*.
- Parse *curasti*.

Style and Theme:

- Discuss the interrelation of style and theme in *vi, copiis, consilio, virtute*.
- How does 'the past' figure in Cicero's argument?
- What are the names of the stylistic devices that Cicero deploys in *postea … quam*? How do they reinforce his argument?

[57]   Tu quae ex fanis religiosissimis per scelus et latrocinium abstulisti, ea nos videre nisi in tuis amicorumque tuorum tectis non possumus: P. Servilius quae signa atque ornamenta ex urbe hostium vi et virtute capta belli lege atque imperatorio iure sustulit, ea populo Romano adportavit, per triumphum vexit, in tabula publica ad aerarium perscribenda curavit. Cognoscite ex litteris publicis hominis amplissimi diligentiam. Recita. RATIONES RELATAE P. SERVILI. Non solum numerum signorum, sed etiam unius cuiusque magnitudinem, figuram, statum litteris definiri vides. Certe maior est virtutis victoriaeque iucunditas quam ista voluptas quae percipitur ex libidine et cupiditate. Multo diligentius habere dico Servilium praedam populi Romani quam te tua furta notata atque perscripta.

Grammar and Syntax:

- Explain the case and the function of *multo* in the phrase *multo diligentius.*

Style and Theme:

- Compare Cicero's coverage of Verres and Servilius. What are the main points of contrast?
- Describe the dramatic effect of Cicero's address to the court clerk (*recita!*) and his use of public records.
- Compile a lexicon of good practice in accounting: what words and expressions does Cicero use to praise the approach of P. Servilius?
- What stylistic devices does Cicero use to underscore the meticulous accounting of P. Servilius?

[58]   Dices tua quoque signa et tabulas pictas ornamento urbi foroque populi Romani fuisse. Memini; vidi simul cum populo Romano forum comitiumque adornatum ad speciem magnifico ornatu, ad sensum cogitationemque acerbo et lugubri; vidi conlucere omnia furtis tuis, praeda provinciarum, spoliis sociorum atque amicorum. Quo quidem tempore, iudices, iste spem maximam reliquorum quoque peccatorum nactus est; vidit enim eos qui iudiciorum se dominos dici volebant harum cupiditatum esse servos.

Grammar and Syntax:

- Define the case and the function of *ornamento* and *urbi foroque*.

Style and Theme:

- Explore how Cicero handles the theme of sight in the paragraph: who sees what with what consequences and emotional reactions?
- Discuss the rhetorical design of the relative clause *eos qui ... esse servos* and situate Cicero's argument in its wider historical context.

[59]   Socii vero nationesque exterae spem omnem tum primum abiecerunt rerum ac fortunarum suarum, propterea quod casu legati ex Asia atque Achaia plurimi Romae tunc fuerunt, qui deorum simulacra ex suis fanis sublata in foro venerabantur, itemque cetera signa et ornamenta cum cognoscerent, alia alio in loco lacrimantes intuebantur. Quorum omnium hunc sermonem tum esse audiebamus, nihil esse quod quisquam dubitaret de exitio sociorum atque amicorum, cum quidem viderent in foro populi Romani, quo in loco antea qui sociis iniurias fecerant accusari et condemnari solebant, ibi esse palam posita ea quae ab sociis per scelus ablata ereptaque essent.

Grammar and Syntax:

- Explain the case and function of *Romae*.
- What is the antecedent of the relative clause *qui sociis iniurias fecerant*?

Style and Theme:

- Explore how Cicero follows up on the keynote (*Socii*) in the rest of the paragraph.
- How does Cicero generate pathos (and sympathy for the plight of Rome's allies)?
- Discuss Cicero's rhetoric of space.

[60]   Hic ego non arbitror illum negaturum signa se plurima, tabulas pictas innumerabilis habere; sed, ut opinor, solet haec quae rapuit et furatus est non numquam dicere se emisse, quoniam quidem in Achaiam, Asiam, Pamphyliam sumptu publico et legationis nomine mercator signorum tabularumque pictarum missus est. Habeo et ipsius et patris eius accepti tabulas omnis, quas diligentissime legi atque digessi, patris, quoad vixit, tuas, quoad ais te confecisse. Nam in isto, iudices, hoc novum reperietis. Audimus aliquem tabulas numquam confecisse; quae est opinio hominum de Antonio falsa, nam fecit diligentissime; verum sit hoc genus aliquod, minime probandum. Audimus alium non ab initio fecisse, sed ex tempore aliquo coepisse; est aliqua etiam huiusce rei ratio. Hoc vero novum et ridiculum est, quod hic nobis respondit cum ab eo tabulas postularemus, usque ad M. Terentium et C. Cassium consules confecisse, postea destitisse.

Grammar and Syntax:

- Parse the case and function of *illum* and of *se* in the opening sentence.

Style and Theme:

- What stylistic device does Cicero use in the phrase *non numquam*?
- Try to describe the tone of the clause *quoniam quidem … missus est*.
- Extrapolate the typology of accounting built into this paragraph: which types of doing accounts does Cicero mention and how does he appraise each?
- Discuss how Cicero brings Verres' father into play.

[61]   Alio loco hoc cuius modi sit considerabimus; nunc nihil ad me attinet; horum enim temporum in quibus nunc versor habeo tabulas et tuas et patris. Plurima signa pulcherrima, plurimas tabulas optimas deportasse te negare non potes. Atque utinam neges! Unum ostende in tabulis aut tuis aut patris tui emptum esse: vicisti. Ne haec quidem duo signa pulcherrima quae nunc ad impluvium tuum stant, quae multos annos ante valvas Iunonis Samiae steterunt, habes quo modo emeris, haec, inquam, duo quae in aedibus tuis sola iam sunt, quae sectorem exspectant, relicta ac destituta a ceteris signis.

Grammar and Syntax:

- Parse the case and function of *cuius modi*.
- What kind of clause is *atque utinam neges*?
- What type of accusative is *multos annos*?
- Parse *emeris* and explain the mood.

Style and Theme:

- Discuss the way in which Cicero describes the fate of the two statues that remain in Verres' house.

[62]   At, credo, in hisce solis rebus indomitas cupiditates atque effrenatas habebat: ceterae libidines eius ratione aliqua aut modo continebantur. Quam multis istum ingenuis, quam multis matribus familias in illa taetra atque impura legatione vim attulisse existimatis? Ecquo in oppido pedem posuit ubi non plura stuprorum flagitiorumque suorum quam adventus sui vestigia reliquerit? Sed ego omnia quae negari poterunt praetermittam; etiam haec quae certissima sunt et clarissima relinquam; unum aliquod de nefariis istius factis eligam, quo facilius ad Siciliam possim aliquando, quae mihi hoc oneris negotique imposuit, pervenire.

Grammar and Syntax:

- What case and function is *quo* (in *quo facilius…*)?
- Explain the case and function of *oneris negotique*.

Style and Theme:

- What is the tone of the opening sentence?
- What stylistic device does Cicero employ in the phrase *plura … vestigia*? What is the rhetorical effect?
- What stylistic device does Cicero employ in reiterating *quam multis*? What is the rhetorical effect?
- What are the thematic links between this and the previous paragraphs?
- Explore Cicero's portrayal of Verres' character: what metaphors does he use to describe the workings of Verres' mind?

[63]   Oppidum est in Hellesponto Lampsacum, iudices, in primis Asiae provinciae clarum et nobile; homines autem ipsi Lampsaceni cum summe in omnis civis Romanos officiosi, tum praeterea maxime sedati et quieti, prope praeter ceteros ad summum Graecorum otium potius quam ad ullam vim aut tumultum adcommodati. Accidit, cum iste a Cn. Dolabella efflagitasset ut se ad regem Nicomedem regemque Sadalam mitteret, cumque iter hoc sibi magis ad quaestum suum quam ad rei publicae tempus adcommodatum depoposcisset, ut illo itinere veniret Lampsacum cum magna calamitate et prope pernicie civitatis. Deducitur iste ad Ianitorem quendam hospitem, comitesque eius item apud ceteros hospites conlocantur. Ut mos erat istius, atque ut eum suae libidines flagitiosae facere admonebant, statim negotium dat illis suis comitibus, nequissimis turpissimisque hominibus, uti videant et investigent ecqua virgo sit aut mulier digna quam ob rem ipse Lampsaci diutius commoraretur.

Grammar and Syntax:

- What – or rather where – is the verb in the sentence *homines autem ipsi … adcommodati*? What is this device called and what is its effect here?
- What is the meaning of *cum* in *cum summe in omnis civis Romanos officiosi…*?
- On what noun does the genitive *Graecorum* depend?

Style and Theme:

- Analyse the stylistic design of the phrase *cum magna calamitate et prope pernicie civitatis*.
- Discuss Cicero's use of the term *homo/ homines* in this paragraph.
- Describe how Verres interacts with his superior-in-charge.
- What are the main features of the character portrayal of Verres that Cicero develops in this paragraph?

[64]   Erat comes eius Rubrius quidam, homo factus ad istius libidines, qui miro artificio, quocumque venerat, haec investigare omnia solebat. Is ad eum rem istam defert, Philodamum esse quendam, genere, honore, copiis, existimatione facile principem Lampsacenorum; eius esse filiam, quae cum patre habitaret propterea quod virum non haberet, mulierem eximia pulchritudine; sed eam summa integritate pudicitiaque existimari. Homo, ut haec audivit, sic exarsit ad id quod non modo ipse numquam viderat, sed ne audierat quidem ab eo qui ipse vidisset, ut statim ad Philodamum migrare se diceret velle. Hospes Ianitor, qui nihil suspicaretur, veritus ne quid in ipso se offenderetur, hominem summa vi retinere coepit. Iste, qui hospitis relinquendi causam reperire non posset, alia sibi ratione viam munire ad stuprum coepit; Rubrium, delicias suas, in omnibus eius modi rebus adiutorem suum et conscium, parum laute deversari dicit; ad Philodamum deduci iubet.

Grammar and Syntax:

- What kind of ablatives are *genere, honore, copiis,* and *existimatione*?
- What kind of ablatives are *eximia pulchritudine* and *summa integritate pudicitiaque*?
- Why is *suspicaretur* in the subjunctive?
- What type of *ut*-clause is *ut statim … diceret velle*?

Style and Theme:

- How does Cicero characterize Philodamus and his family? What aspects will have resonated particularly well with a Roman audience?
- How does Cicero portray the relationship between Verres and Rubrius?

[65]   Quod ubi est Philodamo nuntiatum, tametsi erat ignarus quantum sibi ac liberis suis iam tum mali constitueretur, tamen ad istum venit; ostendit munus illud suum non esse; se, cum suae partes essent hospitum recipiendorum, tum ipsos tamen praetores et consules, non legatorum adseculas, recipere solere. Iste, qui una cupiditate raperetur, totum illius postulatum causamque neglexit; per vim ad eum, qui recipere non debebat, Rubrium deduci imperavit. Hic Philodamus, posteaquam ius suum obtinere non potuit, ut humanitatem consuetudinemque suam retineret laborabat. Homo, qui semper hospitalissimus amicissimusque nostrorum hominum existimatus esset, noluit videri ipsum illum Rubrium invitus domum suam recepisse; magnifice et ornate, ut erat in primis inter suos copiosus, convivium comparat; rogat Rubrium ut quos ei commodum sit invitet, locum sibi soli, si videatur, relinquat; etiam filium suum, lectissimum adulescentem, foras ad propinquum suum quendam mittit ad cenam.

Grammar and Syntax:

- On what word does the genitive *mali* depend, what type is it, and what do you call the stylistic device that Cicero uses here – and to what effect?
- Explain the subjunctive in the relative clause *Iste, qui una cupiditate raperetur*.
- Explain the tense of *laborabat*.

Style and Theme:

- What is the stylistic device Cicero uses in the formulation *humanitatem consuetudinemque suam*?
- Explore the confrontation between Verres and Philodamus: what are the principal qualities exhibited by each?

[66]   Rubrius istius comites invitat; eos omnis Verres certiores facit quid opus esset. Mature veniunt, discumbitur. Fit sermo inter eos, et invitatio ut Graeco more biberetur; hortatur hospes, poscunt maioribus poculis, celebratur omnium sermone laetitiaque convivium. Posteaquam satis calere res Rubrio visa est, 'Quaeso,' inquit, 'Philodame, cur ad nos filiam tuam non intro vocari iubes?' Homo, qui et summa gravitate et iam id aetatis et parens esset, obstipuit hominis improbi dicto. Instare Rubrius. Tum ille, ut aliquid responderet, negavit moris esse Graecorum ut in convivio virorum accumberent mulieres. Hic tum alius ex alia parte, 'Enim vero ferendum hoc quidem non est; vocetur mulier!' Et simul servis suis Rubrius ut ianuam clauderent et ipsi ad foris adsisterent imperat.

Grammar and Syntax:

- What type of infinitive is *Instare*?
- Define the case and function of *moris*.

Style and Theme:

- Discuss Cicero's use of the passive voice in the passage.
- Where at the banquet is Verres?
- Discuss the clash of cultures (Greece vs. Rome) that Cicero portrays here.

[67]   Quod ubi ille intellexit, id agi atque id parari ut filiae suae vis adferretur, servos suos ad se vocat; his imperat ut se ipsum neglegant, filiam defendant; excurrat aliquis qui hoc tantum domestici mali filio nuntiet. Clamor interea fit tota domo; pugna inter servos Rubri atque hospitis; iactatur domi suae vir primarius et homo honestissimus; pro se quisque manus adfert; aqua denique ferventi a Rubrio ipso Philodamus perfunditur. Haec ubi filio nuntiata sunt, statim exanimatus ad aedis contendit, ut et vitae patris et pudicitiae sororis succurreret; omnes eodem animo Lampsaceni, simul ut hoc audierunt, quod eos cum Philodami dignitas tum iniuriae magnitudo movebat, ad aedis noctu convenerunt. Hic lictor istius Cornelius, qui cum eius servis erat a Rubrio quasi in praesidio ad auferendam mulierem conlocatus, occiditur; servi non nulli vulnerantur; ipse Rubrius in turba sauciatur. Iste, qui sua cupiditate tantos tumultus concitatos videret, cupere aliqua evolare, si posset.

Grammar and Syntax:

- Identify the type of *ut*-clause Cicero uses in the first sentence (*ut filiae suae vis adferretur*).
- Explain the mood of *excurrat*.
- What is the meaning of *cum* in *cum Philodami dignitas* etc.?
- Identify the case and function of *noctu*.

Style and Theme:

- Identify the words in the paragraph that refer to Philodamus' household and dwelling – what overall image of the event is Cicero creating?
- Discuss the movements and the action in the paragraph: who does what (from) where? And where in all of this is Verres?

[68]   Postridie homines mane in contionem conveniunt; quaerunt quid optimum factu sit; pro se quisque, ut in quoque erat auctoritatis plurimum, ad populum loquebatur; inventus est nemo cuius non haec et sententia esset et oratio, non esse metuendum, si istius nefarium scelus Lampsaceni ulti vi manuque essent, ne senatus populusque Romanus in eam civitatem animadvertendum putaret; quodsi hoc iure legati populi Romani in socios nationesque exteras uterentur, ut pudicitiam liberorum servare ab eorum libidine tutam non liceret, quidvis esse perpeti satius quam in tanta vi atque acerbitate versari.

Grammar and Syntax:

- Define the form and function of *factu*.
- What kind of genitive is *auctoritatis*?
- What is the case and function of *quidvis*?

Style and Theme:

- How does Cicero present the civic community of Lampsacus to his Roman audience?

[69]   Haec cum omnes sentirent, et cum in eam rationem pro suo quisque sensu ac dolore loqueretur, omnes ad eam domum in qua iste deversabatur profecti sunt; caedere ianuam saxis, instare ferro, ligna et sarmenta circumdare ignemque subicere coeperunt. Tunc cives Romani, qui Lampsaci negotiabantur, concurrunt; orant Lampsacenos ut gravius apud eos nomen legationis quam iniuria legati putaretur; sese intellegere hominem illum esse impurum ac nefarium, sed quoniam nec perfecisset quod conatus esset, neque futurus esset Lampsaci postea, levius eorum peccatum fore si homini scelerato pepercissent quam si legato non pepercissent.

Grammar and Syntax:

- What case is *Lampsaci*?
- Explain the syntax of *sese intellegere hominem illum esse impurum ac nefarium*.

Style and Theme:

- What is the technical term for the stylistic device Cicero uses in the formulations *nomen legationis ~ iniuria legati*?
- Discuss how the use of the comparative (*gravius*, *levius*) figures in the reasoning of the Romans.

[70]   Sic iste multo sceleratior et nequior quam ille Hadrianus aliquanto etiam felicior fuit. Ille, quod eius avaritiam cives Romani ferre non potuerunt, Uticae domi suae vivus exustus est, idque ita illi merito accidisse existimatum est ut laetarentur omnes neque ulla animadversio constitueretur: hic sociorum ambustus incendio tamen ex illa flamma periculoque evolavit, neque adhuc causam ullam excogitare potuit quam ob rem commiserit, aut quid evenerit, ut in tantum periculum veniret. Non enim potest dicere, 'cum seditionem sedare vellem, cum frumentum imperarem, cum stipendium cogerem, cum aliquid denique rei publicae causa gererem, quod acrius imperavi, quod animadverti, quod minatus sum.' Quae si diceret, tamen ignosci non oporteret, si nimis atrociter imperando sociis in tantum adductus periculum videretur.

Grammar and Syntax:

- Identify the case and function of *multo*.
- Identify the case of *Uticae* and of *domi suae*.
- What kind of conditional clause is *Quae si diceret, …*?

Style and Theme:

- What stylistic device does Cicero use in the formulation *flamma periculoque*?
- What rhetorical techniques does Cicero employ to make Verres' close shave with death appear justified?
- Compare and contrast the tone of *quod acrius imperavi* and *nimis atrociter imperando sociis*.

[71]   Nunc cum ipse causam illius tumultus neque veram dicere neque falsam confingere audeat, homo autem ordinis sui frugalissimus, qui tum accensus C. Neroni fuit, P. Tettius, haec eadem se Lampsaci cognosse dixerit, vir omnibus rebus ornatissimus, C. Varro, qui tum in Asia militum tribunus fuit, haec eadem se ipso ex Philodamo audisse dicat, potestis dubitare quin istum fortuna non tam ex illo periculo eripere voluerit quam ad vestrum iudicium reservare? Nisi vero illud dicet, quod et in Tetti testimonio priore actione interpellavit Hortensius – quo tempore quidem signi satis dedit, si quid esset quod posset dicere, se tacere non posse, ut, quam diu tacuit in ceteris testibus, scire omnes possemus nihil habuisse quod diceret: hoc tum dixit, Philodamum et filium eius a C. Nerone esse damnatos.

Grammar and Syntax:

- What case is *Lampsaci*?
- Explain the case and function of *signi*.

Style and Theme:

- Compare and contrast how Cicero presents (the evidence of) his two witnesses, Tettius and Varro.
- Explore how Cicero tries to deflect Hortensius' challenge to his witness during the first *actio*.

[72]   De quo ne multa disseram tantum dico, secutum id esse Neronem et eius consilium: quod Cornelium lictorem occisum esse constaret, putasse non oportere esse cuiquam ne in ulciscenda quidem iniuria hominis occidendi potestatem. In quo video Neronis iudicio non te absolutum esse improbitatis, sed illos damnatos esse caedis. Verum ista damnatio tamen cuius modi fuit? Audite, quaeso, iudices, et aliquando miseremini sociorum et ostendite aliquid iis in vestra fide praesidi esse oportere. Quod toti Asiae iure occisus videbatur istius ille verbo lictor, re vera minister improbissimae cupiditatis, pertimuit iste ne Philodamus Neronis iudicio liberaretur; rogat et orat Dolabellam ut de sua provincia decedat, ad Neronem proficiscatur; se demonstrat incolumem esse non posse, si Philodamo vivere atque aliquando Romam venire licuisset.

Grammar and Syntax:

- What kind of genitives are *improbitatis* and *caedis*?
- What kind of genitive is *praesidi*? On what word does it depend?

Style and Theme:

- What is the rhetorical effect of the sentence that begins *Audite, quaeso*…?
- What stylistic device does Cicero employ in the phrase *aliquid iis in vestra fide praesidi*? What is the rhetorical effect?

[73]   Commotus est Dolabella: fecit id quod multi reprehenderunt, ut exercitum, provinciam, bellum relinqueret, et in Asiam hominis nequissimi causa in alienam provinciam proficisceretur. Posteaquam ad Neronem venit, contendit ab eo ut Philodami causam cognosceret. Venerat ipse qui esset in consilio et primus sententiam diceret; adduxerat etiam praefectos et tribunos militaris suos, quos Nero omnis in consilium vocavit; erat in consilio etiam aequissimus iudex ipse Verres; erant non nulli togati creditores Graecorum, quibus ad exigendas pecunias improbissimi cuiusque legati plurimum prodest gratia.

Grammar and Syntax:

- What type of *ut*-clause is *ut … relinqueret*?
- *qui esset in consilio et primus sententiam diceret*: explain the use of the subjunctives.

Style and Theme:

- Identify the stylistic devices that Cicero uses in *ut exercitum, provinciam, bellum relinqueret* and discuss their rhetorical effect.
- Discuss Cicero's use of the superlative in the paragraph, with special reference to *hominis nequissimi causa, aequissimus iudex ipse Verres, improbissimi cuiusque legati*, and *plurimum prodest*.
- How does Cicero discredit the *consilium* that advised Nero?

[74]   Ille miser defensorem reperire neminem poterat; quis enim esset aut togatus, qui Dolabellae gratia, aut Graecus, qui eiusdem vi et imperio non moveretur? Accusator autem adponitur civis Romanus de creditoribus Lampsacenorum; qui si dixisset quod iste iussisset, per eiusdem istius lictores a populo pecuniam posset exigere. Cum haec omnia tanta contentione, tantis copiis agerentur; cum illum miserum multi accusarent, nemo defenderet; cumque Dolabella cum suis praefectis pugnaret in consilio, Verres fortunas agi suas diceret, idem testimonium diceret, idem esset in consilio, idem accusatorem parasset – haec cum omnia fierent, et cum hominem constaret occisum, tamen tanta vis istius iniuriae, tanta in isto improbitas putabatur ut de Philodamo amplius pronuntiaretur.

Grammar and Syntax:

- *quis enim esset aut togatus*: explain the subjunctive.
- What is the main verb of the sentence beginning with *Cum haec omnia…*?

Style and Theme:

- What is the technical term for Cicero's repeated use of *cum*?
- Analyze the rhetorical effect of Cicero's repetition of *idem*.
- What is the effect of Cicero's repeated use of passives in this paragraph (*adponitur, agerentur, putabatur, pronuntiaretur*)?

[75]   Quid ego nunc in altera actione Cn. Dolabellae spiritus, quid huius lacrimas et concursationes proferam, quid C. Neronis, viri optimi atque innocentissimi, non nullis in rebus animum nimium timidum atque demissum? qui in illa re quid facere potuerit non habebat, nisi forte, id quod omnes tum desiderabant, ut ageret eam rem sine Verre et sine Dolabella. Quicquid esset sine his actum, omnes probarent; tum vero quod pronuntiatum est non per Neronem iudicatum, sed per Dolabellam ereptum existimabatur. Condemnatur enim perpaucis sententiis Philodamus et eius filius. Adest, instat, urget Dolabella ut quam primum securi feriantur, quo quam minime multi ex illis de istius nefario scelere audire possent.

Grammar and Syntax:

- Explain the subjunctives in the sentence *quicquid esset sine his actum, omnes probarent*.
- What are the case and function of *securi*?

Style and Theme:

- What do you call the stylistic device Cicero uses in the phrase *non nullis in rebus*? What is the rhetorical effect?
- Analyse the stylistic features and the rhetorical effect of *Adest, instat, urget Dolabella*.
- Discuss the seemingly awkward formulation *quam minime multi* – what, exactly, is Cicero trying to convey by it?

[76]   Constituitur in foro Laodiceae spectaculum acerbum et miserum et grave toti Asiae provinciae, grandis natu parens adductus ad supplicium, ex altera parte filius, ille quod pudicitiam liberorum, hic quod vitam patris famamque sororis defenderat. Flebat uterque non de suo supplicio, sed pater de fili morte, de patris filius. Quid lacrimarum ipsum Neronem putatis profudisse? quem fletum totius Asiae fuisse, quem luctum et gemitum Lampsacenorum? securi esse percussos homines innocentis nobilis, socios populi Romani atque amicos, propter hominis flagitiosissimi singularem nequitiam atque improbissimam cupiditatem!

Grammar and Syntax:

- Explain the case and function of *natu*.
- Explain the case and function of *lacrimarum*.

Style and Theme:

- Analyse the arrangement of *sed pater de fili morte, de patris filius*. What is the rhetorical effect of Cicero's chosen design?
- What are the means by which Cicero generates pathos?

[77]   Iam iam, Dolabella, neque me tui neque tuorum liberorum, quos tu miseros in egestate atque in solitudine reliquisti, misereri potest. Verresne tibi tanti fuit ut eius libidinem hominum innocentium sanguine lui velles? Idcircone exercitum atque hostem relinquebas ut tua vi et crudelitate istius hominis improbissimi pericula sublevares? Quod enim eum tibi quaestoris in loco constitueras, idcirco tibi amicum in perpetuum fore putasti? nesciebas ab eo Cn. Carbonem consulem, cuius re vera quaestor fuerat, non modo relictum sed etiam spoliatum auxiliis, pecunia, nefarie oppugnatum et proditum? Expertus igitur es istius perfidiam tum cum ipse se ad inimicos tuos contulit, cum in te homo ipse nocens acerrimum testimonium dixit, cum rationes ad aerarium nisi damnato te referre noluit.

Grammar and Syntax:

- Explain the case and function of *tanti*.
- Explain the grammar and syntax of *nisi damnato te*.

Style and Theme:

- Collect all instances of personal pronouns and possessive adjectives in the paragraph and explore their role in Cicero's rhetoric.
- Describe the tone in which Cicero attacks Dolabella.
- How does Cicero employ Roman political norms and recent history against Verres and Dolabella?

[78]   Tantaene tuae, Verres, libidines erunt ut eas capere ac sustinere non provinciae populi Romani, non nationes exterae possint? Tune quod videris, quod audieris, quod concupieris, quod cogitaris, nisi id ad nutum tuum praesto fuerit, nisi libidini tuae cupiditatique paruerit, immittentur homines, expugnabuntur domus, civitates non modo pacatae, verum etiam sociorum atque amicorum ad vim atque ad arma confugient, ut ab se atque a liberis suis legati populi Romani scelus ac libidinem propulsare possint? Nam quaero abs te circumsessusne sis Lampsaci, coeperitne domum in qua deversabare illa multitudo incendere, voluerintne legatum populi Romani comburere vivum Lampsaceni? Negare non potes; habeo enim testimonium tuum quod apud Neronem dixisti, habeo quas ad eundem litteras misisti. Recita hunc ipsum locum de testimonio. TESTIMONIUM C. VERRIS IN ARTEMIDORUM. NON MULTO POST IN DOMUM.

Grammar and Syntax:

- Parse *concupieris, cogitaris,* and *deversabare.*

Style and Theme:

- Explore the function of Verres' *libido* (or *libidines*) in Cicero's argument.
- Compare and contrast the style of the first half of the paragraph (*Tantaene … propulsare possint?*) with the second half (*Nam quaero … IN DOMUM*).

[79]   Bellumne populo Romano Lampsacena civitas facere conabatur? deficere ab imperio ac nomine nostro volebat? Video enim et ex iis quae legi et audivi intellego, in qua civitate non modo legatus populi Romani circumsessus, non modo igni, ferro, manu, copiis oppugnatus, sed aliqua ex parte violatus sit, nisi publice satis factum sit, ei civitati bellum indici atque inferri solere.

Grammar and Syntax:

- Parse *conabatur* and explain the significance of the tense.

Style and Theme:

- Analyse the rhetorical design of the relative clause *in qua civitate … violatus sit* and discuss how design reinforces theme.

[80]   Quae fuit igitur causa cur cuncta civitas Lampsacenorum de contione, quem ad modum tute scribis, domum tuam concurreret? Tu enim neque in litteris quas Neroni mittis, neque in testimonio causam tanti tumultus ostendis ullam. Obsessum te dicis, ignem adlatum, sarmenta circumdata, lictorem tuum occisum esse dicis, prodeundi tibi in publicum potestatem factam negas: causam huius tanti terroris occultas. Nam si quam Rubrius iniuriam suo nomine ac non impulsu tuo et tua cupiditate fecisset, de tui comitis iniuria questum ad te potius quam te oppugnatum venirent. Cum igitur quae causa illius tumultus fuerit testes a nobis producti dixerint, ipse celarit, nonne causam hanc quam nos proposuimus cum illorum testimonia tum istius taciturnitas perpetua confirmat?

Grammar and Syntax:

- What type of ablative is *a nobis*?

Style and Theme:

- Explore how Cicero operates with the word *causa* in this paragraph.

[81] Huic homini parcetis igitur, iudices, cuius tanta peccata sunt ut ii quibus iniurias fecerit neque legitimum tempus exspectare ad ulciscendum neque vim tantam doloris in posterum differre potuerint? Circumsessus es. A quibus? A Lampsacenis. Barbaris hominibus, credo, aut iis qui populi Romani nomen contemnerent. Immo vero ab hominibus et natura et consuetudine et disciplina lenissimis, porro autem populi Romani condicione sociis, fortuna servis, voluntate supplicibus: ut perspicuum sit omnibus, nisi tanta acerbitas iniuriae, tanta vis sceleris fuisset ut Lampsaceni moriendum sibi potius quam perpetiendum putarent, numquam illos in eum locum progressuros fuisse ut vehementius odio libidinis tuae quam legationis metu moverentur.

Grammar and Syntax:

- What types (pl.!) of ablative are *condicione sociis, fortuna servis, voluntate supplicibus*?

Style and Theme:

- Discuss the factors that, according to Cicero, shape the character and the actions of the Lampsacenes, both normally and in the situation of crisis triggered by Verres.

[82]   Nolite, per deos immortalis, cogere socios atque exteras nationes hoc uti perfugio, quo, nisi vos vindicatis, utentur necessario! Lampsacenos in istum numquam ulla res mitigasset nisi eum poenas Romae daturum credidissent: etsi talem acceperant iniuriam, quam nulla lege satis digne persequi possent, tamen incommoda sua nostris committere legibus et iudiciis quam dolori suo permittere maluerunt. Tu mihi, cum circumsessus a tam inlustri civitate sis propter tuum scelus atque flagitium, cum coegeris homines miseros et calamitosos quasi desperatis nostris legibus et iudiciis ad vim, ad manus, ad arma confugere, cum te in oppidis et civitatibus amicorum non legatum populi Romani, sed tyrannum libidinosum crudelemque praebueris, cum apud exteras nationes imperi nominisque nostri famam tuis probris flagitiisque violaris, cum te ex ferro amicorum populi Romani eripueris atque ex flamma sociorum evolaris, hic tibi perfugium speras futurum? Erras: ut huc incideres, non ut hic conquiesceres, illi te vivum exire passi sunt.

Grammar and Syntax:

- What kind of condition is *Lampsacenos in istum numquam ulla res mitigasset nisi eum poenas Romae daturum credidissent*?

Style and Theme:

- Analyse the design of the sentence *Tu mihi … speras futurum?*

[83]   Et ais iudicium esse factum te iniuria circumsessum esse Lampsaci, quod Philodamus cum filio condemnatus sit. Quid, si doceo, si planum facio teste homine nequam, verum ad hanc rem tamen idoneo – te ipso, inquam, teste docebo te huius circumsessionis tuae causam et culpam in alios transtulisse, neque in eos, quos tu insimularas, esse animadversum. iam nihil te iudicium Neronis adiuvat. Recita quas ad Neronem litteras misit. EPISTULA C. VERRIS AD NERONEM. THEMISTAGORAS ET THESSALUS –. Themistagoram et Thessalum scribis populum concitasse. Quem populum? Qui te circumsedit, qui te vivum comburere conatus est. Ubi hos persequeris, ubi accusas, ubi defendis ius nomenque legati? in Philodami iudicio dices id actum?

Grammar and Syntax:

- What kind of construction is *teste homine nequam*?

Style and Theme:

- Analyse the rhetorical design of *Ubi hos persequeris, ubi accusas, ubi defendis ius nomenque legati?*
- Explore Cicero's use of documentary evidence.

[84]   Cedo mihi ipsius Verris testimonium: videamus quid idem iste iuratus dixerit. Recita. AB ACCUSATORE ROGATUS RESPONDIT IN HOC IUDICIO NON PERSEQUI: SIBI IN ANIMO ESSE ALIO TEMPORE PERSEQUI. Quid igitur te iuvat Neronis iudicium, quid Philodami damnatio? Legatus cum esses circumsessus, cumque, quem ad modum tute ad Neronem scripsisti, populo Romano communique causae legatorum facta esset insignis iniuria, non es persecutus: dicis tibi in animo esse alio tempore persequi. Quod fuit id tempus? quando es persecutus? Cur imminuisti ius legationis, cur causam populi Romani deseruisti ac prodidisti, cur iniurias tuas coniunctas cum publicis reliquisti? Non te ad senatum causam deferre, non de tam atrocibus iniuriis conqueri, non eos homines qui populum concitarant consulum litteris evocandos curare oportuit?

Grammar and Syntax:

- Parse *videamus*.

Style and Theme:

- Explore the stylistic design of the *cum*-clause *Legatus cum … insignis iniuria*.

[85]   Nuper M. Aurelio Scauro postulante, quod is Ephesi se quaestorem vi prohibitum esse dicebat quo minus e fano Dianae servum suum, qui in illud asylum confugisset, abduceret, Pericles Ephesius, homo nobilissimus, Romam evocatus est, quod auctor illius iniuriae fuisse arguebatur: tu, si te legatum ita Lampsaci tractatum esse senatum docuisses ut tui comites vulnerarentur, lictor occideretur, ipse circumsessus paene incenderere, eius autem rei duces et auctores et principes fuisse, quos scribis, Themistagoram et Thessalum, quis non commoveretur, quis non ex iniuria quae tibi esset facta sibi provideret, quis non in ea re causam tuam, periculum commune agi arbitraretur? Etenim nomen legati eius modi esse debet quod non modo inter sociorum iura, sed etiam inter hostium tela incolume versetur.

[86]   Magnum hoc Lampsacenum crimen est libidinis atque improbissimae cupiditatis: accipite nunc avaritiae prope modum in suo genere non levius…

Grammar and Syntax:

- What construction is *M. Aurelio Scauro postulante*?
- Parse *incenderere*.

Style and Theme:

- Explore the similarities and differences in Cicero's portrayal of the incident involving M. Aurelius Scaurus and of Verres' handling of the Lampsacus affair.

Commentary

§ 53

Cicero's main aim in this paragraph is to illustrate the magnitude of Verres' greed, in particular how it manifests itself in comprehensive looting. The contrast between what Cicero will *not* say and what he *is* saying (*non dicam – hoc dico*), made more forceful by the demonstrative pronoun *hoc*, is between selective thieving and systematic plunder. The paragraph thus continues themes that are prominent throughout Cicero's portrayal of Verres: complete lack of self-control, resulting in the uninhibited indulgence in excessive behaviour, especially where objects of art and sex are concerned.

A key theme in the paragraph is Cicero's depiction of public and private space: the town of Aspendos, with its richly adorned temples and civic spaces, is set in contrast to the location where the treasures end up: the house of Verres. Note, too, how in the course of the paragraph Cicero alternates his addressees: he begins with a gesture to the judges (*scitis*), then switches to Verres (named in the vocative), before concluding with a sentence in third-person reporting mode (*sustulit … posuit*), which, however, includes a relative clause that is again addressed directly to the judges (*de quo … audistis*).

Aspendum vetus oppidum et nobile in Pamphylia scitis esse, plenissimum signorum optimorum. Non dicam illinc hoc signum ablatum esse et illud. hoc dico, nullum te Aspendi signum, Verres, reliquisse: Cicero uses *homoioteleuton as a stylistic device to connect three main themes of the paragraph: (i) the town of Aspendos, (ii) its rich treasure of statues, and (iii) their plunder by Verres. Even after the climactic *nullum signum*, the ending -*um* continues Cicero's habit of underscoring thematic coherence by means of stylistic coherence: in his discussion of the one item of art singled out for special attention, that is the introspective cithara-player, *homoioteleuton recurs (*illum Aspendium citharistam; illum ipsum*). Some may consider a recurrent *um*-ending plodding, or even cacophonous in principle, but here it produces an *onomatopoetic effect that enhances Cicero's feeling of outrage at Verres' misdeeds.[43]

Aspendum: located on the Southern coast of Turkey on the right bank of the river Eurymedon (between the modern tourist hotspots Antalya and Alanya), Aspendos was a significant centre of trade in ancient times, especially for salt, oil, grain, and wool; after the battle of Magnesia in 190 BC, it became part of the kingdom of Pergamum, which King Attalus III, at his death without heir, bequeathed to Rome in 133 BC. Still, it is unclear whether all members of Cicero's Roman audience would have been able to locate the town securely on a map.

Aspendi: a locative ('in Aspendos').

vetus: Cicero may allude to Greek traditions according to which the city was founded by 'the Argives', perhaps in the aftermath of the Trojan war. The evidence is murky.[44] In 44 BC, when he wrote the *de Divinatione*, Cicero was familiar with local lore (*Div.* 1.88: *Amphilochus et Mopsus Argivorum reges fuerunt, sed iidem augures, iique urbis in ora maritima Ciliciae Graecas condiderunt*), but this is just the sort of information he could have picked up during his pro-consulship in Cilicia in 51 BC.

nobile: the attribute strikes a note of pathos and, also from an etymological point of view [*nosco + bilis*], points forward to *scitis*: the city, Cicero claims, is so renowned that its prestige and location can count as common knowledge.

Pamphylia: a region on the Southern coast of Asia Minor, between Lycia in the West and 'rough' Cilicia in the East; at the time of the trial it was part of the Roman province of Cilicia, though until recently it had also served as a stronghold of pirates – suppressed in 77 BC by Publius Servilius Vatia Isauricus (see below § 56).

43. Hofman, J. B., Szantyr , A. (1965), *Lateinische Syntax und Stilistik*, vol. 2, Munich, 707: 'the frequent use of -*um* is cacophonous'.
44. See Scheer, T. (1993), *Mythische Vorväter: Zur Bedeutung griechischer Heroenmythen im Selbstverständnis kleinasiatischer Städte*, Munich, 203–11.

scitis: To what extent that was indeed the case is difficult to ascertain; but the deliberate over-estimation of the degree of insight and knowledge of the audience on the part of an orator is a well-known technique of currying favour by means of flattery, or, in Latin, *captatio benevolentiae*. Cicero, at any rate, typically characterized his audience as being more knowledgeable than it most likely was. See also the note on *de quo saepe audistis* below.

scitis ... te..., Verres: the second person plural addressing the judges, the deictic pronoun, and the vocative are all features that produce and sustain the illusion of a life-performance: Cicero wants his audience to re-imagine the courtroom setting and him turning to and directly addressing the main parties involved in the trial: here he makes a gesture to the judges before turning to the defendant. (For deixis and the adjective 'deictic', which comes from the Greek *deiktikos*, meaning 'able to show, showing directly' see Morwood (1999) 151: 'the use of words or expressions to *point* to some feature of a situation. Pronouns ... and words of place ... and time tell us such things about a situation as who is involved in it, and where or when it takes place.' Throughout his corpus of speeches, which reproduce in written form a past or imagined performance, Cicero retains deictic features to recreate the dramatic setting: he wishes to generate the impression for his audience that they are actually there.)

plenissimum: Cicero is very fond of 'extreme' expressions, such as superlatives (as here; see also *optimorum* and *intimis*) or adjectives that articulate extremes or a sense of totality, such as *nullus* and *omnis* (which in this paragraph alone occurs three times): see next note.

hoc signum ... et illud ... nullum ... signum ... omnia: The sentence explains what happened to the richness of the city. Cicero contrasts a selective removal of 'this or that statue' with Verres' approach to plunder, which is meticulously comprehensive: '*none* was left, *all* were taken'. By varying the verbs (*reliquisse*; *evecta exportataque esse*), Cicero manages to apply both of the antithetical poles 'none' and 'all' to Verres' despoilment of Aspendos, in keeping with his preference for 'extreme' expressions (see note on *plenissimum* above).

Non dicam: 'an effective form of *comparatio*, rising from a lesser variety of wrongdoing to a greater': Mitchell (1986) 185.

hoc dico…: Latin authors frequently add a demonstrative pronoun to verbs of thinking and stating that introduce an accusative + infinitive construction to give special emphasis to the indirect statement: '*This* I say, namely that you…' The feature gains in force and prominence here by way of contrast to the *non-dicam* clause, where Cicero does not use it.

nullum te Aspendi signum, Verres, reliquisse, omnia ex fanis, ex locis publicis, palam, spectantibus omnibus, plaustris evecta exportataque esse: Cicero builds up carefully towards this quick-fire sentence, with its notably *asyndetic style. Contrast the 'leisurely' and exactly parallel constructions *vetus oppidum et nobile* and (with added *hyberbaton) *hoc signum … et illud* with the absence of connectives here: Cicero uses none between *reliquisse* and *evecta exportataque esse*, *ex fanis* and *ex locis publicis*, or *palam, spectantibus omnibus*, and *plaustris*. Other rhetorical features energize Cicero's 'rhetorical pouncing': the switch from the (retarding) future *non dicam* to the much more immediate present *dico*; the use of the demonstrative pronoun *hoc* (see previous note); the switch from a generalizing passive construction in the indirect statement after *non dicam* (*signum ablatum esse*) to the active *reliquisse* with a specific agent (*te*), reinforced by a direct address (*Verres*); and the expansion of the idea of 'carrying away' from the single *ablatum esse* to the *alliterative *pleonasm *evecta exportataque esse*. Note also the crescendo from one accusative object (*omnia*) to two prepositional phrases in the ablative, the second with an attribute (*ex fanis, ex locis publicis*), to three phrases indicating modalities of removal: *palam* (an adverb), *spectantibus omnibus* (an ablative absolute), *plaustris* (an instrumental ablative).

Aspendium citharistam … quem omnia 'intus canere' dicebant: The cithara was a musical instrument similar to a lyre. *Aspendioi kitharistai* – that is, cithara-players of Aspendos – were known for their custom of playing the instrument, designed for both hands, with their left hand only, which was placed between the cithara and the player (hence *intus*), without using the right hand that held the plectron and was placed 'outside', facing the audience. Pseudo-Asconius' commentary on this passage is worth quoting in full since it brings out an otherwise obscure nuance of Cicero's text:[45]

> *cum canunt citharistae, utriusque manus funguntur officio. Dextra plectro utitur, et hoc est foris canere; sinistrae digiti chordas carpunt, et hoc est intus canere. Difficile*

---

45. Stangl, T. (1964), *Ciceronis Orationum Scholiastae*, Hildesheim (photographic reprint of 1912 edition).

est autem quod Aspendius citharista faciebat: ut non uteretur cantu utraque manu, sed omnia, id est universam cantionem, intus et sinistra tantum manu complecteretur. Unde omnes quotquot fures erant a Graecis Aspendii citharistae in proverbio dicebantur, quod, ut ille carminis, ita isti furtorum occultatores erant. Valet hoc proverbium et in eos qui multum intestinis suis commodis consulunt praeter honestatem. (When cithara-players perform, they make use of both hands: the right hand uses the plectron and this is called 'to perform outside'; the fingers of the left hand pluck the strings and this is called 'to perform inside'. But what the cithara-player of Aspendos is wont to do is difficult: for he does not use both hands in a performance, but does everything, that is, the entire performance, 'inside' and with the left hand only. This is the reason why the Greeks proverbially called all thieves 'Aspendian cithara-players': he concealed his music-playing, just as these concealed their thefts. This proverb also applies to those who look much after their own personal interests at the expense of moral rectitude.)

In the light of this observation, Cicero seems to be cracking a complex joke here: in addition to the analogy between the 'hiding away' performed by the statue and by Verres (the former shielding his playing of music from the audience, the latter concealing his plunder from public viewing), the statue itself is proverbially associated with thievery, which means that Verres imitates and outdoes his looted artwork. This nuance, however, which Cicero does not explicitly emphasize in the text itself, would only have been apparent to those members of Cicero's audience familiar with the Greek proverb, and it is by no means certain that all (or any) of them were (see also next note, *de quo saepe audistis*).

de quo saepe audistis: the knowledge of a Roman court audience is difficult to calibrate but the assumption that many of the senators that sat in judgement at Verres' trial had frequently heard of a piece of proverbial commentary based on a specific type of Greek statuary is probably no more than that – an assumption. By turning it into a fact, Cicero both flatters and bullies the audience: since no one likes to appear ignorant, presumably even those members of the audience (most likely the majority) who had never heard of either the statue or the proverb would have nodded knowingly. The problem is of course less acute when we imagine the context of reception to be not an oral performance during a public trial, but a private reading session at a villa: in that case, any reader unfamiliar with the proverb and interested in ascertaining its wider significance could have found out by quizzing one of his learned Greek slaves.

quem omnia 'intus canere' dicebant: the antecedent of *quem* is *citharistam*; the relative pronoun *quem* is the subject accusative of the indirect statement introduced by *dicebant*; *omnia* is accusative object of *canere*. The (fairly frequent) phenomenon of a relative pronoun assuming a twofold syntactic function is best illustrated by rephrasing the relative clause as a main clause: *eum omnia 'intus canere' dicebant* – 'they used to say that he played all of his music inside'. It is impossible to reproduce this construction literally in English: one can either turn the relative clause into a main clause or add the verb in apposition, i.e. 'who, as they used to say, played all of his music inside'.

intus canere: as discussed above, the expression refers to a technique of playing only that side of the cithara which is turned away from the audience: Cicero quips that Verres has outdone the activity represented by the statue by hiding it away in the innermost part of his house. This is in direct antithesis to the emphasis on the public despoiling (*palam*), which everyone witnessed as onlookers (*omnibus spectantibus*).

intus – intimus: a *paronomasia; Cicero plays with the fact that the two words are etymologically related.

§ 54

Building on the themes and the idiom of the previous paragraph, Cicero increases the intensity of his condemnation. Particularly aggressive features are: (a) the emphasis on a specific and highly venerable shrine (inclusive of its cult statue), that Verres violated, in contrast to the generic reference to shrines (*ex fanis*) in § 53; (b) the use of verbs from the sphere of warfare and military plunder (see esp. *spoliare* and *invadere*) to characterize Verres' 'collections' of artworks; and (c) the inclusion of an emotive exclamation (*quae, malum, est ista tanta audacia atque amentia!*) that gives the impression that Cicero has reached the limits of his rhetoric – Verres' actions are depraved beyond words.

The contrast between public and private continues: Cicero argues that military commanders displayed the spoils of their victory in the public spaces of Rome, rather than using them to adorn their personal estates. It is worth stressing that the picture he draws is highly idealized. Roman generals had much leeway over how to dispose of booty: they could distribute it among their soldiers, keep it for themselves, or hand it over to the public treasury (or any combination thereof). In general, the handling of booty was a highly controversial issue throughout the Republic.[46] The famous quip of Cato the Elder that thieves of private property are put into shackles and fetters, whereas 'public thieves' (i.e. Roman generals) lead a life in wealth and luxury arguably offers a more realistic perspective, at cross-purposes to the one evoked by Cicero (see Aulus Gellius, *Attic Nights* 11.18.18: *fures privatorum furtorum in nervo atque in compedibus aetatem agunt, fures publici in auro atque in purpura*): personal enrichment through war spoils was a prime source of financial and symbolic capital in Roman politics, especially during the last two centuries of the Republic.

What Cicero passes over in silence is that Verres could apparently rely on the help of local collaborators. Thus he mentions in a later speech that an inhabitant of Perge, a doctor with the name Artemidorus, acted as Verres' executor and mastermind in the despoilment of his own native town and subsequently became Verres' personal doctor and a member of his entourage under the name Cornelius. See *Ver.* 2.3.54: ... *Cornelium – is est Artemidorus Pergaeus, qui in sua patria dux isti quondam et magister ad spoliandum Dianae templum fuit*; and 2.3.68 where Cicero again calls Artemidorus a temple-robber and takes exception to his 'sudden' assumption of a Roman name. Here, Cicero mentions none of this since it would have enfeebled his attempt to brand Verres as the lone culprit.

Pergae: the capital of Pamphylia. The form is the locative ('in Perge').

fanum ... Dianae: Perge was famous for its temple of Artemis (the Greek equivalent to Diana), the second most distinguished site of worship of the goddess in Asia Minor outside Ephesus. In the cult practice of Asian Greeks, Artemis was not primarily the virgin goddess of the hunt (her dominant image in much of Greek mythology), but the mother goddess who represented natural fertility.[47] Cicero is distinctly disinterested in

---

46. For a good discussion of the topic see Shatzman, I. (1972), 'The Roman General's Authority Over Booty', *Historia* 21, 177–205. The most recent treatment is a French-German edited collection: M. Coudry, M. and Humm, M. (eds.) (2009), *Praeda. Butin de guerre et société dans la Rome républicaine / Kriegsbeute und Gesellschaft im republikanischen Rom*, Stuttgart.
47. For discussions of Artemis, see Burkert, W. (1985), *Greek Religion*, trans. by J. Raffan, Cambridge, Mass., 149–52; Vernant, J.-P. (1991), *Mortals and Immortals: Collected Essays*, ed. by F. I. Zeitlin, Princeton, 195-257; Ferguson, J. (1970), *Religions of the Roman East*,

these religious nuances, though he may play on the association of Diana with chastity and virginity (see note on *nudatum ac spoliatum*).

antiquissimum et sanctissimum: Cicero continues in superlative mode, here rightly so: the cult site *was* very ancient and sacred.

scimus: in variation to the *scitis* and *audistis* in § 53, Cicero here uses the first person plural, thereby constituting a community of knowledge that includes himself and the judges. See also §§ 55 (*videmus*), 59 (*audiebamus*), 60 (*audimus*, two times), 61 (*considerabimus*), 84 (*videamus*).

id quodque ... esse dico: in the course of this sentence, Cicero picks up *fanum ... Dianae* in two ways: he proceeds from the shrine itself to its centre, that is the cult statue, and in doing so he renders the abstract divinity material and concrete – ready for the taking.

nudatum ac spoliatum: as in § 53 (the *assonance *evecta *exportataque*), Cicero describes Verres' actions by pairing two verbs: see also *detractum atque ablatum*. The same stylistic habit is on display in his exclamatory comment *ista tanta audacia atque amentia* (again reinforced by assonance), the phrase *sociorum atque amicorum*, the description of Verres' legal status (*legationis iure et nomine*), the hypothetical scenario of warfare (*cum exercitu imperioque*) and his description of the spoils (*signa atque ornamenta*).

spoliatum esse, ex ipsa Diana ... ablatum esse dico: Cicero *asyndetically juxtaposes the two indirect statements depending on *dico*. The effect is jarring, especially because of the switch in the subject accusative from *id* (that is, *fanum*) to *[id] quod habebat auri*. (See further below on *auri*.)

ex ipsa Diana: the formulation has considerable shock value: Cicero's formulation deliberately blurs the distinction between the goddess and her cult statue, thus suggesting that Verres does not shy away from laying hands on the deity, and his earlier use of *nudatum* may proleptically introduce a sexual aspect to this act of aggression. In Rome, Diana is famed for her chastity and commitment to virginity, though her cultic significance in Perge will have focused on different aspects (see above on

---

Ithaca, NY, 21-22; for the cult site at Perge in particular: Pace, B. (1923), 'Diana Pergaea', in W. H. Buckler and W. M. Calder (eds.), *Anatolian Studies presented to Sir William Mitchell Ramsay*, Manchester, 297–314 (in Italian).

fanum .... Dianae.) As such, the accusation here complements an earlier section in the speech, where Cicero described Verres' theft of the cult statue of Apollo at Delos (2.1.46–48). In contrast to the rather detailed and colourful explication of the episode at Delos, which includes a reference to the wrath of the god and much mythological detail (such as comments on Delos as the birthplace of Apollo and Diana), Cicero avoids specifics here: while his imaginary audience was most likely able to relate to general points about Delos and the mythology of Apollo and Diana, in the context of the trial it would hardly have been interested in the religious practices and believes of a city in Asia Minor. In a later speech, he recalls the incident as part of a recapitulation of the divinities whom Verres committed sacrilege against in the course of his career (*Ver.* 2.4.71): *Miramur Athenis Minervam, Deli Apollinem, Iunonem Sami, Pergae Dianam, multos praeterea ab isto deos tota Asia Graeciaque violatos, qui a Capitolio manus abstinere non potuerit?* ('Are we astonished that Minerva at Athens, Apollo at Delos, Juno at Samos, Diana at Perge, and many further gods all over Asia and Greece suffered sacrilege on the part of this man here who could not keep his hands away from the Capitol?')

auri: partitive genitive depending on *quod*. The antecedent of the relative clause *quod habebat auri* (namely *id*), which is also the subject accusative of the second half of the indirect statement, is elided.

Quae, malum, est ista tanta audacia atque amentia!: an exclamation of extreme irritation, reinforced at the sound level by the *homoioteleuton *ista tanta* and the *assonance *audacia atque amentia*.

audacia: for the meaning and rhetorical function of *audax* and *audacia* in the political discourse of the late republic, see Wirszubski, C. (1961), '*Audaces*: A Study in Political Phraseology', *Journal of Roman Studies* 51, 12–22, who gives the following definition (p. 15): 'If I were to define, in Roman terms, who is *audax* in a political sense, I would say that he is a man, notably a public man, who dared in public life to do what no good man would think of doing.'

amentia: 'insanity' is a favourite charge in the late-Republican rhetoric of abuse in general and in the oratory of Cicero in particular. Verres is the first victim of his tendency to turn his adversaries into madmen; Catiline and his ilk, Clodius, and Mark Antony were to follow. Frequently (as here), the charge of madness occurs in a context of religious significance. The proverb

Quos deus vult perdere dementat prius ('Those whom a god wishes to destroy he strikes with madness first') perfectly sums up Cicero's approach, especially in this particular speech. The theme of divinely induced madness is present from the outset, and indeed underwrites the very fiction of the second *actio*: Cicero presents Verres' (entirely imaginary) appearance in court as an act of insanity, caused by supernatural forces keen on exacting retribution for Verres' religious and political crimes, not least on behalf of Rome's civic community. Consider 2.1.6: *de impudentia singulari, quod adest, quod respondet, sunt qui mirentur. Mihi pro cetera eius **audacia atque amentia** ne hoc quidem mirandum videtur; multa enim et in deos et in homines impie nefarieque commisit, quorum scelerum poenis agitatur et a mente consilioque deducitur* ('some wonder about his unparalleled shamelessness in being present in court and facing trial. To me, however, given his overall impudence and insanity, not even this seems to be cause for astonishment; for he perpetrated many unholy and wicked deeds against both gods and humans and he is haunted by the avenging spirits of these crimes and is deprived of his mind and reason'). Being *a mente*, i.e. deprived of his rational mind and judgment, manifests itself in *amentia*, i.e. madness, and, in Cicero's logic of crime and punishment, entails the perpetration of further crimes and insane actions (such as Verres' appearance in court, despite the fact that everyone knows him to be guilty) in an inexorable movement towards justice. The theme of madness also dominates Cicero's conclusion of the Delos episode (2.1.48): *Hoc tu fanum depopulari, homo improbissime atque **amentissime**, audebas? Fuit ulla cupiditas tanta quae tantam exstingueret religionem?* ('You dared to plunder this shrine, you most wicked and utterly insane human? Was there ever any desire of such magnitude as to overcome such a degree of religious scruple?').[48]

Quas enim … deportasses: *Quas* is a connecting relative; *deportasses* is the main verb of the sentence – 'a pluperfect subjunctive used in a jussive sense to indicate what should or should not have been done': Mitchell (1986) 186. Both relative clauses (*quas enim…*; *quae signa…*) are 'out of place' as it were – Cicero places them ahead of the clauses into which they belong and includes the two antecedents (*urbis* and *signa atque ornamenta*) within the relative clauses. The relative clauses are, respectively, picked up by the demonstrative pronouns *in eas* and *haec*. The placing of the first

---

48. See further Gildenhard (2011) 99–124, esp. 113–16 ('Criminal Insanity'), which includes an analysis of Cicero's portrayal of Verres as someone who is criminally insane and explores his insanity as one factor in a larger cosmic scheme that brings him to justice.

relative clause at the beginning of the sentence makes sense thematically: it states what Cicero says actually happened and thus serves as foil for the unfulfilled condition *si...invasisses, ...deportasses*. Cicero may have repeated the anticipation of the relative clause in the main clause to produce a parallel syntactic pattern between *protasis* (*si*-clause) and *apodosis* (main clause). Rewritten without Cicero's rhetorical emphases, the sentence would run: *Si enim in sociorum atque amicorum urbis, quas adisti legationis iure et nomine, vi cum exercitu imperioque invasisses, tamen, opinor, signa atque ornamenta, quae ex iis urbibus sustulisses, non in tuam domum neque in suburbana amicorum, sed Romam in publicum deportasses.*

sociorum atque amicorum urbis: Cicero's usage of the terms 'allies' (*socii*) and 'friends' (*amici*) is very fluid and varies from context to context. In the stretch of text under consideration here, he employs the phrase 'allies and friends' (the former carrying technically legal, the latter emotive connotations) to refer to the non-citizen inhabitants of the Roman provinces in Asia Minor. (Indeed, some define the status of *socius* in the context of Rome's international diplomacy as comprising anyone who was not a citizen (*civis*) or an enemy (*hostis*).) The positive associations of the phrase ensured that it was tailor-made for rhetoric in the extortion court since it portrayed the victims of Roman exploitation on the lexical level as integral parts of the Roman world rather than subjects and dependents. Throughout the *Verrines*, Cicero calls the Sicilians and other provincials *socii* (91 times) or *socii et amici* (29 times).[49]

vi cum exercitu imperioque: generally speaking, *vis* denotes the application of physical force; in a civic context, *vis* is unequivocally negative – it refers to illegitimate use of violence. Cicero's gloss *cum exercitu imperioque* makes it clear that in his hypothetical scenario (the sack of the city in the context of war) the violence involved is authorized and sanctioned – in direct contrast to the *vis* that Verres brings to bear upon friends and allies of the Roman people. The phrase here is the first in a series of similar formulations in the following paragraphs, designed to establish the distinction between legitimate and illegitimate use of violence: see § 55 (*vi ac virtute*); § 56 (*vi, copiis, consilio, virtute*); and § 57 (*vi ac virtute*).

---

49. This note is based on material kindly made available to me by Myles Lavan. It forms part of his forthcoming book (provisionally titled *Slaves to Rome*) on Roman conceptions of empire.

suburbana: a *suburbanum* is a country seat near a city, here of course Rome.

non (a) **in tuam domum neque** (b) **in suburbana amicorum, sed** (b) **Romam** (a) **in publicum**: Cicero concludes this paragraph on the same theme as the previous one, the contrast between Verres' private enterprise and Rome's public sphere. The arrangement is *chiastic: Cicero contrasts Verres' *domus* with the public spaces of Rome (*in publicum*), and he contrasts the city of Rome with the country houses (*suburbana*), which are removed from the urban settings in which the senate and the people of Rome interact with one another (law courts, the forum). (a) *tuam* (b) *domum* also forms a *chiasmus with (b) *suburbana* (a) *amicorum* as Cicero emphasizes the personal enrichment of Verres and his cronies. In contrast, *Romam in publicum* is utterly laconic and to the point.

amicorum: Cicero's reference to Verres' friends recalls his technical use of the word at the beginning of the sentence: Verres despoils friends of the Roman people for the benefit of his buddies.

deportasses: here in the specific sense 'to bring back to Rome from the provinces': *OLD* s.v. 2a.

§ 55

Cicero here produces a catalogue of rhetorical questions, each focusing on a landmark battle and commander in the context of Rome's imperial expansion. With one exception, the list is arranged chronologically and traces significant military encounters in Sicily and the Greek East from the late third century to the middle of the second: i.e. exactly those regions of the Mediterranean in which Verres was active – but also those that produced the most spoils for the coffers of generals and the treasury. Spain was a much less attractive theatre of operation in this respect; but the omission of Carthage – sacked in the same year as Corinth – indicates that Cicero chooses those *exempla* of particular relevance to the case at hand. Despite the itemizing, Cicero endows his list with a sense of ring-composition, insofar as the list of conquest starts with a city (Syracuse) moves on to region & king (Asia and Antiochus) and king & region (Philip and Macedonia) to king only (Perses) before concluding with one named and many unnamed cities (Corinth and the cities of Achaia and Boeotia more generally).

At the end of the paragraph, Cicero draws his conclusion and establishes a double contrast between the precedents set by the ancestors and the conduct of Verres: their family homes shone with symbolic prestige and excellence but were otherwise unadorned since they put on display their spoils in the public spaces of the city of Rome and all of Italy. With Verres, the exact opposite is the case: the houses of himself and his friends are crammed full with plundered items (yet, by implication, devoid of *honos* and *virtus*), whereas the general public in Rome and Italy benefits not at all.

Lists of items can easily become monotonous. This is not the case here. While sticking to a basic 'subject–object–verb-of-conquest structure' throughout, Cicero alters details and constructs the overall list climactically. The ensuing effect combines the desirable relentlessness (a long list of ancestral precedents, outstanding figures and their deeds, of which Verres has fallen pitifully short) with the equally desirable variety (to maintain interest and suspense):

- Marcellus: *Syracusas, urbem ornatissimam, cepit*: one verb, one direct object with an amplification in apposition. Claudius Marcellus (consul 222, 215, 214, 210, 208) sacked Syracuse in 212 – it is perhaps not a coincidence that an event in Sicily inaugurates the catalogue. See also *Ver.* 2.4.120–1.

- Scipio: *bellum in Asia gessit Antiochumque, regem potentissimum, vicit*: two verbs, two direct objects, the second with an amplification in apposition. L. Cornelius Scipio Asiaticus (consul 190, proconsul 189) beat King Antiochus III in the battle of Magnesia in 190.

- Flamininus: *qui regem Philippum et Macedoniam subegit*: one verb, two direct objects in *chiastic order to the king (Antiochus) and the theatre of operation (Asia) in the previous sentence; there is no amplifying attribute, but the shift from an adverbial specification of place (*in Asia*) to direct object (*Macedoniam*) ensures an increase in imperial pressure. T. Quinctius Flamininus (consul 198) defeated king Philip of Macedon in the battle of Cynoscephalai in 197. It is difficult to say why Cicero presents this *exemplum* out of chronological order. Perhaps he wanted to touch on the two geographic regions of greatest pertinence to the case at hand (Sicily and Asia) first, before adding three examples all to do with mainland Greece? Or perhaps he simply wanted the two great battles against Macedon (at Cynoscephalai and Pydna: see next item) to follow on one another?

- Paulus: *qui regem Persen vi ac virtute superavit*: Paulus' success is located in the same theatre of operation as Flamininus' (Macedonia). Cicero underscores the personal quality of the general epitomized by the term *virtus*, which he here uses in its basic sense of 'military prowess'. The *alliterative *paronomasia *vis* ~ *virtus* ~ *superavit* implies an inherent connection between the three words. L. Aemilius Paullus Macedonicus (consul 182 and 168), father of Scipio Aemilianus, defeated Perses of Macedon in the battle of Pydna in 168.

- Mummius: *qui urbem pulcherrimam atque ornatissimam, Corinthum, plenissimam rerum omnium, sustulit, urbisque Achaiae Boeotiaeque multas sub imperium populi Romani dicionemque subiunxit*: after his pithy restraint with the first four figures, Cicero opens the floodgates of his rhetoric: two superlatives modifying *urbs*, the name of the city in apposition, with a further superlative (*plenissimam*) and a totalizing expression (*rerum omnium*) attached to it. L. Mummius Achaicus, as consul, sacked Corinth in 146, when he was in charge of the war against the Achaean Confederacy. Elsewhere, Cicero is highly critical of the devastation he wrought: see *de Officiis* 1.35 and 3.46.

ego … loquar: the subject and verb of each of the *quid*-questions, but elided after the first.

ornatissimam … potentissimum … pulcherrimam atque ornatissimam … plenissimam: this paragraph too amply illustrates Cicero's fondness for the superlative.

cepit? … vicit? … subegit? … superavit? … sustulit, … subiunxit?: Each of the verbs places the emphasis on the act of military conquest; the subsequent despoiling of the conquered cities and territories is elided, though at the end of the paragraph Cicero, in praising the civic spirit and personal modesty that informs the public display of war spoils in Rome and Italy, makes it clear that these generals took as much as Verres did, if not more. The fact of plunder is not the issue, but rather the terms and motivations for it.

urbisque: the *-que* links *sustulit* and *subiunxit*.

Boeotiaeque: the *-que* links *Achaiae* and *Boeotiae*.

sub imperium populi Romani dicionemque: this is the Roman language of power and military conquest. As in the previous paragraph, Cicero voices no objections to the violent extension of Roman rule; rather, he disapproves of the abuse of diplomatic functions for personal enrichment.

dicionemque: the *-que* links *imperium* and *dicionem*.

Quorum domus: a connecting relative: 'their houses'

honore ac virtute: the formulation recalls the phrase *vi ac virtute* in §§ 55 and 57. Cicero celebrates the combination of recognition in Rome and (martial) excellence abroad, outstanding achievement based on military leadership and courage in battle, and commitment to a code of conduct that meant that the ensuing riches and spoils resulted in acts of public munificence (see *dona*), rather than private display. *Honos* also means 'public office'; the attainment of public office was the only way to enter into the collective memory of one's kin group (*familia* or *gens*) and the *res publica* at large. The core of Rome's ruling elite, the so-called nobility, consisted of families that produced office-holders, especially consuls, across many generations and their offspring were expected to live up to the standards of achievement set by their ancestors, by entering upon the so-called *cursus honorum*, i.e. being voted into (ever more important) magistracies in the running of the *res publica*. Rome's memorial culture awarded former office holders with a wax mask (*imago*) upon their death and celebrated their achievements with a public funeral; these aristocratic funerals included a procession (the so-called *pompa funebris*) from the house of the deceased to the forum, consisting of the corpse and an entourage of actors who had donned the wax-masks and official garb of former family members who had received similar distinctions. In the forum, a son or other close relative of the deceased delivered a funeral oration (*laudatio funebris*), praising his deeds in the context of those of his ancestors. The wax-masks were stored in little shrines put on display in the atrium, together with *stemmata* and *tituli* that indicated genealogical connections, the public career, and the most outstanding military deeds of the person thus honoured.[50]

signis et tabulis pictis: an ablative of separation depending on *vacuae*. *signa* are statues, *tabulae pictae* are paintings; the two often go together:

---

50. See in detail Flower, H. (1996), *Ancestor Masks and Aristocratic Power in Roman Culture*, Oxford.

see below § 60: *mercator signorum tabularumque pictarum*; Cicero, *de Oratore* 1.161: *tabulis et signis propalam conlocatis*; Livy 42.63.11. Apart from a wooden panel used for painting as here, *tabula* designated more generally any object with a flat surface, which could be of various types of material (wood, stone, metal). *Tabulae* played an extraordinarily important role in Roman culture: apart from paintings, they could feature permanent inscriptions (the law code of the 'Twelve Tables' is the most famous example), or could be used for the temporary display of information (such as the *tabula dealbata* used by the pontiffs to record significant events throughout the year). *Tabula* could also mean 'writing-tablet' (in its simplest form a board coated with wax), and *tabulae* (pl.) could designate 'account books' (the meaning of the term in § 57 below).[51] In the present context, Cicero seems to be referring to paintings plundered from Greek cities; but he may also have had in mind the 'victory paintings' that offered a pictorial record of the deeds of the general and his army and were carried through the streets of Rome during the triumph, before finding a place of permanent display.[52]

urbem totam ... omnisque Italiae partes: the attributes *totam* and *omnis* are two further examples of Cicero's penchant for 'totalizing' expressions. He presents the places that feature war spoils in a *climactic *tricolon that moves from the city, to the dwelling places of the gods (*templa deorum*) to all of Italy.

templaque deorum: this destination is particularly pointed, since the adornment of temples by Rome's successful generals stands in direct contrast to Verres' practice of despoiling temples. Cicero of course suppresses the fact that generals also plundered sites sacred to the people they conquered.

videmus: the switch to the first person plural present indicative underscores the lasting importance of the achievements and the generosity of the illustrious forebears mentioned and their continuing presence within Rome's civic community ('all of us see their munificence').

---

51. See further Meyer, E. A. (2004), *Legitimacy and Law in the Roman World: Tabulae in Roman Belief and Practice*, Cambridge.

52. See further Holliday, P. J. (2002), *The Origins of Roman Historical Commemoration in the Visual Arts*, Cambridge, with the review by Hölkeskamp, K.-J. (2005), 'Images of Power: Memory, Myth and Monuments in the Roman Republic', *Scripta Classica Israelica* 24, 249–71.

§ 56

After adducing figures from the period 212 – 146 BC in the previous paragraph, Cicero suddenly pauses to voice the fear that his grand sweep of *exempla* from the more or less distant past will be deemed 'ancient history', that is, lacking pertinence in the present context. After an attempt to explicate the reason for his apprehension, he homes in on a contemporary figure, P. Servilius, whose conduct in office he explores in detail as a positive foil for Verres in both this and the subsequent paragraph.

nimis antiqua et iam obsoleta: this is a surprising point of view in a culture that placed a premium on tradition and often equated antiquity with authority. As recent studies have shown, however, the Roman attitude towards their own past in general and Cicero's handling of *exempla maiorum* in particular defy easy simplifications.[53] Two points are worth bearing in mind: (i) *exempla* and exemplary figures were often hotly contested, especially during the late Republic: was Scipio Nasica, who killed Tiberius Gracchus in 133 BC, a cold-blooded murderer who ought to be executed or a heroic killer of a potential tyrant who deserved the gratitude of the senate and the people of Rome? Opinion on this differed according to political persuasion. But struggles over the meaning of history were co-existent with Roman Republican history (and, of course, beyond). An example from an earlier period is the controversy around the historical significance of outstanding individuals: a prime example is the above-mentioned Claudius Marcellus, whose reputation was slandered by his opponents after he died ignobly in an ambush.[54] (ii) All this adds up to the second point, namely that Cicero never simply invokes *exempla* as if they pre-existed as readily available facts; rather, he *construes* them for the rhetorical purpose at hand.

---

53. A German dissertation by Bücher, F. (2006), *Verargumentierte Geschichte. Exempla Romana im politischen Diskurs der späten römischen Republik*, Stuttgart, has shown that the overwhelming majority of historical precedents that Cicero brings into play belong to the fairly recent past (the book comes with a CD-Rom that includes tables of all *exempla* that Cicero uses in his speeches); and van der Blom, H. (2010), *Cicero's Role Models: The Political Strategy of a Newcomer*, Oxford, offers a nuanced overview of the current state of research on Rome's memorial culture and Cicero's place within it.

54. See Flower, H. (2003), 'Memories of Marcellus: History and Memory in Roman Republican Culture', in U. Eigler, U. Gotter, N. Luraghi, U. Walter (eds.), *Formen römischer Geschichtsschreibung von den Anfängen bis Livius: Gattungen – Autoren - Kontexte*, Darmstadt, 1-17.

videantur ... videatur: Cicero here develops a *hypothetical* scenario, reinforced by the use of *forte* ('conceivably', 'perhaps') and *quispiam* ('an unspecified person', 'someone').

haec laus ... esse videatur: another interesting line of thought, which builds on the notion of the *exempla* just listed being potentially out of date. The sentence is meant to explain *why* Cicero fears that some may consider his precedents obsolete (see *enim*). The explanation is quite contrived, presupposes a great deal, and is therefore not entirely easy to untangle. The aspects that make up the argument are as follows: (i) Cicero implies that the praise and admiration that his exemplary ancestors nowadays attract is a retrospective phenomenon; during their lifetime, they would not have appeared extraordinary since everyone was equally excellent; (ii) in the absence of degrees of excellence, the praise belongs not (just) to individuals, but (also) to the period;[55] this presupposes that the excellence of specific individuals did not owe itself to any personal qualities – rather, it was simply the result of the good luck of living at a good moment in history; (iii) times have changed, and the behavioural patterns that were once common (and now elicit praise) have become obsolete; note that for this inference to make sense Cicero presupposes for the sake of the argument that human beings are by and large creatures of the period in which they happen to live – a notion that, apart from doing away with personal agency and responsibility, would seem to eliminate the past as a meaningful reservoir of norms, values, and exemplary conduct; (iv) a consequence of the presupposition that we are creatures of our times is that the negative comparison of Verres with figures of the past is by the way – since times have changed, so the implied argument, past paragons of virtue (who anyway did nothing more than act in the spirit of their period) possess no authoritative value. What Cicero leaves unexplained in all this is why the current generations of Romans should attach *laus* to times past (and specific historical figures): this implies, after all, that they did perceive a difference between ancient excellence and the current state of affairs – though his hypothetical adversary could have argued, from within his model of historical determinism, that the perception and evaluation of historical difference is one thing and drawing consequences for current practice quite another. Cicero of course does not endorse this hypothetical line of reasoning at all; for him the past remains a meaningful

---

55. The notion of praise belonging to a period rather than to specific individuals who lived within it recurs elsewhere in Cicero's *oeuvre*, notably in *de Officiis* 3.

resource of precedents and normative benchmarks. But why does he go to such length to refute the potential objection that his historical *exempla* could be dismissed as irrelevant? Perhaps we here capture a mainstay of defences in extortion trials, namely the argument that the behaviour of the defendant did not differ from that of fellow-Romans, that he simply acted like his contemporaries. One way of countering this objection was to cite a contemporary figure who exhibited what some considered outdated excellence; and this, of course, is exactly what Cicero does: he devotes the remainder of § 56 and all of § 57 to a comparison between Verres and P. Servilius, who, conveniently, was part of the jury.

hominum ... temporum illorum: genitives of possession depending on *esse*

temporum illorum: *illorum* is ambiguous: it could mean either 'their times', i.e. referring back to *hominum* (pronominal use of *ille*), or 'those times' (adjectival use of *ille*).

Olympum: a city in Cilicia (that is, the very region where Verres served as legate), which served as basis for pirates; the sack yielded a significant amount of booty.

P. Servilius: P. Servilius Vatia Isauricus (*consul* 79, proconsul in Cilicia 78–77) fought the pirates of the Eastern Mediterranean and local tribes of Asia Minor as proconsul from 78–74. (One of the tribes were the Isauri, inhabitants of Isauria, a region of Asia Minor on the borders of Pisidia and Cilicia, hence his triumphant epithet *Isauricus*; for the custom of attaching a geographical moniker to a name to signal military involvement in a region one can compare Lawrence of Arabia or Earl Mountbatten of Burma.) In Cicero's *oeuvre*, Servilius and superlatives (or alternative markers of distinction) go hand-in-hand: in addition to *clarissimus* and *fortissimus* as here, we find *gravissimus, amplissimus, sanctissimus, ornatissimus, constantissimus* and such formulations as *in senatu princeps erat, amabatur a populo*.[56] Servilius was one of the most distinguished jurors sitting in judgement at Verres' trial, and Cicero names him repeatedly in the *Verrines*. They remained close political allies until Servilius' death as nonagenarian in 44 BC.

---

56. References in Münzer, F. (1923), '93) P. Servilius Vatia Isauricus', *Real-Encyclopädie* 2.4, 1812–17 (1815).

vir clarissimus: at the time of Cicero, the adjective *clarus* tended to be used of senators, but it was not yet a technical term that designated senatorial rank (as it became under the empire): see Berry, D. H. (1996), *Cicero, Pro P. Sulla Oratio, edited with introduction and commentary,* Cambridge, 136 (on *Sul.* 3.2).

vi, copiis, consilio, virtute: an intricate quadruple: whereas *alliteration links *vi* with *virtute* and *copiis* with *consilio*, in thematic terms *vi* goes with *copiis* (the troops) and *consilio* with *virtute* (the general).

laturus: Mitchell (1986) 187 points out that this 'is the only example in Cicero of the use of the future participle to convey the idea of purpose.'

Recens: placed first for emphasis; it stands in implied antithesis to the *nimis antiqua et iam obsoleta* of the opening sentence.

profero: the verb can have the legal sense 'to produce (documents, etc.) in evidence' and, more generally (as here), 'to bring up (a fact, circumstance, etc.) in support of a contention, adduce, put forward for consideration': *OLD* s.v. 5.

nam postea Servilius imperator populi Romani Olympum urbem hostium cepit quam tu in isdem illis locis legatus quaestorius oppida pacata sociorum atque amicorum diripienda ac vexanda curasti: Cicero's report of Servilius' achievements recalls the idiom used to enumerate the *exempla maiorum* in the previous paragraph: subject – object – verb of conquest, with subject and object being developed in precise parallel. Here *Servilius* corresponds to *Olympum*, *imperator* to *urbem*, and *populi Romani* to *hostium*. Cicero's laconic precision in recounting the deed of Servilius ('he sacked the hostile city Olympus') contrasts with his verbose description of the activities of Verres. *imperator populi Romani* contrasts with *legatus quaestorius* (by adding the qualification 'of the Roman people' Cicero reinforces the theme of rightful entitlement and action taken on behalf of the entire commonwealth), just as *urbem hostium* stands in sharp *antithesis to *oppida pacata sociorum atque amicorum*. The rhetoric (understatement in one case, hyperbole in the other) misrepresents the facts: whatever Verres may have done, he hardly inflicted more suffering on the locals with his thievery than Servilius did with his military operations – though this is precisely what Cicero implies with *diripienda ac vexanda*, two verbs that belong in the context of warfare and, in particular, looting.

postea ... quam: Cicero elaborates on *recens* by stressing (not leas\
of the *tmesis and the massive *hyperbaton which allow him to p\
prominently at the beginning of the sentence) that he now brings into play
events so recent that they happened *after* Verres' stint as legate. *'Postea ...
quam* brackets the main clause and signals the upcoming temporal clause':
Mitchell (1986) 187. Note that there is a slight inconcinnity in Cicero's
argument here: because he wishes to emphasize the recent nature of the
exemplum and the fact that Servilius and Verres acted in the same geographic
region (*in isdem illis locis*), we have the seemingly paradoxical situation that
at the time of Verres the region was full of pacified towns and friends and
allies of the Roman people, yet several years later, during Servilius'
pro-consulship it had somehow turned into an enemy stronghold. One
wonders how 'pacified' and 'friendly' Cilicia truly was when Verres was legate.

curasti: syncopated form of *curavisti*; Cicero is being highly ironic, while
setting up the non-ironic use of *curare* in the following paragraph.

§ 57

The paragraph continues the contrast between Verres and Servilius, with a
particular emphasis on their respective practices of accounting.

Tu quae ... perscribenda curavit: The sentence contains a comparison
between Verres and Servilius that combines precise parallels on the level of
syntax with diametrical opposition on the level of theme. The correlations
can be tabulated as follows:

(i) Subject	*Tu*	*P. Servilius*
(ii) Relative Clause recounting the removal of treasures	*quae ... abstulisti*	*quae signa atque ornamenta ... sustulit*
(iii) Within the Relative Clause: specification of the place from which treasures were taken	*ex fanis religiosissimis*	*ex urbe hostium vi et virtute capta*

(continued)

(continued)

(iv) Within the Relative Clause: the manner and the terms on which the removal took place	*per scelus et latrocinium*	*belli lege atque imperatorio iure*
(v) What happened with the treasures in Rome	*ea nos videre nisi in tuis amicorumque tuorum tectis non possumus*	*ea populo Romano adportavit, per triumphum vexit, in tabula publica ad aerarium perscribenda curavit.*

Thus (i) Verres (ii) perpetrated (iii) blasphemous (iv) thievery (v) for private gain; in contrast, (i) Servilius (ii) performed (iii) a heroic conquest (iv) according to military law (v) for the public benefit.

Tu quae ~ ea nos: the *antithesis, arranged in a *chiasmus, with *Tu* in the exposed, initial position, generates a contrast between Verres and his ilk and the expansive 'we' that Cicero adopts, including both him and the Roman populace at large. (Note that from the point of view of Latin grammar, neither the *Tu* nor the *nos*, are strictly speaking, necessary.) That Verres' shenanigans are entirely for private benefit is reinforced by the *polyptoton *Tu, tuis, tuorum* – which is picked up at the end of the paragraph by *te tua furta*.

per scelus et latrocinium: the criminal tribunal dealing with illegal conduct on the part of magistrates or jurymen (*quaestio de repetundis*) policed, among other things, the distinction between 'criminal' and 'acceptable' exploitation of the provinces. But the court setting also provided an ideal context for rival politicians to pursue personal or political agendas by means of criminalizing their opponents. Cicero was arguably more radical than most in demonizing his adversaries as hardened criminals and he often split the political field in Rome – which featured many shades of grey – into black and white, the wicked (*improbi*) and the good (*boni*). When Cicero accuses Verres (and other aristocratic adversaries, such as Catiline) of banditry (*latrocinium*), he uses the term metaphorically; the effect is a rhetorical disenfranchisement – the individual so labelled ceases to be a Roman citizen or, indeed, member of Rome's ruling elite, living within the legal order of the commonwealth and abiding by its laws; instead he becomes a criminal figure at the margins of society, an 'outlaw', who threatens to undo order and stability.[57]

in tuis amicorumque tuorum tectis: mimetic word order: the syntax reproduces the theme of something locked inside a house, with *in tuis* and *tectis* framing and embracing the reference to Verres and his friends. The *-que* links *tuis* and *amicorum tuorum*, which are both dependent on *tectis*.

nos videre nisi ... non possumus: Cicero delays the final, powerful negative (*non*) for great effect, with *nisi* functioning as a retarding element, specifying the exception; the alliteration *nos ~ non* (with *nisi* providing variation) and the *homoioteleuton *tuis ... tectis* endow the sentence with coherence on the sound-level. While Verres' plunder simply disappears from public view, the opposite is the case with Servilius' war spoils (see below).

vi et virtute: as the *vi ac virtute* in § 57, this is an abbreviated repetition of *vi, copiis, consilio, virtute* in § 56 and anticipating the formulation *virtutis victoriaeque iucunditas* later on in the paragraph.

triumphus: the Roman ritual of victory, which has received much scholarly discussion in recent years.[58] Many aspects of modern reconstructions of this ancient ritual are controversial, but the point that matters for our purposes is reasonably straightforward: protocols that governed the distribution of spoils existed, even if they were constantly in dispute, evolved over time, and were not codified in law. Cicero simplifies to gain rhetorical purchase on his adversary: he wants a stark and easily intelligible opposition between public spirited commanders who gained their spoils through effort and excellence, on behalf and for the benefit of the Roman people and a criminal who, under the cover of a minor Roman magistracy, operates for private gain and acquires his plunder by means of thievery

---

57. T. Habinek defines bandits thus: 'bandits are criminals who operate in the spaces that are claimed by the political authorities but are not well integrated into the social, economic, and cultural life of mainstream society.' (*The Politics of Latin Literature: Writing, Identity, and Empire in Ancient Rome*, Princeton, 1998, Chapter 3: 'Cicero and the Bandits', 69–87, here 69, with reference to Shaw, B. (1984), 'Bandits in the Roman Empire', *Past and Present* 105, 3–52.) For monographic treatment of *latrones*, see Grünewald, T. (1999), *Räuber, Rebellen, Rivalen, Rächer*, Stuttgart [translated by J. Drinkwater as *Bandits in the Roman Empire: Myth and Reality*, London and New York, 2004]; he notes that, in the (late) Roman jurists, *latrocinium* refers to 'heavy gang criminality in the dimension of irregular warfare', but can also be used for 'crime' more generally (25).
58. See e.g. Beard, M. (2007), *The Roman Triumph*, Cambridge/ MA, or Östenberg, I. (2009), *Spoils, Captives and Representations in the Roman Triumphal Procession*, Oxford.

for the exclusive enjoyment of himself and his friends. From a different point of view, one could argue that P. Servilius and the culture of military triumphs and Verres and the exploitation of the provinces are two aspects of the same phenomenon.

belli lege atque imperatorio iure: the rules of war and the privileges that come with military command – this has nothing to do with the Geneva convention, but rather the fact that the spoils belong to the victor.

ea ... adportavit ... vexit ... curavit: whereas the part of the sentence dealing with Verres contains a surprising break in subject between the relative clause (*tu*) and the main clause (*nos ... non possumus*), the same is not the case in the half devoted to Servilius: he remains the subject throughout, not least in the highly ordered, *asyndetic *tricolon *adportavit, vexit, curavit*, which details the action of 'bringing spoils to the city', 'displaying them publicly during a triumph', and 'entering them into the civic records afterwards'.

populo Romano ... in tabula publica ... ex litteris publicis ... praedam populi Romani: Cicero stresses the public presentation and the public record for the people (*populus*) of Rome. The correlation of *publicus* and *populus* lies at the very heart of the political culture of the Roman Republic, which was grounded in the principle that members of the ruling elite performed outstanding deeds for the benefit of the people (or the *res publica*), who in turn rewarded them with public recognition in the form of further magistracies (*honores*), social standing (*dignitas*) and fame (*gloria*). This ideology underwrites Cicero's famous definition of '*res publica*', i.e. commonwealth, from which derives the English term 'republic', at *de Republica* 1.39, which links *res publica* and *populus* by suggesting a (fake) etymological relation: *est igitur ... res publica res populi, populus autem non omnis hominum coetus quoquo modo congregatus, sed coetus multitudinis iuris consensu et utilitatis communione sociatus*. ('A commonwealth, therefore, is the property of the people. But a people is not every kind of human congregation, brought together in whatever manner, but the congregation of a large number united by consensual commitment to law and community of interest.'). Verres goes against the very principles that hold the Roman commonwealth together, i.e. public accountability and ownership, recognition of law, and shared utility. (The organic interlocking of Cicero's vision of Rome's political culture and his political philosophy, which operates with categories derived from Greek political thought, is a dimension of his *oeuvre* that remains underappreciated.)

aerarium: here refers to Rome's public treasury, which was located in the temple of Saturn.

perscribenda (also end of paragraph, **perscripta**): *perscribere* is a technical term of Roman accounting, and means 'to enter a detailed record of official transactions in an account-book'.

curavit: picks up the ironic *curasti* in § 56.

Recita: such orders to the clerk and gestures to documentary material reinforce the illusion that the speech is the record of an actual performance. Se also §§ 79, 83, and 84.

RATIONES RELATAE P. SERVILI: the phrase serves as a place-holder, indicating the moment when Cicero would have stopped speaking and a court clerk would have read out the accounts registered by P. Servilius. See *OLD* s.v. *refero* 5 for *rationes referre* = 'to render an account of one's actions'.

vides: after an address to the judges (*cognoscite*) and an order to the court clerk (*recita*), Cicero turns straight to Verres, forcing him to confront the evidence of how his aristocratic peer handled his accounts.

Certe ... cupiditate: this reads almost like a marginal gloss that has intruded into the text; it certainly interrupts the train of thought, separating the report of Servilius' conduct from the punchline, i.e. the damning comparison between him and Verres. In contrast, this sentence is about moral philosophy and consists of the assertion that the wellbeing that attends good deeds and outstanding achievements surpasses the pleasure derived from fulfilling illicit passions and desires. Not everyone would agree with the assertion. Yet the Latin is unexceptionally Ciceronian and the sentence reinforces one of Cicero's major lines of attack in the *Verrines*, i.e. the portrayal of Verres as a (ultimately subhuman) creature who lives on passionate and wicked lusts and instincts; it also sets up *servos cupiditatum* in the following paragraph.

virtutis victoriaeque: the logical step after *vi et virtute*, with *virtus* functioning as connecting pivot between military violence (*vis*) and victory (*victoria*).

(a) **numerum** (b) **signorum** ... (b) **unius cuiusque** (a) **magnitudinem, figuram, statum**: the *chiastic structure of decidedly unequal length helps to produce wording of mimetic force: after a straightforward reference to the overall number of statues (*numerum signorum*), Cicero honours (and stylistically re-enacts) Servilius' punctilious itemization of each piece included in the tally with an elaborate *asyndetic *tricolon, of descending numbers of syllables (5, 3, 2).

(a) **praedam** (b) **populi Romani** ~ (b) **tua** (a) **furta**: a *chiastic arrangement designed to bring out the *antithesis between legitimate spoils of war and Verres' criminal thievery; it revolves around the contrast between *praeda* and *furta*. The two nouns recall the opening contrast between spoils of war after the sack of a city and illicit plunder (*latrocinium*).

notata atque perscripta: the participles go both with *praedam* and *furta*, but grammatically correspond to the nearest noun, i.e. *furta*. Cicero tolerates the apparent paradox in his claim that stolen items ought to be correctly entered in public accounts.

§ 58

In this paragraph Cicero changes tack, as he anticipates (note the future *dices*) and counters the potential objection by Verres that, far from hiding away his plundered treasures, he put them on public display at the centre of the city. It is not entirely clear what occasion Cicero refers to. As Mitchell (1986) 185 points out, 'it was customary for aediles to decorate the *comitium* and the forum for major festive occasions, and they often had to resort to borrowing works of art from friends and from provincial and allied communities to secure the necessary adornments' (with reference to our passage, as well as Ver. 2.3.9, 2.4.6, and 2.4.126). Pseudo-Asconius suggests that Verres helped Hortensius and the Metelli brothers in that way (*nam aedili atque praetori Hortensio et item Metellis rapta ex provinciis signa ad ornandum forum et comitium commodaverat Verres*). Along those lines, P. A. Brunt has more recently argued that Hortensius' otherwise inexplicable devotion to Verres derived from the fact that he was a prime beneficiary of Verres' extortions.[59]

---

59. Brunt, P. A. (1980), 'Patronage and Politics in the *Verrines*', *Chiron* 10, 273–89, 280: 'But why was Hortensius so devoted to Verres? He had long been a leader of the bar; he

As for dates: Hortensius was aedile in 75 and praetor in 72; Quintus Caecilius Metellus Creticus (in 70 consul designate, together with Hortensius) canvassed for the praetorship in 75 (and must have held it in one of the following years given his application to the consulship in 70); L. Caecilius Metellus was praetor in 71; and Marcus Caecilius Metellus was praetor designate in 70. (We do not have information about the *cursus honorum* of a fourth brother, C. Caecilius Metellus.) Alternatively, Cicero may be recalling (*memini*) the year 74 when Verres was himself urban praetor and hence responsible for the *ludi Apollinares*. Most likely, however, he deliberately avoids specifying the precise occasion, leaving it up to the audience in joining him 'to think back' to any one occasion when Verres' plundered artworks adorned the public spaces of Rome. As far as Cicero was concerned, Verres was damned if he did as well as when he did not: the public spectacle he generated out of his large-scale thievery for himself or for others might have been magnificent to behold, but the sight saddened anyone endowed with thought and feeling. In the second half of the paragraph, however, Cicero makes it clear that this by no means included all sightseers. Quite the contrary: Verres had occasion to observe (*vidit*) the reaction of fellow senators to his spectacle, and what he saw was appreciative greed. Cicero reproachfully identifies this experience of implicit encouragement from his peer group as providing the stimulus for Verres to perpetrate further crimes of a similar nature in future.

ornamento urbi foroque … fuisse: a double dative: *urbi* and *foro* are in the dative of advantage (*dativus commodi*); *ornamento* is a dative of purpose (*dativus finalis*)

Memini: highly ironic: 'don't tell me, I remember very well!'

comitium: an open space adjacent to the forum, used for assemblies.[60]

adornatum ad speciem magnifico ornatu, sed ad sensum cogitationemque acerbo et lugubri: a contorted and *pleonastic way to describe the complex and contradictory response of those who saw Verres' displays: they were

---

had been elected to the consulship with the minimum interval after his praetorship. How could such a man have any need of Verres? I find it hard to resist acceptance of Cicero's imputations: Hortensius was an accessory after the fact in Verres' extortions' (with reference to our passage, among others).

60. For a good, basic account of Roman assemblies see Beard, M. and Crawford, M. (1985), *Rome in the Late Republic*, Ithaca, NY.

indeed splendid to look upon (a point reinforced by the **figura etymologica adornatum ~ ornatu*, which picks up *ornamento* in the opening sentence of the paragraph); but whatever awe the splendour was designed to inspire was overpowered by thoughts and emotions of grief. Cicero again enacts the point stylistically, achieving emphasis through quantity of verbiage: *ad speciem* is dwarfed by *ad sensum cogitationemque*, and the single qualifier *magnifico* is outdone by the two qualifiers *acerbo et lugubri*.

magnifico: both *magnifico* and *acerbo et lugubri* are in the predicative position. The forum and the comitium were adorned (*adornatum*) with ornamentation (*ornatu*), which was spectacular (*magnifico*) to behold (*ad speciem*), but bitter and distressing (*acerbo et lugubri*) to feeling and thought (*ad sensum cogitationemque*).

lugubri: Cicero returns to the theme of distress and grief caused by Verres' public displays in more detail in the following paragraph.

vidi ... vidi ... vidit: Cicero stages an intricate drama of sight. In the first half of the paragraph he describes his own experience, which, he implies, coincided with the experience of the Roman people (*vidi simul cum populo Romano*); in the second half, he focuses on what Verres sees, namely senators looking at his display in rampant greed. Cicero fingers their admiration and approval as the stimulus for future crimes on Verres' part. In essence, he here implicates much of Rome's senatorial elite in Verres' crimes and his personality defects. This aggressive strategy recurs throughout the *Verrines* and has its flipside in Cicero's repeated reminders that the jury can rid itself of suspicions of complicity with Verres (and regain at least a minimal reputation for righteousness and integrity) by deciding the case in his favour.

furtis tuis, praeda provinciarum, spoliis sociorum atque amicorum: a *climactic *tricolon of instrumental ablatives, with each colon dramatically increasing in size on account of the attributes. Further stylistic touches include the *homoioteleuton *furtis tuis* and the *alliterations *praeda provinciarum* and *spoliis sociorum*.

iudiciorum ... dominos ... cupiditatum ... servos: a powerful *antithesis – the group of established aristocrats who think like Verres want to be *masters* of the lawcourts, but they are in fact *slaves* of their desires. Cicero here reactivates a theme that he pursues through the entire corpus of the *Verrines*: the deep-seated corruption of the senate in the aftermath of Sulla's reforms, which had put senators in charge of the law courts. (Control of the courts would revert to the knights soon after the case against Verres.) It is unlikely that senators openly wanted to be called 'masters of the court' – outside the context of the *familia* and master-slave relationships, *dominus* comes close to being an insult: it implies the abuse of power.

§ 59

Cicero here elaborates on the idea he introduced obliquely in the previous paragraph, with the formulation *ornatu … acerbo et lugubri*. The scenes he pretends to remember are as emotionally moving as they are implausible: ambassadors from all over Greece and Asia spending their days in Rome worshipping in front of cult statues that Verres had plundered from their shrines and displayed in the forum or gazing tearfully on other statuary and precious objects. Cicero's creative writing manifests itself in an overwrought, emphatic idiom; notable stylistic features include the conjuration of a historical watershed (*tum primum*), the series of superlative, totalizing or 'absolute' phrases (*spem omnem*; *plurimi*; *Quorum omnium*; *nihil*), and highly dramatic images and expressions (*spem omnem … abiecerunt*; *lacrimantes*; *de exitio*). Some imaginative touches add colour to the scene that Cicero here invokes: features to savour include the disingenuous *casu* (for which see below) and the delayed *plurimi* ('there happened to be Greek ambassadors in Rome – a whole crowd of them').

In the course of the paragraph, Cicero moves from an emphasis on practice and sight (*venerabantur*, *intuebantur*) to hearsay and reflection (*sermonem*, *audiebamus*); there is an analogous movement from a concern with objects of spiritual and material value (*rerum ac fortunarum suarum*, *deorum simulacra*, *signa et ornamenta*) to more abstract considerations of life and death (*de exitio*), the principles of international relations and justice (or its perversion). All this is designed to set up the punch-line of the paragraph: the same public spaces of the city that were previously used to bring crimes against the allies to justice now serve to celebrate them. The end of § 59 thus harks back to and elaborates on the end of § 58: if in the previous paragraph, we got the reaction of Verres' aristocratic peers to his public displays, namely emulative greed of other prospective perpetrators along with further encouragement of Verres, here we get the perspective of the victims: utter despair. (Cicero underscores the correlation on the lexical level: see below on *spem omnem*.)

Socii vero nationesque exterae: Cicero distinguishes between civic communities within a Roman province and people not subjected to Roman rule. The *socii* here are the first item in a magnificent *polyptoton: after the initial nominative, we get the allies in the genitive (*sociorum*), the dative (*sociis*) and the ablative (*ab sociis*). The foreign peoples, on the other hand, drop from view.

vero … spem omnem … abiecerunt: the formulation works in antithesis to *spem maximam* at the end of the previous paragraph, with the adversative *vero* functioning as pivot. The highly promising prospect of future criminal exploitation for Verres correlates with the utter loss of hope among the provincials.

rerum ac fortunarum suarum: an emphatic *pleonasm ('their property and possessions'). Cicero here touches upon an issue that continues to resonate forcefully today in the sphere of international diplomacy and justice: to whom do objects of plunder and exploitation belong? Cicero's *Verrines* have assumed archetypal importance in western thinking on the subject: see the highly accessible analysis by Miles M. M. (2008), *Art as Plunder: The Ancient Origins of Debate about Cultural Property*, New York, who explores Greek precedents, devotes a significant part of her discussion to Cicero's *Verrines*, and outlines continuities and changes in practice and the terms of the debate from late antiquity to modern times.

propterea quod casu legati ex Asia atque Achaia plurimi Romae tunc fuerunt: given the vagueness of Cicero's temporal indications (see introduction to the previous paragraph) it is difficult to ascertain the precise year Cicero had in mind and why there happened to be a large number of envoys from Asia and Achaia in Rome at the time. But the period in question falls in the wake of Sulla's war against Mithradates, after which he burdened the province of Asia with the enormous penalty of 20,000 talents. Many cities were unable to collect sufficient taxes and had to lend money at exorbitant interest-rates, not least from Roman creditors, to meet their obligations, a vicious cycle that drove them gradually to ruin, necessitating envoys to Rome to plead their cause. In the light of all this, Cicero's use of *casu* ('by chance') is utterly disingenuous: the envoys were in Rome because the provinces suffered inordinately from systemic Roman exploitation. This, however, was not something he was keen to emphasize given his strategy of portraying the Roman system of government as essentially sound, well-liked, and beneficial, with only the occasional rotten apple, such as Verres or Dolabella. See also below on § 73 (*togati creditores*).

Romae: a locative ('in Rome').

simulacra … sublata: the two words are linked by *alliteration.

deorum simulacra … venerabantur: the religious spirit of the provincials contrasts sharply with the materialist attitude of Verres: what for the latter are objects of plunder are cult-images of the gods for the former, i.e. objects of worship that retain their numinous power and link with the supernatural beings they represent even outside their usual abode in temples.[61]

cetera signa: that is, further, non-religious statuary.

cetera signa et ornamenta cum cognoscerent: the postponement of *cum* puts special emphasis on *cetera signa et ornamenta*; note the harsh *alliteration *cetera - cum - cognoscerent*, which contrasts in sound with the subsequent plaintive *alia alio in loco lacrimantes*.

lacrimantes intuebantur: *lacrimantes* is a circumstantial participle ('while weeping', 'in tears').

nihil esse quod: 'there is no reason why': *OLD* s.v. *nihil* 5a.

cum quidem viderent … ereptaque essent: this sentence functions as Cicero's explanatory gloss on why the talk of the allies was all about doom and death. As Mitchell (1986) 188 notes, 'the indicatives *fecerant* and *solebant* show this is Cicero's own comment, not part of what the allies said.'

qui sociis iniurias fecerant: the antecedent (*ii*) needs to be supplied.

---

61. Steiner, D. (2002), *Images in Mind: Statues in Archaic and Classical Greek Literature and Thought*, Princeton, offers a wide-ranging discussion of the varying significance of statues in ancient Greek culture.

in foro populi Romani – quo in loco – ibi: *in loco* and *ibi* are strictly speaking unnecessary and are added to underscore Verres' perversion of a public space for his private displays: the very location in which Roman courts in the past dispensed justice for allies now serves as a showcase of criminal exploitation.

§ 60

In this and the following paragraph, Cicero considers the possibility that Verres, rather than having stolen his artworks, bought them – as Verres himself seems to have claimed. In which context, how, and with what frequency Verres insisted on the legal acquisition of his treasures remains unclear. Cicero argues that it has happened often (see *solet, non numquam*), but the information on which he relies is mere hearsay (and marked as such by Cicero by means of the hedge *ut opinor*: Verres never seems to have made this claim in Cicero's presence) without any legal value. Still, Cicero gets a lot of rhetorical mileage out of subjecting the notion to scrutiny. He first ridicules the idea of a Roman official travelling east to buy up art and then dismisses the claim as a bare-faced lie: not one of the artworks once on display in Verres' house had ever been entered into either his own account books or those of his father. The topic of account books offers Cicero the opportunity to introduce an aside which is not strictly pertinent to the early stages of Verres' career under consideration here, but of great importance for Verres' conduct in Sicily: apparently, Verres, in the run-up to the trial, declared that he had ceased to keep accounts after his year as praetor (74 BC), meaning that no account book existed for this time in Sicily (73–71 BC). Cicero is alluding to this claim here and by means of comparison with other possibilities exposes this approach towards accounting as ludicrous. But the looting of Greece and Asia falls into the period during which Verres kept accounts.

Hic: the adverb (with a long i), rather than the demonstrative pronoun *hic*; the meaning here is either 'At this point (in my speech)' or, more likely, a retrospective 'In the light of what I've just said'.

ego: emphatic use of the personal pronoun ('I, for one')

arbitror illum negaturum ... se ... habere: two indirect statements, the first (*negaturum*, with *illum* as subject accusative) depending on *arbitror*, the second (*habere*, with *se* as subject accusative) depending on *negaturum*.

signa se: the placing of *se* after *signa* produces an *alliterative association between the statues and Verres.

signa … plurima, tabulas pictas innumerabilis: again a climactic arrangement, where Cicero reinforces the step from 'a whole lot' to 'countless' by the increasing number of syllables (5:11) and the quantity of the vowels (*signa plurima* are all short, whereas the last syllables of *tabulas* and *pictas* are long and *innumerabilis* contains three long syllables: - v v - v -). Cf. § 57 above on *numerum signorum*.

solet … dicere se emisse: a word order that builds up suspense. After the non-descript main verb (*solet*: Verres used to … do/say what?) Cicero establishes the facts in the intervening relative clause before providing the infinitive that completes *solet*; the punchline of what Verres is wont to say is saved for last: the indirect statement (depending on *dicere*) *se emisse*. In delivery, one can imagine Cicero hesitating just a moment after *dicere* before delivering the coup de grâce. The absurd lie or euphemism *se emisse* is designed to trigger hilarity in the audience.

non numquam: double negation (not never); the technical term for this rhetorical device is *litotes.

quoniam quidem: after eliciting laughter by means of *se emisse*, Cicero elaborates on the joke. The particle *quidem* after *quoniam* helps to keep the tone light, placing a notional 'as if!' over the clause.

in Achaiam, Asiam, Pamphyliam: *asyndetic *tricolon that covers the geographical area of Verres' exploits. As in § 55, Cicero gives his audience a grand, geopolitical sweep. But rather than military expansion as in § 55, here he traces a trail of illegal looting.

(a) sumptu (b) publico et (b) legationis (a) nomine: the arrangement is *chiastic. The phrase as a whole underscores the crucial point that Verres travelled to Asia in an official capacity – a reminder that sets up the punchline of the sentence, that is, the contrast between Verres' actual status and the role he foolishly claimed for himself (see next note).

mercator signorum tabularumque pictarum missus est: here we have the *reductio ad absurdum* of Verres' apology that he 'bought' his work of art – as if the Roman people had sent him on a special mission as a *mercator*, a merchant or trader, a profession utterly irreconcilable with the dignity of a Roman magistrate. Cicero here draws out the implications of Verres' apology that he bought the artworks, making it seem preposterous.

Habeo et ipsius et patris eius accepti tabulas omnis: there is a textual difficulty here. The manuscripts have *accepi* (I have received) rather than *accepti* (the genitive of *acceptum*, i.e. 'the receipt side of an account'). This generates an undesirable *tautology with *habeo* (I have). *accepti tabulas omnis*, the reading found in Pseudo-Asconius and printed here, is a somewhat cumbersome way of saying 'all the accounting books'. Another way of solving the difficulty is to read *accepi* and to delete *habeo*. In his *Oxford Classical Text*, W. Peterson prints the elegant *et istius et patris eius accepi tabulas omnis*.[62]

et ipsius et patris eius … patris … tuas: another *chiastic arrangement: Cicero begins and ends with Verres *filius*. *ipsius* (or *istius*) and *eius* are contemptuous and distance Verres emotionally from his father (preparing the ground for their diverse morals and habits of accounting), an effect enhanced by Cicero's sudden shift to *tuas* and his direct address to Verres in *ais*.

patris eius … patris, quoad vixit: Verres' father, who had the same name as his son, was a senator still alive at the end of 72 BC, as *Ver.* 2.2.95 shows, where Cicero recalls his intervention on behalf of his son when complaints about Verres' maladministration in Sicily came to the attention of the senate. He must have died shortly before the trial. Whereas Cicero thinks nothing of slandering Verres' son, whom he proclaims to be as morally depraved as his father (see 2.1.32), he is noticeably more respectful of Verres' father.

diligentissime: Cicero repeats the adverb, which he here uses of himself in an act of self-promotion designed to impress the judges, with reference to Antonius a few lines later (*nam fecit diligentissime*). Their exacting standards serve as positive foil for Verres' careless and unsystematic approach to record-keeping.

legi atque digessi: the basic sense of *digerere* [*dis-* + *gerere*] is 'to scatter, disperse' and the *OLD* lists our passage s.v. 4a 'to lay or set out, dispose'. But what Cicero most likely means is that he 'took them apart', that is, studied them in depth.

---

62. Cf. Peterson, W. (1903), 'Emendations of Cicero's *Verrines*', *The Classical Review* 17, 198–202 (201–02).

confecisse: *conficere* in the sense 'to keep accounts or records': *OLD* s.v. 3b. Cicero uses the verb six times in the paragraph: of Verres (*confecisse*), twice of Antonius (first the compositum *confecisse*, then the simplex *fecit*), twice of anonymous (first the simplex *fecisse*, then the compositum *confecisse*), and finally again of Verres (*confecisse*). The pattern is *chiastic: a_1 a_2 b_2 b_3 a_3 a_1, with a = compositum, b = simplex, and a_1 = Verres, a_2/b_2 = Antonius, and b_3/a_3 = anonymous. Keeping accounts (and different ways of doing so) is of course the main theme of the paragraph and Cicero takes care that his use of the key word generates a symmetrical pattern that gives structure and coherence on the formal level. The dot on the i in this artful arrangement is the fact that *conficere* has to be supplied mentally for a seventh time right at the very end of the paragraph, as infinitive complement to *destitisse* (i.e. 'he ceased', sc. 'to keep records'). The absent presence is of course thematically fully appropriate: Verres' records are shockingly incomplete.

Nam in isto, iudices: after his direct address to Verres, Cicero instantly re-establishes distance by turning back to the judges: the phrase *in isto* resounds with mocking disgust, as Cicero exposes Verres like a disagreeable insect to the inspection of the audience: what they will find is unprecedented, indeed scandalous (*hoc novum reperietis*). The direct address is a particularly powerful technique to encourage the audience to engage with the point made by the speaker.

(a) hoc novum ... (b) Audimus ... (b) Audimus ... (a) Hoc vero novum et ridiculum est: Cicero first announces something new, but then delays specification of what '*hoc novum*' actually is by first rehearsing other possible ways of doing accounts. These serve as foils for his climactic return to *hoc novum* and give added force to the further attribute *ridiculum*. On the lexical level, the pattern is again *chiastic; but note that Cicero subsumes *two* different *genera* of keeping accounts under the first *Audimus*: by alluding to the mistaken opinion about Antonius' record keeping he is able to contrast his exacting punctiliousness throughout with keeping no records at all. After sketching out the best and the worst (marked by the two superlatives *diligentissime* and *minime*), Cicero adds the middling type under the second *Audimus*, i.e. those who weren't quite on the ball from the start, but at some point got their act together and then kept at it. Verres, in contrast, falls outside this spectrum of 'reasonable' possibilities: his way of doing accounts, i.e. to have begun, but then to have ceased abruptly and arbitrarily, is unprecedented (*novum*) and makes no sense at all: it is laughable (*ridiculum*).

quae est ... diligentissime: *quae* is a connecting relative; for Cicero's argument, this information, which is presented as if it were in parenthesis, may at first sight look like a marginal gloss, not least since it disrupts an otherwise perfectly symmetrical arrangement. Consider the text without it:

(i) *audimus* (ii) *aliquem* (iii) *tabulas* <u>numquam</u> *confecisse*; [*quae ... diligentissime*] (iv) *verum sit hoc genus aliquod, minime probandum.*

(i) *audimus* (ii) *alium* (iii) <u>*non ab initio*</u> *fecisse,* <u>*sed ex tempore aliquo*</u> *confecisse*; (iv) *est aliqua etiam huiusce rei ratio.*

Put differently, Cicero opens anaphorically with the same verb (i: *audimus*), before identifying an anonymous representative of the respective approach (ii: *aliquem/ alium*); he then specifies the vital criterion for his attack on Verres, namely the duration of the record keeping, when it began and ended, if at all (iii: *numquam/ non ab initio, sed ex tempore aliquo*); and concludes with an appraising comment (iv). The mention of Antonius on the other hand breaks the anonymity and has the odd effect that Cicero gives, and then instantly invalidates, an example of the first approach; we also do not hear anything of when Antonius began keeping his accounts and for how long he continued, though the implication is clearly that he started when he should have and kept it up throughout his public career; still a strategic *semper* or something similar would not have come amiss. On the other hand, as pointed out above, Cicero gets some rhetorical purchase out of including Antonius, not least the full spectrum of more or less 'rational' possibilities, marked by the two superlatives *minime* and *diligentissime*.

Antonio: Marcus Antonius (*cos.* 99), one of the interlocutors in Cicero's *de Oratore* (completed in 55). For a recent account of his public career see Fantham, E. (2004), *The Roman World of Cicero's De Oratore*, Oxford, 26–48.

verum sit hoc genus aliquod, minime probandum: 'but may this be [in the sense of: count as] one possible approach, though in no way to be approved.'

usque ad M. Terentium et C. Cassium consules: i.e. 73 BC in our reckoning. Romans of the Republic dated their years according to the consuls in office ('the annalistic scheme'). The alternative dating 'ab urbe condita' was a later invention. (Imagine referring to years past by American Presidents and British Prime Ministers: 'in the first year of Clinton's second term in office and Blair's first'; '1997' is far more convenient.)[63] Verres, in other words, maintained that he had kept accounts during the initial phase of his public career (up till the end of his praetorship in 74 BC), but discontinued doing so afterwards: this piece of information is vital for the years during which he governed Sicily as pro-magistrate (73–71 BC), but irrelevant in the present context: for his time as legate in Asia, account books apparently existed.

§ 61

After looking into Verres' (lack of) accounting during his pro-praetorship, which will much preoccupy him in later books of the second *actio*, Cicero calls himself to order and sets aside the topic for further treatment in future (see *alio loco* hoc cuius modi sit considerabimus). During his years in the Greek East, after all, it is Verres' keeping of accounts that Cicero uses as basis for his attack: the records prove that none of the statues and artworks that he brought back to Rome was properly bought.

Alio loco ... nunc: Cicero now concedes that his mockery of Verres' way of accounting at a later stage of his career has no relevance to the issue at hand.

cuius modi sit: an indirect question.

Plurima signa pulcherrima, plurimas tabulas optimas: four superlatives; the two phrases are constructed in precise parallel.

Atque utinam neges!: *neges* is present subjunctive expressing a wish. Both the conjunction *atque* (as an emphatic introduction) and the particle *utinam* reinforce the intensity of the wish. With this wish Cicero submits that, on the basis of the account books, Verres would have been better off denying that he brought any artwork to Rome rather than claiming that he bought any. The fact that such a denial is itself an absurd impossibility (see the previous sentence: ... *te negare non potes*) underscores how ridiculous the claim of legal acquisition in Verres' case truly is.

❧

---

63. For more on ancient dating systems see Feeney, D. C. (2007), *Caesar's Calendar: Ancient Time and the Beginnings of History*, Berkeley.

Unum ostende: an imperative and hence a direct challenge to Verres. *unum* is the subjective accusative of the indirect statement depending on *ostende*, but Cicero's word order initially gives the impression that it is a direct object.

quae nunc ad impluvium tuum stant, quae multos annos ante valvas Iunonis Samiae steterunt: two *asyndetic relative clauses that, by means of precise parallelisms, establish a laconic contrast between past and present: *nunc ~ multos annos; ad impluvium tuum ~ ante valvas Iunonis Samiae; stant ~ steterunt*. Within these indications of time, location, and placement Cicero has embedded an outrageous change in ownership, from Samian Juno (*Iunonis Samiae*) to Verres (*tuum*).

impluvium: specifically, the quadrangular basin in the floor of the atrium of a Roman house that received the rain water from the roof; more generally, the entire open space of the atrium.

valvas: the folding doors of the temple.

Iunonis Samiae: The island of Samos became part of the province of Asia in 84 BC; it boasted a famous Heraion, i.e. temple of Hera (the Greek counterpart to the Roman Juno), which featured masterpieces from various famous sculptors (Polycletus, Praxiteles, Myron). Cicero here harks back to his account at 2.1.49–51. Lactantius (c. 250 – c. 320) quotes Varro (116 – 27 BC) as saying that the island was called 'Parthenia' since it was where Juno grew up and also married Jupiter. He refers to her temple there as *nobilissimum et antiquissimum* and discusses her cult statue – it was apparently dressed up as a bride, and the annual worship centred on nuptial rites (*Divine Institutes*, 1.17.8). One of Juno's spheres of responsibility was the wellbeing of women and marriage. By recalling Verres' manhandling of statues associated with her temple here, Cicero obliquely reminds his audience of Verres' debauchery, the character trait that received brief mention in *praeteritio* in his account of Verres' youth (2.1.32–33) and will dominate his version of what happened at Lampsacus (§§ 63–9).

habes [sc. *ostendere*] **quo modo emeris**: *habes* here means 'to have the wherewithal, be in a position (to)': *OLD* s.v. 12c. Cicero elides the complementary infinitive, which is understood from the previous sentence.

quo modo emeris: an indirect question; *emeris* is second person singular perfect subjunctive.

haec, inquam, duo … a ceteris signis: Cicero endows the two statues with human qualities: they experience loneliness (*sola*), await what lies in store for them (*exspectant*), and feel sadness as if the other statues (*ab statuis*: ablative of the agent) had abandoned them (*relicta ac destituta*). He feels compassion for the last two (*duo … sola*) remaining pieces of plunder left over from the great many (*plurima*) that Verres started out with.

sector: from *seco*, to cut or slice; here: 'One who buys up captured or confiscated property at a public auction, with a view to reselling it' (*OLD* s.v. 2). Cicero employs the term quite frequently to abuse an adversary as a profiteer of injustice and slaughter.

relicta ac destituta a ceteris signis: apparently, as long as Verres thought that the trial could be delayed to ensure a favourable outcome, he retained possession of his plunder; but once he realized that Cicero had pushed through his own schedule, he cleared his house of all statuary, except these two from Samos. See 2.1.51 (the section where he describes Verres' ravaging of the island of Samos, a particularly rich hunting ground): … *nullum signum domi reliquisti praeter duo quae in mediis aedibus sunt, quae ipsa Samo sublata sunt*? ('… did you not leave no other statue in your house except two that stood in the middle of it, and even those were taken from Samos?'). *relicta ac destituta* is a *pleonasm.

§ 62

A transitional paragraph, in the course of which Cicero shifts the focus from Verres' illicit desire for works of art to his sexual licence. The common theme is his uncontrollable lust: he is a man ruled by his passions, whatever they are. His disrespect for the female deities Diana (§ 53) and Juno (§ 61) anticipate his maltreatment of human women.

At, credo: a parenthetical opening that endows what follows with an ironic force: see *OLD* s.v. *at* 12 and s.v. *credo* 8c.

in hisce solis rebus: *-ce* is an enclitic, deictic particle, attached to the ablative plural (*his*) of the demonstrative pronoun *hic, haec, hoc*. Its use here reinforces the irony that Cicero introduced with *At credo*, by putting special stress on *solis*. What Cicero is actually saying is something like 'You are not foolish enough to believe that the lust for artworks was Verres' one and only passion, judges, are you?' The locked word order, in which the two attributes *hisce* and *solis* are framed by the preposition *in* and their referent *rebus*, reproduces iconically the notion of a confined or limited problem – in contrast to *indomitas cupiditates atque effrenatas*, where the way in which Cicero adds on the synonymous second attribute *atque effrenatas* enacts the idea of passions being out of control.

indomitas cupiditates atque effrenatas: etymologically, *in-domitus* means 'untamed' (*dominari*) and hence incapable of living within a human household (*domus*); Latin authors use it predominantly of beasts, though Cicero is fond of applying it metaphorically to human beings as well, either specific individuals, whom he deems to be in the thrall of irrational (that is, beastly) passions and desires, or a certain segment of the population, namely the people/masses, whom social elites throughout history have frequently portrayed as acting on instincts, just as animals: see, for instance, *de Republica* ('On the Commonwealth') 1.9, 1.49 and 1.68. The notion of desires that are out of control implies as a corollary that they have come to dominate the person (and his rational self), who harbours them. The idea that, within an individual, reason has to restrain the passions underwrites much moral philosophy from Plato onwards and also informs other literary genres (such as tragedy, comedy, historiography, or oratory) concerned with the representation of human beings and their motivations for action (see note on *ratione aliqua aut modo*). The upshot of Cicero's abuse is that Verres' agency emerges as severely compromised: he is not a dignified senator who controls his desires and hence has the right to govern Rome and the world, but a subhuman creature, in the thrall of passions, who acts out his animal-instincts. *Effrenatus* (*ex + frenum*) is the perfect passive participle of *effreno* (though the *Thesaurus Linguae Latinae* s.v. moots the possibility that the finite form was derived from the participle). It is synonymous with *indomitus* (with an even stronger, literal link to the animal sphere) and one of Cicero's favourite terms of abuse, usually linked to a noun from the domain of the passions: *cupiditates* (as here), but also *libido, audacia*, or *furor*. The ensuing image is of a person 'gone wild', behaving utterly out of control, unleashed from any civilizing inhibitions, which is not unlike the effect of charging Verres with insanity (*a-mentia*: see above § 54).

ceterae libidines: Cicero uses *cupiditates* and *libidines* synonymously; both are non-technical words for desires or passions (in contrast to the philosophical, and specifically Stoic, *affectus*, which Cicero uses in his philosophical writings, but not in his speeches).

ratione aliqua aut modo: *modus* is the consequence of *ratio*; it is possible to see the phrase as a *hendiadys, in the sense of 'rational moderation'.

Quam multis … quam multis … existimatis?: the emotive *anaphora of the interrogative proverb *quam* and the indiscriminate *multis* prepares Cicero's punchline that Verres' transgressions are countless. The question is clearly rhetorical.

ingenuis … matribus familias: Cicero singles out two categories of victims: freeborn individuals (*ingenuus, ingenua*; in the dative plural the gender remains unspecified) and wedded mothers who preside over the household (*familia*). Put differently, Verres' conduct tears apart the normative fabric of society, turning free people into slaves of his passion and violating those who sustain society by means of reproduction (*matribus*) and oversight of a key social institution (*familias*). (Note that *familias* is an archaic form of the genetive singular.)

stuprorum flagitiorumque: the original meaning of *stuprum* was 'disgrace'; in the sexual arena it refers to an illicit act, on the grounds of adultery or violence.[64] Here it picks up the claim in the previous sentence that Verres was a serial rapist of married women, i.e. perpetrated adulterous violence on a large scale. *Flagitium* does not have a technical sexual sense.

taetra atque impura: *taeter* means 'morally offensive, abominable, foul' and carries connotations of monstrosity – it is one of Cicero's favourite attributes of abuse and lowers the person thus labelled to a subhuman level. *impurus* means 'morally foul, esp. in regard to sexual conduct' (*OLD* s.v. 2) and can carry connotations of religious pollution. It, too, features frequently in Ciceronian invective, and is an attribute that accompanies Verres throughout the *Verrines*: see e.g. 2.1.32 and 2.2.192.

… reliquerit?: another rhetorical question.

Ecquo in oppido: *ec-* is a prefix that gets attached to interrogatives with intensive or indefinite force, hence the interrogative adjective *ecqui, -ae/a, -od*

---

64. See Adams, J. (1982), *The Latin Sexual Vocabulary*, London, 200–1.

'is there any?' Cicero uses it to underscore the indiscriminate and random trail of outrage and violence that Verres left behind wherever he went. See also *ecqua virgo sit* at the end of § 63.

Ecquo in oppido pedem posuit ubi non plura stuprorum: the opening of the sentence contains a variety of sound effects: the rhyme *ecquo ~ oppido*, the *alliteration in *pedem posuit* (prepared for by *oppido* and continued by *plura*), and the assonance of 'p', 'u' and 'r' in *plura ~ stuprorum*.

plura ... vestigia: a remarkable *hyperbaton (from Greek *huperbaino*, that is, 'to step over'); Cicero may even be punning on the technical term of the rhetorical device he is using, given that he here comments on where Verres put his feet or left traces, both literally and metaphorically. Likewise, Cicero enacts the hyperbolic claim that Verres' acts of transgression outnumber his footprints in the respective length of the two genitive phrases that depend on *vestigia*: *stuprorum flagitiorumque suorum* has 12 syllables, *adventus sui* 5.

adventus sui: genitive of *adventus, -us*, m., depending on *vestigia*; its technical meaning is 'arrival'.

vim attulisse: also below § 67. For oratorical decorum in sexual matters, see Adams, J. N. (1982), *The Latin Sexual Vocabulary*, Baltimore and London, 222–23.

omnia quae ... praetermittam; haec quae ... relinquam; unum aliquod ... eligam: the last sentence is built as a *tricolon, with the first two items serving as foil for the third (see next note). Cicero marks the contrast syntactically, using an accusative object + attached relative clause for the first two units and an accusative object only for the third. The effect is a heightened sense of drama, as Cicero diminishes the length but increases the rhetorical force. The way he sets up his choice of illustrative example implies that denial of its truth is impossible: as a matter of course he does not touch upon anything in doubt (*omnia quae negari poterunt praetermittam*), and only chooses one instance from among those transgressions that are well established and notorious.

praetermittam ... relinquam: Cicero here employs the rhetorical device of *praeteritio, which works according to the principle of having your cake and eating it at the same time – by mentioning omission, he ensures that what is omitted nevertheless registers with the audience. Often, *pi* is cast in such a way (as here) that its use is advertised as being motivated by consideration for the audience or a sense of duty and thereby heightens appreciation for the orator's sense of decorum ('of what is appropriate'): Cicero could if he wished spend several days detailing the sexual exploits and outrages of Verres – he won't, limiting himself to one instance only in order to press on with the real business.

de nefariis ... factis: *nefarius* is an adjective derived from *nefas*, 'what is not *fas*', that is, in violation of divine law. Its basic meanings are 'immoral' or 'wicked' and it carries connotations of sacrilege. It continues the theme of Verres as a religious criminal who does not shy away from plundering shrines of the gods and manhandling their cult-statues.

oneris negotique: a *hendiadys; the phrase is a partitive genitive depending on *hoc*.

pervenire: the infinitive complements and completes *possim*; Cicero again uses *hyperbaton (see above on *plura*), and again the stylistic device mirrors the theme, that is, the distance that Cicero's speech needs to cover before arriving at its final destination, Sicily. Despite his commitment to economy of coverage (see above on *praetermittam ... relinquam*, here recalled by means of *facilius*, which picks up the announcement that Cicero will choose one deed only for further comment), the path is long (see *aliquando*: 'finally') – even though he has decided to take shortcuts through the terrain of Verres' crimes before his governorship of Sicily.

§ 63

The events at Lampsacus, which was located in the Roman province of Asia, will preoccupy Cicero until the beginning of § 86. This is a fairly self-contained unit of text. Mitchell (1986) 188 calls Cicero's account of what happened at Lampsacus 'one of the finest examples of his skill in *narratio*' – and, as one could add with reference to Catherine Steel's study, spin.[65] For in order to appreciate the text in all of its nuances it is of vital importance to bear in mind that we are not getting an objective record of

---

65. Steel, C. (2004), 'Being Economical with the Truth: What Really Happened at Lampsacus?', in J. Powell and J. Paterson (eds.), *Cicero the Advocate*, Oxford, 233–51.

what actually happened, but what Cicero wants his audience to believe has happened. He accordingly manipulates the available information (or facts) in such a way as to capture the attention of his audience by means of a fascinating story that portrays Verres in the worst possible light. In Cicero, narration always has the double function of report *and argument*. Indeed, the facts that can be established with reasonable certainty from Cicero's text (our only source) boil down to: (i) during Verres' stay at Lampsacus, a commotion broke out at a dinner party that the highranking Lampsacene citizen Philodamus organized and which was attended by several members of Verres' entourage (not by Verres himself); (ii) during this commotion, Cornelius, one of Verres' lictors, was killed; (iii) at the subsequent trial, over which Dolabella presided, Philodamus and his son were sentenced to death and summarily executed. Everything else remains unsubstantiated and circumstantial – we have to take Cicero's word for it, even though in § 71 he mentions his informants (P. Tettius and C. Varro, who belonged to the staff of C. Nero, the governor of Asia at the time). Cicero's purpose is obvious: he construes his tale in such a way that Verres emerges as the mastermind behind the commotion at the dinner party, driven on by lust and lechery; that Philodamus and his son are the innocent and upright victims of Roman aggression; and that the court proceedings were skewed by Verres and his supporters, meaning that the Roman provincial governors of Cilicia (Dolabella) and Asia (Nero) perpetrated judicial homicide to protect Verres. A good way to approach this portion of the text is to ask at every step what techniques Cicero employs to endow his version of the story with plausibility: how does he enhance the appearance of veracity? What parts of his story do not stand up to scrutiny? How does he brush over details that suggest a different explanation of what happened? What is the balance between argument and appeal to the emotions, logic and outrage, that Cicero aims for? Are you, in the end, convinced that Cicero has actually told us what *really* happened at Lampsacus?

In terms of structure, the story itself falls into two parts, roughly equal in length: §§ 63–69 give an account of what happened in Lampsacus; §§ 70–76 deal with the judicial aftermath, i.e. the trial and the execution of Philodamus and his son. This is followed by a lengthy attempt to discredit Verres' version of the story (§§ 77–85). The strategy is telling: Cicero first advances his own account and then uses it as foil to question Verres' 'official' version of the story.

In § 63, Cicero sets the scene. He begins in an ethnographic vein, introducing the inhabitants of the city and their key traits, before detailing how it came about that Verres paid a visit to the city. The final part of the paragraph details what Verres initiated upon his arrival at Lampsacus; Cicero makes it out that he is reporting 'standard operating procedure' (see esp. *ut mos erat istius*), thereby underscoring his earlier point that he chose this episode *exempli gratia*: it stands in for countless similar events that Cicero is passing over in silence. The claim that we are witnessing 'routine business' adds to the plausibility of the tale – but it may not be more than a claim.

autem: in its basic sense, it expresses a contrast 'without any pronounced adversative sense' (*OLD* s.v. 1) – here it is between the qualities of the town (fame and renown) and the qualities of the inhabitants (peace-loving and dutiful).

clarum et nobile: a surprising, and perhaps slightly ironic, choice of attributes: in Rome, public recognition derived from political and, especially, military success; the so-called *nobiles* were those who belonged to aristocratic families with a distinguished record of past achievement in politics and warfare, including at least one consulship. Here Cicero uses *nobile* in the generic, non-technical sense of 'renowned' or 'famous', as if he wishes to underscore cross-cultural differences between Greece and Rome: if in Rome, renown derives first and foremost from strenuous feats of public endeavour, in the Greek-speaking East, a lifestyle of leisure seems capable of ensuring a famous reputation – though it is important to bear in mind that Cicero, strictly speaking, applies the attributes to the town, not its inhabitants. Alternatively, 'the description of the city itself as *clarum et nobile* may be meant to indicate that it is not democratic, and therefore not in thrall to the lower classes': Steel (2004) 243.

homines … ipsi Lampsaceni: technically speaking, the *homines* here is superfluous – Cicero could simply have refered to the *Lampsaceni*, that is, the inhabitants of Lampsacus; but contrasting different types of *human beings* is one of his favourite ploys: Gildenhard (2011) 50–73. His account of the events at Lampsacus offers a perfect case study in his 'anthropological rhetoric' insofar as Cicero uses his version of the events to highlight what type of human being (or rather non-human monster) Verres is. In the paragraph here, he contrasts the gentle human beings who live in Lampsacus with the human beings that make up Verres' entourage and who are utterly wicked and sinful: see *nequissimis turpissimisque <u>hominibus</u>* towards the end of the paragraph. It is important to bear in mind that the generic portrayal of the inhabitants that Cicero offers has no *historical* value.

officiosi ... sedati et quieti ... accommodati: In each case the verb (*sunt*) is implied. Cicero assumes the point of view of the ethnographer who informs his Roman audience of the characteristics of the inhabitants of Lampsacus. Three qualities stand out: they are particularly well predisposed towards Roman citizens; they have an extraordinarily calm disposition; and they value a life of leisure even more than the rest of the Greeks. The *ellipsis results in a more concentrated focus on the attributes of the Lampsacenes that Cicero wishes to highlight.

prope: 'almost', 'virtually'; Cicero often slips in qualifications (such as *quasi, paene*, or, as here, *prope*, 'which expresses the idea of falling short by a little': *OLD* s.v. 6) to put some perspective on his *hyperboles or take the edge off an excessively outrageous statement.[66] In this paragraph, he uses *prope* twice.

Graecorum: *apo koinou*: the genitive is shared between *praeter ceteros* and *otium*.

cum ... tum: coordinating two co-existing circumstances, with a special emphasis on the second: *OLD* s.v. *cum* 14.

summe ... maxime ... ad summum ... otium: Cicero again operates in superlative mode: the two adverbs (*summe, maxime*) and the one attribute (*summum*) suggest that the inhabitants of Lampsacus are so peaceful as to be all but comatose.

ad summum Graecorum otium: Romans (and in particular Cicero) stereotypically portrayed Greeks as fond of leisure – in contrast to the Romans, who were busy conquering and governing the world. In Cicero, this ethnic difference manifests itself paradigmatically in the two figures of the Greek philosopher, who lives a life of leisure in idle speculations of a theoretical nature, and the Roman statesman, who is fully preoccupied with the administration of public (and military) affairs at home and abroad. Cicero here extends a highly tendentious view of the life-style choices of cultural elites to entire ethnic groups, in an attitude of appreciative and

---

66. See Gildenhard (2011) 266–67.

jovial benevolence: here, for once, the Greeks are 'the good guys', the victims of Roman oppression. The stereotypes to which he resorts when the Greeks are 'the bad guys' are more insidious.[67]

potius quam ad ullam vim aut tumultum: violence (*vis*) and unrest (*tumultum*), the antithesis of *otium*, are of course precisely the eventual outcome of Verres' visit to the city. The formulation thus has a proleptic force: it obliquely alerts the audience to what will happen. But initial characterization of the Lampsacenes suggests that violent unrest in their city is the most unlikely turn of events, indeed a perversion of their nature, and thus it prepares the ground for his argument that the responsibility for what was to come rests entirely with Verres.

Accidit ... ut ... veniret: after setting the scene, Cicero turns to the plot; the impersonal main verb *accidit* takes the exposed, front position, whereas the complementary *ut*-clause is much delayed (*accidit ut* + subjunctive means 'it happens or comes about that', 'it is the case that': *OLD* s.v. 7a.): in-between (from *cum iste...* to *adcommodatum depoposcisset*) Cicero inserts the requisite background information that explains how Verres happened to visit Lampsacus. This syntax does not translate easily into English.

a Cn. Dolabella efflagitasset: *flagito*, as well as the intensive *efflagito*, means 'to ask imperiously'; Verres in other words behaves rudely towards his superior in charge; later on in the paragraph Cicero portrays Verres as a man ruled by his disgraceful desires (*libidines flagitiosae*: see below), which sheds retrospective light on the reasons for his outrageous conduct: he is a man ruled by his disgraceful passions.

Cn. Dolabella: Cn. Cornelius Dolabella was praetor in 81 BC, before becoming governor of the province Cilicia (80–79 BC). Verres served him first as legate and, after the death of his quaestor C. Malleolus, as pro-quaestor. Shortly after Dolabella's return to Rome, he was successfully prosecuted on the charge of extortion by M. Aemilius Scaurus and sentenced to exile in 78 BC.[68] A prime witness for the prosecution was none other than Verres, who took this opportunity to blame any mismanagement and misdeed

---

67. The topic of ethnic stereotypes in ancient thought has recently received a new monograph treatment: see Gruen E. (2010), *Rethinking the Other in Antiquity*, Princeton.
68. For a discussion of the events, see Gruen, E. (1966), 'The Dolabellae and Sulla', *American Journal of Philology* 87, 385–99.

that happened during his time in Asia Minor on his superior-in-command. Cicero makes heavy weather of this act of treachery at various moments in the *Verrines*, notably at 2.1.44–45, that is, shortly before our present passage and again in § 77 (where he addresses Dolabella directly).

ad regem Nicomedem regemque Sadalam: Nicomedes IV Philopator was king of Bithynia, Sadalas a Thracian king. As Mitchell (1986) 190 points out, 'embassies to allied or client states could be highly profitable' – on account of the lavish gifts and hospitality that such kings parcelled out to get on good terms with their Roman visitors. Steel (2004) 241 n. 18, however, cautions us to take Cicero's insinuations at face value: 'given the delicate situation of the whole region following the first Mithradatic War, we do not have to follow Cicero in his suggestion that there was no pressing public interest which could justify the embassy.'

cumque: the *-que* connects the two *cum*-clauses.

iter hoc: the phrase correlates *chiastically with *illo itinere* in the subsequent clause.

sibi: the dative of advantage (*dativus commodi*) is strictly speaking unnecessary, but nicely reinforces *ad quaestum suum* and more generally the utterly selfish nature of Verres' motivation.

depoposcisset: 'to demand peremptorily' – as with *ef-flagitasset*, Cicero intensifies the meaning of the verb by opting for a composite form (*de-poscere*).

magis ad ... quam ad ... adcommodatum: with slight variation, Cicero uses the same construction of Verres as he just did of the Lampsacenes (*ad ... potius quam ad ... adcommodati*). The different positions of the comparatives *magis* and *potius* serve to emphasize the positive in the case of the Lampsacenes and the negative in the case of Verres. Note also the shift in focus from the Lampsacenes themselves (*accommodati*) to an aspect of Verres' doings (*accommodatum* modifies *iter*).

ad (a) **quaestum** (b) **suum ... ad** (b) **rei publicae** (a) **tempus**: the arrangement is *chiastic. With *tempus* Cicero signals that Verres is wasting his time in office – a short and precious resource – that he ought to spend in seeing to the public interest for his personal gain and pleasure.

cum magna calamitate et prope pernicie civitatis: *cum* here means 'with as a consequence, with resulting': *OLD* s.v. 12; *civitatis* modifies both *calamitate* and *pernicie* (that is, it is used **apo koinou*) and constitutes a shocking end to the question as to who has suffered the calamity: nothing less than the entire citizen community. Again, Cicero proclaims the outcome at the beginning. The phrase is well balanced in terms of syllables and assonance: *magna calamitate* (2:5), *prope pernicie* (2:4); but it also sports variation: *magna* is an attribute, *prope* an adverbial qualification. The arrangement is *climactic, moving from terrible disaster (*calamitas*) to complete destruction (*pernicies*). Cicero here falls out of his reporter's logic – it almost sounds as if Verres, the subject of the two *cum*-clauses as well as the purpose-clause – demands to travel by way of Lampsacus *in order to* visit death and destruction upon its community. This, of course, is not the case. Yet by his anticipation of the consequences of Verres' visits (whatever his intentions), Cicero manages to imply that *calamitas* and *pernicies* are inevitable byproducts of Verres' approach to provincial administration.

Deducitur iste … comitesque … conlocantur: verbs and subjects form a *chiasmus, whereas *ad Ianitorem quendam hospitem* and *apud ceteros hospites* are construed in parallel fashion. Note the switch into the historic present.

Ut mos erat istius, atque ut eum suae libidines flagitiosae facere admonebant: the imperfect tense here indicates iteration: Cicero recounts routine business. *Libidines flagitiosae* harks back to his earlier discussion of Verres' lustfulness. Note how Cicero's choice of grammar helps portray Verres as a plaything of his passions: it is not he who is in control of his own passions, his passions are in control of him; they are in the nominative and are the subject of *admonebant*, whereas Verres is the accusative object, the person whom they govern (*eum*). The combination of this figure of thought with a reference to habit (*mos*), i.e. a customary practice, generates a particularly insidious effect: it suggests that passionate, i.e. unpredictable, irrational, un-Roman, and despicable, actions that fall short of standards of rational and socially acceptable behaviour are the norm, rather than the exception, with Verres. Not unlike the reference to *voluptas*, *libido*, and *cupiditas* in § 57, the clause *atque ut … admonebant* thus constitutes a piece of spiteful ethopoiea not strictly necessary for the advancement of the plot.

iste … comitesque eius: Cicero's account targets both Verres and his cronies. See the introduction for some comments on the entourage of Roman officials.

nequissimis turpissimisque hominibus: two further abusive superlatives; as elsewhere Cicero characterizes Verres' entourage from an anthropological perspectives: in the apposition, he specifies what kind of *human beings* (*hominibus*) follow him.

ecqua virgo sit aut mulier: the formulation recalls § 62, where Cicero also used a form of *equis* (*ecquo in oppido*) and a reference to two types of women (*ingenuae* and *matres familias*) to underscore the arbitrary, indiscriminate, and hence comprehensive nature of Verres' sexual crimes. The stylistic and rhetorical reminiscences reinforce Cicero's claim that he has quite randomly chosen one specific example to illustrate a countless number of transgressions. If the omission of *familias* after *mulier* downgrades the outrage (though broadens the remit of the order), the switch from *ingenuae* to *virgo* heightens the premonition that the sex-monster Verres is about to rape an innocent virgin, aided by his vile companions.

digna: highly ironic – as if Verres were particularly choosy concerning his victims.

quam ob rem: also written as one word (*quamobrem*), it is an interrogative or relative adverbial phrase: 'for which reason, for the sake of which, why': *OLD* s.v. 2.

quam ob rem ipse Lampsaci diutius commoraretur: Cicero insidiously suggests that the quality of the city's 'female resources', rather than any concern for public business, are Verres' only reason to linger.

§ 64

After the generic references in § 63 (*ut mos erat istius, negotium dat illis suis comitibus, ecqua virgo sit aut mulier*), Cicero now zooms in on specifics: in this particular case, the companion who came up with the goods was one Rubrius, who, being particularly talented for this sort of thing, learned from hearsay that one high-ranking citizen in Lampsacus called Philodamus had an outstandingly beautiful daughter known for her chastity. (We never learn her actual name.) This piece of information, so Cicero submits, was all it took to inflame Verres with an all-consuming passion to have his way with the woman. A tragic farce begins to play itself out. Comic elements include the role of Rubrius, who acts as scout and pimp; Verres' instant outburst into passion upon hearing news of Philodamus' daughter; the speaking name of Ianitor, Verres' host; and hyperbolic statements such as the use of excessive force (*summa vi*) by which Ianitor is trying to prevent Verres from moving house. (The notion that a chap called 'Porter' gets into a pushing and pulling match with a Roman official to keep him lodged in his house borders on the absurd – it is a scene more at home in dramatic and literary genres, such as comedy or love elegy, than in Roman provincial administration.) The assimilation of the narrative to a farce or mime is further aided by Cicero's generic use of *homo* to refer to the protagonists.

Rubrius quidam; Philodamum ... quendam: *quidam* means 'a certain' – Cicero uses the tag to introduce characters of the tale otherwise unknown to his audience. 'Nothing is known about Rubrius apart from what emerges in this passage; but given his position, as part of the entourage of a legate, it is probable that he was a young man who was in the provinces, quite possibly for the first time, to gain experience as a preliminary to a political career': Steel (2004) 240 n.14. Philodamus, on the other hand, whose name means something akin to 'fond (*philo-*) of the people (*damos*)', clearly belonged to the citizen-elite of Lampsacus, in terms of wealth, social rank, and willingness to undertake civic obligations, not least those imposed by Rome.[69] Cicero recognizes his status as a local aristocrat, but then concentrates on his private role as father and family man.

homo [i.e. Rubrius] **factus ad istius libidines ... . Homo** [i.e. Verres], **ut haec audivit, sic exarsit... . ... hominem** [i.e. Verres] **summa vi retinere coepit:** Cicero continues his 'anthropological idiom', which transposes the events from Roman history into a narrative about human types, from the good to the depraved.

rem istam: the accusative object of *defert*, which proleptically sums up, and finds explication in, the indirect statements *Philodamum esse quendam ...*; *eius esse filiam, ... ; eam ... existimari.*

---

69. For the life of leading citizens in the Greek cities of Asia Minor in Hellenistic and Roman times, see Quaß, F. (1993), *Die Honoratiorenschicht in den Städten des griechischen Ostens. Untersuchungen zur politischen und sozialen Entwicklung in hellenistischer und römischer Zeit*, Stuttgart.

genere, honore, copiis, existimatione: four ablatives of respect, in *asyndetic sequence that refer to different areas of distinction: descent (*genus*), rank in the community (*honos*), wealth (*copiae*), and reputation (*existimatio*).

filiam ... cum patre ... virum ... mulierem: Cicero here reports what Rubrius reported to Verres. This raises the question of focalization – is the idiom that of Rubrius or that of Cicero? Whereas the first three nouns (*filia, pater, vir*) are value-neutral, *mulier* ('a woman who is married or has had sexual experience (opp. *virgo*'): *OLD* s.v. 2) here surprises: from Cicero's point of view one would have expected rather *virgo*. He may have opted for *mulier* to convey a sense of Rubrius' crudity: he calls her a *mulier* to suggest that this female wants a male, that is Verres. Another possibility is that the daughter of Philodamus was indeed a *mulier*, rather than a *virgo*, perhaps because she had once been married, before returning to live with her father (as widow or divorcee?).

eximia pulchritudine; summa integritate pudicitiaque: ablatives of description, the first referring to natural endowment, the second to her moral character and reputation. Cicero submits that it is the tension between utmost desirability and utter unattainability that sets Verres' perverse mind afire. Note again Cicero's predilection for extreme diction: *eximia, summa*. His rhetoric colours everything as brightly and graphically as possible.

sic exarsit [ad id quod non modo ipse numquam viderat, sed ne audierat quidem ab eo qui ipse vidisset], **ut statim ...** : the *sic* sets up the consecutive *ut*-clause; the intervening *quod*-clause, which heightens the sense of Verres being utterly out of control (he is set on fire by mere hearsay), finds confirmation in his demand for instant action (*statim*).

exarsit ... coepit ... coepit ... dicit ... iubet: Cicero again switches from the perfect to the 'historical present' to make his narrative more vivid.

ab eo qui ipse vidisset: not Rubrius, but a hypothetical 'someone' who (unlike Rubrius) had actually seen Philodamus' daughter with his own eyes. The perfect subjunctive is generic ('... from a person of the kind that he had seen it himself').[70]

---

70. Morwood (1999) 100, Nr. 5 and 8.

Ianitor, qui nihil suspicaretur: Ianitor is a so-called 'speaking name', that is, a name that carries a meaning beyond designating an individual. In this case, the meaning ('Porter', 'Gatekeeper') is closely related to what Ianitor is doing, namely preventing Verres from leaving the house. Cicero most likely invented the name for the occasion to enhance the tragi-comic appeal of his narrative. (That an inhabitant of a Greek city should have a Latin name tailour-made for the yarn that Cicero is here spinning staggers belief.) The subjunctive in the relative clause has causal force.

ne quid: after *si, nisi, ne* and *num*, *ali-* disappears; here *(ali)quid* functions adverbially, in the sense of 'somehow'.

Rubrium, delicias suas, in omnibus eius modi rebus adiutorem suum et conscium, parum laute deversari dicit: Cicero, who here reports what Verres said, includes two phrases in apposition in the indirect statement: (a) *delicias suas*; (b) *in omnibus eius modi rebus adiutorem suum et conscium*. This again raises the question of focalization: are we supposed to imagine these phrases as having been part of what Verres allegedly said at the time or are they rather Cicero's observations, added to provide a commentary on Verres' utterance? Whereas (b) is clearly Cicero's point of view since it could not have been part of Verres' statement, the case is less clear cut with (a): in many ways, focalization via Verres produces a more vicious meaning, with Cicero putting the following into Verres' mouth: 'Rubrius, my darling, suffers in a substandard accommodation – have him transferred to Philodamus.' As Steel (2004) 239 n. 10 puts it: 'Is this markedly colloquial phrase, *delicias suas*, simply Cicero's description of Rubrius? Or does Cicero want us to think that Verres is so far gone in shamelessness that he could reveal such a liaison to a provincial?'

delicias suas: literally, *deliciae* means 'pleasures' or 'delights' and it is then used as an endearing expression of a 'delightful person' (in the sense of 'sweetheart' or 'pet'), most frequently in direct addresses. It is a mannerism of Roman New Comedy, but here constitutes an inappropriate endearment in several respects: in contrast to the Greek personnel of the genre, Verres is a Roman magistrate; his relationship to Rubrius should not follow any New-Comic pattern or habit of speech; the phrase, which is erotically charged, hinting at sexual delight, feminizes Rubrius by suggesting that he was Verres' 'toyboy'; and if the generic connotations of comedy resonate, the plot that unfolds here is tragic. (Cf. § 76, which describes the heart-wrenching and tear-inducing *spectaculum* – the public execution of Philodamus and his son – that brings the affair to a sorry end.)

deversari: 'to have lodgings'.

Iste, qui ... reperire non posset, ... coepit: Cicero here portrays Verres in a hilarious fisty-cuff battle with a stubborn provincial, who is loath to see his distinguished visitor go and hence manhandles him. Being at a loss of how to extricate himself from the unwanted hospitality of Ianitor, Verres, so Cicero notes with sarcastic undertone, in his shrewdness devises a Plan B. Note the lexical and syntactical parallels between this and the previous sentence, in which Cicero described Ianitor: *Hospes Ianitor* corresponds to *Iste*, in each case the subjects are further described by a relative clause with causal force, and both sentences have *coepit* as main verb. Cicero thereby assimilates Verres to a character in a comic plot, at the same level as his stereotypical Ianitor.

§ 65

The paragraph recounts the encounter between Verres and Philodamus, when the latter tries to register a protest against the indignity of being forced to quarter a low-ranking Roman over and above his regular hospitality duties, which he so far had met without fail. He emerges as courageous and courteous, full of dignity, and conscious of his rank and standing within his city, yet at the same time well-disposed to a fault towards the Romans. He calmly and rationally presents his case to Verres, yet once he realizes that there is nothing to be done, he graciously accepts defeat and tries to make the best of an unpleasant situation. In contrast, Verres appears as the stereotype of the arrogant Roman: he imperiously disregards Philodamus' legitimate objection, driven as he is by his consuming passion for sexual gratification by whatever means necessary. At the same time, if one sets aside Cicero's portrayal of the two characters and only looks at the facts, some oddities emerge: in particular, Philodamus' dinner plans look over the top – as well as terribly naive. Why did he become so utterly self-effacing as to give Rubrius a free hand in organizing the dinner? Why did he not simply hand over the house, if he was so inclined, but asked for a place for himself? Why did he send away his son? All of these actions turn him retrospectively into an unwitting facilitator of Verres' criminal ambitions (as construed by Cicero), but it raises the question whether Cicero's account of the social dynamics behind the dinner arrangements actually captures the truth.

tametsi: *tam* + *etsi* – introduces a concessive clause ('even though').

quantum … mali: *mali* is a partitive genitive depending on *quantum*. The *hyberbaton underscores the extent of the evil that lies in wait for Philodamus.

iam tum: the phrase reinforces the idea of premeditation: Cicero makes it out that Verres and his cronies hatched a detailed plan of how to achieve the rape of Philodamus' daughter. The motivation that determines the sequence of events is Verres' beastly lust; Cicero never allows for the possibility that other factors (such as chance) may have played a role.

munus … cum suae partes essent hospitum recipiendorum: a *munus* is a (public) duty or obligation. In addition to official taxation, pro-magistrates in charge of provinces, as well as members of their entourage, could demand a certain amount of supplies and entertainment to be provided by the local population. The Romans passed some legislation designed to curb excessive use of this form of exploitation, but in practice much must have depended on the attitude and expectations of individual magistrates.[71]

praetores et consules, non legatorum adseculas: Philodamus' phrasing implies that even Verres (who was a *legatus*) falls short of the required rank: his hospitality usually extends only to high magistrates of the Roman people (praetors or consuls), not to any lesser official, and hence *a fortiori* not to mere members of the entourage.

adseculas: *adsecula, ae* (m.) means 'follower'.

---

71. See for more details Lintott, A. (1993), *Imperium Romanum: Politics and Administration*, London and New York, 92–5; Richardson, J. S. (1994), 'The Administration of the Empire', *Cambridge Ancient History* 9 (2nd edn), Cambridge, 572–84; laconically and to the point Steel (2004) 239 n. 11: 'Officials abroad regularly abused their rights to lodging and entertainment.'

postulatum causamque: possibly a *hendiadys: 'legitimate grievance'. This is the only hint in Cicero's account that Philodamus may have overstepped the tightly circumscribed boundaries within which provincials could object to the demands of their Roman superiors.

per vim ... imperavit. Hic: Cicero has conjured a moment of crisis: we have reached a point in the narrative where a resort to violence (*per vim*) looms. Verres is beyond reason and ready to enforce his will by any means necessary. But the physical confrontation is averted since Philodamus gives in: 'at this point' (*hic*, with a long i), that is, when he sees that he will not be able to attain what is his right (*ius*), he wishes to save face and make the best of an unpleasant situation. Thus he counters the threat of force with obliging kindness: the contrast between the *vis* of Verres and the *humanitas* of Philodamus could not be sharper; in Cicero's thought, it coincides with the distinction between barbarity and civilization. Yet whereas normally provincials or foreigners are associated with barbarity and the Romans with civilization, here the affiliations are inverted.

imperavit ... noluit ... comparat ... rogat ... mittit: as in the previous paragraph, Cicero starts out to narrate events in the perfect tense, before switching to the more vivid present.

laborabat: the imperfect tense here signifies 'attempt' – the so-called 'conative' use of the imperfect (from *conari*, to try, attempt).

humanitatem consuetudinemque suam: a *hendiadys, best rendered by turning the second noun (*consuetudo*) into an adjective ('usual'), such as 'usual human kindness' or 'standards of civilized conduct'. *Humanitas* is one of Cicero's favourite nouns, with a range of meanings, including compassion, human kindness, (Roman) civilization, and Roman-elite, yet Greek-educated urbanity. See Gildenhard (2011) 201–16.

Homo, qui semper hospitalissimus amicissimusque nostrorum hominum existimatus esset...: that Cicero uses *homo* twice right after mentioning Philodamus *humanitas* is no coincidence: he construes a group of human beings that includes the provincial Philodamus and all right-minded Romans (*nostri homines*) on the grounds of shared human values, such as hospitality, urbanity, respect for the law, and the disinclination to use violence, but excludes Verres and his entourage. Throughout the *Verrines*, Cicero pursues a systematic campaign of portraying his adversary as subhuman.

magnifice et ornate: Steel (2004) 240 questions whether the banquet really was of the 'splendidly lavish scale' that Cicero makes it out to be. She argues that it was most likely a relatively minor affair, which would explain in part why Philodamus sent away his son – he 'had better things to do than have dinner with some unimportant Romans'. This interpretation chimes well with Philodamus' grievance that he was used to entertaining much more important persons than legates (let alone the riff-raff in a legate's entourage) and why he did not invite any other local dignitary or even neighbours, but decided to deal with the unpleasant situation by himself (see *locum sibi soli*).

copiosus: wealthy – the attribute picks up *copiis* in § 64.

copiosus, convivium comparat: the adjective, the noun, and the verb are linked both by *alliteration and thematically. Note, with reference to the following paragraph, that Philodamus organizes a (Roman) *convivium*, rather than a (Greek) *symposion* (for the difference see below).

ut quos ei commodum sit invitet: the antecedent of *quos* (*eos*), which is also the accusative object of *invitet*, is left out.

§ 66

Cicero describes the banquet that Philodamus put on in honour of his guest, emphasizing the hybrid nature of the event, in which elements of the Roman *convivium* (a dinner-party) and the Greek *symposium* (a drinking party) get mixed. The etymologies of the two terms underscore the different emphases of the two get-togethers: *convivium* comes from *con-vivo*, i.e. to live together, spend one's time in company, and hence dine together, with a stress on conviviality, that is, the enjoyment of one another's company and the social dimension of the affair; *sym-posion* comes from *sun-poteo*, that is, to drink together, which, while also highlighting the social aspect of the activity with the prefix *sun-* ('with, together' – the Greek equivalent of Latin *cum*), focuses on alcohol consumption. What starts out as an orderly Roman dinner party ends up as a rowdy Greek *symposium*. One significant difference in the social etiquettes that governed the Roman *convivium* and the Greek *symposium* concerned the role of women: while ladies of the household could be present at the former (though they tended to sit on chairs, or were often represented as doing so, rather than to recline on couches), the only females present at the latter were courtesans. The occasion was strictly off-limits to women of the household, especially unmarried and hence supposedly virginal daughters.[72]

Strikingly, Cicero does nowhere say that Verres himself was actually present at the banquet, though some of his formulations are designed to generate the (erroneous) impression that he was. But the sentence *Rubrius istius comites invitat* makes it clear that Verres himself was not invited – even though Cicero instantly follows up this piece of information by saying that Verres briefed the invitees before they went to dinner (*eos omnis Verres certiores facit quid opus esset*). Steel (2004) 237 is surely right in arguing that Cicero would have made much more of it if Verres had participated in the banquet: 'quite apart from his role in the supposed kidnap, allegations of misbehaviour in sympotic contexts are a recurrent feature of Cicero's invective against Verres elsewhere in the *Verrines*, and against his other forensic opponents and political enemies.'[73] As it is, the care Cicero takes to assert Verres' involvement, if not to suggest his presence, without ever committing himself to an explicit statement concerning his whereabouts, would seem to imply that his absence from the banquet was too well-established a fact to bend it much.

Why did the brawl break out? Cicero overlays two scenarios, which are not mutually exclusive: (i) a cross-cultural misunderstanding concerning the presence of women at a party that got out of hand: see Steel (2004) 240, who moots the possibility that 'Rubrius simply did not understand how offensive and inappropriate his request was, and that the incident was a cultural misunderstanding and not the start of a premeditated attack'; or (ii) a carefully devised plot, hatched and masterminded by Verres and Rubrius before the dinner even started. (ii) is clearly the scenario that

---

72. See further the collection of papers edited by J. Donahue and B. K. Gold (2005), *Roman Dining*, Baltimore, especially that by M. Roller, 'Horizontal Women: Posture and Sex in the Roman Convivium', 49–94, which challenges the view that 'respectable' women dined seated until the Augustan era. On the Greek symposion, see e.g. Murray, O. (ed.) (1994), *Sympotica: A Symposium on the symposion*, Oxford; and Davidson, J. (1997), *Courtesans and Fishcakes: The Consuming Passions of Classical Athens*, HarperCollins.
73. With reference to Corbeill, A. (1996), *Controlling Laughter: Political Humor in the Late Republic*, Princeton, 128–43.

Cicero presupposes and tries to render plausible, while building aspects of scenario (i) into his account. But we have to ask ourselves: does scenario (i) not suffice to explain what happened – or indeed constitute, by itself, the more plausible scenario? Is it really likely that Verres devised a scheme that would have him wait elsewhere until his henchmen brought him his prey? Could Roman magistrates count on abducting a random woman from the household of their hosts to have their way with her and expect to get away with it? Would it not have made more sense for Verres to join the party (after all, according to Cicero, Rubrius was at liberty to invite anyone he wanted) and to see what would transpire? In short, should we not rather reckon with a version of scenario (i), namely chance circumstances that turned awry on the spot, owing to cross-cultural misunderstandings and the inebriation of the participants, which Cicero then embeds within the freely invented scenario (ii)? These are fraught questions: a dinner party getting out of control is one thing, a violent abduction to perpetrate premeditated rape quite another.

Rubrius invitat; Verres certiores facit; veniunt; discumbitur; fit sermo; invitatio ut … biberetur; hortatur hospes; poscunt; celebratur … convivium; … Rubrio visa est: after setting up Rubrius and Verres as masterminds of the whole affair, Cicero describes the proceedings without reference to specific actors, using the impersonal third person singular (*discumbitur*, *biberetur*) and anonymous third person plurals (*veniunt*, *poscunt*), an effect reinforced by the passive *celebratur* and the deponent *fit*. The only identifiable subject in this stretch is Philodamus who, as host (*hospes*), sees to it that a good time is had by all. Then, when the decisive moment has come, Cicero returns to naming Rubrius (and by implication Verres).

Rubrius istius comites invitat; eos omnes Verres certiores facit quid opus esset: Cicero here both acknowledges and obfuscates the rather crucial fact that Verres himself was not present at the banquet.

sermo: small-talk, easy-going conversation, often involving wit and urbanity; in contrast to the protocols of alcohol consumption the party adopted (see *invitatio ut Graeco more biberetur*), it is a markedly Roman term.

ut Graeco more biberetur: *Graeco more* could either refer to the habit of drinking to the health of the person to whom the cup is then passed or the practice of imbibing the wine undiluted with water.

Homo, qui … esset: the relative clause has causal meaning, hence the subjunctive.

et summa gravitate et iam id aetatis et parens: *a polysyndetic sequence: Cicero gives three weighty reasons why Philodamus was taken aback by Rubrius' suggestion. *summa gravitate* is an ablative of description, *id aetatis* a partitive genitive.

Homo … obstipuit hominis improbi dicto: again we have a sharp, anthropological contrast between one type of human being and another, underscored on the lexical and stylistic level by the *polyptoton *homo – hominis*. *Improbus* ('wicked') is a favourite attribute of abuse in Cicero: he routinely contrasts 'the good' (*boni*) with 'the wicked' (*improbi*).

poscunt maioribus poculis: a complementary infinitive such as *bibere* (to drink) is to be supplied after *poscunt*.

Instare Rubrius: Cicero uses an infinitive in place of the finite verb (*instat*) to enhance vividness. Philodamus is shocked into silence, but Rubrius rudely presses on.

ut aliquid responderet: a purpose clause – the emphasis is on *aliquid*: Philodamus is still under shock, but makes a dignified effort to say *something*.

moris esse Graecorum: *moris* is a genitive of characteristic; in ancient Greek society the men and the women of the household mixed far less than in Rome's aristocratic milieu.[74] Philodamus tries his best to explain some basic cross-cultural differences to his guest, obviously to no avail.

ut in convivio virorum accumberent mulieres: following up on his reference to Greek customs, Philodamus now spells out the gender protocols that he insists on upholding at an event such as this, using the *antithesis *virorum – mulieres* for clarity. (Note that Philodamus too is presented as referring to his daughter as *mulier*.)

---

74. Bibliography on the Greek and Roman family and gender issues includes: Lacey, W. K. (1968), *The Family in Classical Greece*, Ithaca; Pomeroy, S. B. (1975), *Goddesses, Whores, Wives and Slaves*, New York; Treggiari, S. (1991), *Roman Marriage. Iusti Coniuges from the Time of Cicero to the Time of Ulpian*, Oxford.

Hic tum alius ex alia parte: the seemingly synchronized response by everyone present generates the impression of prior coordination: everyone appeared to know exactly what to do and reacted right on cue.

simul servis suis: emphatic initial position, reinforced by the s-alliteration, to indicate how quickly Rubrius acted; Cicero thereby again reinforces, however obliquely, his charge of premeditation.

§ 67

The paragraph focuses on the events that unfold in Philodamus' house, and how the dwelling becomes the centre of attention for the entire town. For the news spread fast: first the son, informed of the outrage, rushes back, then all of the inhabitants of Lampsacus come together at the house. In his description of the fighting, Cicero foregrounds Rubrius and Philodamus and the slaves, and rather sidelines the fact that a Roman lictor (Cornelius) was killed in the melee. The paragraph concludes with an unexpected glimpse of Verres: he seems not to have been present at the banquet (at least Cicero never gives him an active part in the turmoil) and it remains unclear where precisely he was; but, Cicero submits, he somehow stayed abreast of developments and realized what he had caused.

Quod: connecting relative.

servos suos ad se vocat – his imperat ut se ipsum neglegant: the *alliteration underscores the telling dynamic of Philodamus summoning his slaves to him only to tell them to disregard his own safety.

ut se ipsum neglegant, filiam defendant: the *asyndeton (no *et* or equivalent after *neglegant*) conveys something of the breathlessness and urgency with which Philodamus issues his orders.

excurrat: subjunctive – syntactically, Cicero continues the *ut*-clause introduced by *imperat*. Just as the *asyndeton (see previous note), the disjointed, *elliptic language underscores the stress Philodamus experiences.

domestici mali ... tota domo ... domi suae: Cicero emphasizes by means of a *figura etymologica* and the *polyptoton *domo – domi* that the commotion takes place not in public spaces but a private dwelling – this is not a riot of provincials, but an attack carried out by Romans on what ought to be a sanctuary of peace for the owners. The domestic motif continues with *ad aedis contendit* and *ad aedis ... convenerunt.*[75]

pugna inter servos Rubri atque hospitis: Cicero elides the verb; it is either *est* or *fit* (from the previous sentence).

iactatur domi suae vir primarius et homo honestissimus: Cicero's syntax enacts the confusion he depicts – the subject comes at the end (rather than the beginning) and the verb (*iactatur*) at the beginning (rather than the end).

vir primarius et homo honestissimus: Cicero uses an elaborate paraphrasis of Philodamus that combines the generic terms *vir* and *homo* with superlative attributes and a climactic increase of syllables (1:4 :: 2:5); the *alliteration *homo honestissimus* reinforces the overall effect of pathos and outrage at the Romans' utter disregard for the respectability and social standing of their host.

... Philodamus perfunditur: again, the subject is effectively delayed until the very end; the two words go well together at the sound level (perhaps enacting the drenching?), not least since all five vowels feature (i-o-a-u + e-u-i-u).

Haec ubi filio nuntiata sunt: there is a minor inconcinnity in Cicero's account: for the violence against the father, of which the son is notified here, occurred after Philodamus' orders to his slaves to fetch his son (see *excurrat aliquis*); so either the slaves waited to witness the further developments or we have to reckon with two messengers.

exanimatus: literally, *exanimatus* (the participle of *ex-animo*) means 'deprived of one's soul/ life (*anima*)', hence killed, but it is also used figuratively to signify 'paralyzed with fear or passion'. This metaphorical usage is particularly widespread in New Comedy; Cicero, too, uses *exanimatus* frequently in this sense to heighten the drama of a situation.

lictor istius Cornelius: Roman magistrates were accompanied by attendants who helped them carry out their official duties; they famously carried the

---

75. Secondary literature on Greek houses includes Jameson, M. (1990), 'Private Space in the Greek City', in O. Murray and S. Price (eds.), *The Greek City from Homer to Alexander*, Oxford, 171–98; and Nevett, L. (1999), *House and Society in the Ancient Greek World*, Cambridge.

fasces, which symbolized the right and the power to command and exercise jurisdiction. The number of lictors varied according to office: a Roman consul had twelve, a legate two.[76] The presence of the lictor, at an advanced stage of the fighting, comes as somewhat of a surprise. Cicero gives the impression that he had been there from the start, and was supposed to play a key role in the abduction plot. But another scenario, suggested by Steel (2004) 241, is equally plausible: that he was 'summoned once the fight began'. The brawling, after all, went on for some time: if Philodamus was able to dispatch messengers to recall his son (and the entire town to gather around Philodamus' house at the news of the commotion), Verres, too, must have become aware of the disorder in the city – and sending a lictor in the first instance to see that order was observed would have been an obvious thing to do.

Cornelius … occiditur; servi … vulnerantur; ipse Rubrius … sauciatur: in all three passive constructions, Cicero studiously suppresses the agent – in contrast to his earlier specification that Philodamus was drenched in boiling water 'by Rubrius' (*a Rubrio ipso Philodamus perfunditur*). The killing and the wounding occur in the wake of the son rushing (*contendit*) to the house to aid his father and sister and the Lampsacenes coming together (*convenerunt*) in outrage, but Cicero passes over in silence what these parties actually did upon arrival. He thereby elegantly sidesteps the issue of who was actually responsible for the death of a Roman official.

quasi in praesidio ad auferendam mulierem conlocatus: a paradoxical formulation: *praesidium* usually occurs in scenarios of protection, not abduction. As often when he experiments conceptually, Cicero here hedges with the modifier *quasi*, which puts imaginary scare-quotes around *in praesidio*, thus signalling the irony.

Iste … qui … videret: Cicero here describes Verres' reaction to the turmoil *as if* he were an eye-witness (clearly the impression he wished to generate among members of the jury). But *videre* can also have (as here) the more abstract meaning, 'perceive', 'come to understand'. As Steel (2004) 238 points out 'Cicero is not saying something obviously false, and the alert reader will see that he must mean that Verres wished that he were no longer in Lampsacus.'

---

76. See further Marshall, A. J. (1984), 'Symbols and Showmanship in Roman Public Life: the *Fasces*', *Phoenix* 38, 120–41.

cupere: Cicero uses the historic infinitive, instead of a finite verb form, to enhance the vividness of his account.

§ 68

Cicero here details the reaction of the civic community on 'the morning after': we get an image of ordered proceedings, but also a firm commitment to basic principles of fairness and justice. There is, then, a decisive shift in register and tone, away from the sordid affairs and the private lusts of Verres into the public sphere and collective decision-making within a civic setting. The turn at the end from the specific case at hand to general views about Roman (mal-)administration in the provinces implicitly highlights the wider significance of Verres' misbehaviour and the importance of bringing him to justice. Cicero here gives a very partial and incomplete account of what happened in the aftermath of the fateful banquet. In particular, he leaves out any mention of the two inhabitants whom Verres would later on identify as the ringleaders of the uprising, namely Themistagoras and Thessalus (see §§ 83 and 85). The selective reporting has a rhetorical purpose: Cicero generates the impression of a collective moral outrage of all the inhabitants of Lampsacus, which nevertheless manifests itself at least initially in ordered political procedure, an impression that the naming of specific individuals responsible for instigating others into violent action would have weakened significantly.

in contionem ... auctoritatis plurimum ... ad populum loquebatur: Cicero projects familiar elements of Rome's political culture onto the Greek city: a *contio* is a meeting devoted to public deliberation that consists of speeches by members of the elite to the assembled populace (in contrast to voting meetings, which were called *comitia*); *auctoritas* is a Roman term that denotes respect and recognition granted on the basis of rank, standing, and achievement and carried much weight in Roman politics; and *populus* refers to a civic community held together by law. The use of the term here sets up an inherent affinity with the senate and the people of Rome, which are mentioned right afterwards. These are all markers of civilization and proper political procedure, the exact opposite of a raging mob of unruly provincials. Pseudo-Asconius perceptively comments on the ethnographic subtext in Cicero's account: *adeo non Graeca levitate res gestae sunt, sed agitato consilio defensa libertas*. *levitas* ('fickleness') was a standard stereotype that the Romans ascribed to the Greeks, and Cicero does his best to obviate any charge that the Lampsacenes acted rashly (as Greeks were, from a Roman perspective, wont to do). Pseudo-Asconius attribute *Graeca* sets up the second half of an implicit antithesis: the defence of liberty after due consideration (*agitato consilio*) resonates in a Roman key.

pro se quisque ... in quoque: a *polyptoton designed to underscore that the opinion of each individual add up to one collective view of the matter. Cicero's depiction of the transformation of a plurality of voices into the unanimous outlook of the entire civic community is far more damning for Verres than Verres' own account of the affair, which Cicero supplies only much later (§§ 83 and 85).

loquebatur: the imperfect stresses duration – the Lampsacenes, so Cicero implies, took their time to come to a considered view of the affair.

quid optimum factu sit: *factu* is an ablative supine: 'what is best in the doing', i.e. 'what is best to do'.

et sententia et oratio: the nouns set up a complicated indirect statement that falls into two parts. The two verbs are (i) *non esse metuendum*; (ii) *esse satius*. (i) *non esse metuendum* is followed by a fear clause (*ne ... putaret*) that also forms the apodosis of a conditional clause (Cicero has put the protasis *si ... ulti ... essent*, which logically belongs into the *ne*-clause, ahead of it). (ii) *esse satius* is also the apodosis of a conditional clause (with *quodsi ... uterentur* as protasis); it takes two complementary infinitives: (*quidvis*) *perpeti* and (*in tanta vi atque acerbitate*) *versari*. Overall, the indirect statement specifies the two core ideas (one optimistic, the second – a default position – pessimistic) that emerged from the deliberations of the Lampsacenes: first, they believe that they have actually nothing to fear from the senate and the people of Rome if they avenged the injustice they suffered at the hands of Verres; and secondly, if Rome were to endorse Verres' behaviour, then violent resistance would anyway be the only course of action.

ulti ... essent: the third person plural pluperfect subjunctive of *ulciscor*. As Steel (2004) 246 n. 28 points out, the 'vengeance' in question could refer either to an act in the past (the death of the lictor) or the future (the riot that is about to start), depending on whether the pluperfect subjunctive in the indirect statement represents an original past tense or a future perfect.

in eam civitatem animadvertendum: *animadvertere* + *in* + acc. means, in an absolute sense, 'to take punitive action (against)', 'to inflict (capital) punishment on': *OLD* s.v. 8b. Here it is part of an indirect statement dependent on *putaret*, with *esse* to be supplied: '...that punitive action ought to be taken against this citizenry'.

hoc iure: bitterly ironic. The paradox of *ius* functioning as the basis of oppression is heightened by the adversative force of *in socios nationesque exteras*.

legati populi Romani: *legati* is nominative plural (the subject of *uterentur*), *populi Romani* genitive singular.

pudicitiam liberorum servare ab eorum libidine tutam: a carefully constructed phrase that features *chiasmus, i.e. (a) *pudicitiam* (b) *liberorum* (b) *eorum* (a) *libidine*, *alliteration (*liberorum, libidine*), and *hyperbaton (*pudicitiam* – *tutam*), with the predicative attribute *tutam* coming as an emphatic surprise since it is strictly speaking superfluous.

quidvis esse perpeti satius: *satius esse* is syntactically at the same level as *non esse metuendum* and expresses the second, complementary opinion that emerged from the meeting of the Lampsacenes. See above on *et sententia et oratio*. *perpeti* is a complementary infinitive depending on *satius esse*, and *quidvis* ('anything') is the accusative object of *perpeti*.

in tanta vi atque acerbitate: a *hendiadys – what is so bitter is the kind of violent oppression the Lampsacenes suffer, which involves destruction of their nearest and dearest and the disrespect of everything they value.

§ 69

The shift from considered deliberation to violent action is swift and unanimous. If in the previous paragraph Cicero described the (impressively measured) proceedings on the basis of which the Lampsacenes opted for a course of violent self-defence to redress the injury suffered, he now details the outcome: because of Verres, the peace-loving inhabitants of the city have turned into a determined crowd of enemies. (The flip from lethargic lovers of peace and victims of exploitation into a mob set on physical violence reminds one of the meeting of the Ents and its outcome in J. R. R.

Tolkien's *The Lord of the Rings*, Chapter 'Treebeard', *The Two Towers*.) The Roman citizens who convince the Lampsacenes to desist from violence, however, leave no doubt that Rome will deem such violent uproar an unacceptable transgression and retaliate, especially if Verres should suffer harm or indeed be killed. Aggression against a Roman magistrate, however justified, almost inevitably set Rome's military machine into motion.

omnes – omnes: Cicero emphasizes the unanimity with which the Lampsacenes acted in the matter.

sensu ac dolore: a *hendiadys ('feeling of grief', 'grievance').

caedere ianuam saxis, instare ferro, ligna et sarmenta circumdare ignemque subicere: the list of actions contains four units, which Cicero has arranged chiastically: verb (*caedere*) – nouns (*ianuam saxis*), verb (*instare*) – noun (*ferro*) :: nouns (*ligna et sarmenta*) – verb (*circumdare*), noun (*ignem*) – verb (*subicere*). But if one focuses on Cicero's use of connectives, a tripartite structure emerges, which proceeds *climactically from stones to swords to fire: the unit from *caedere* to *circumdare* forms an *asyndetic *tricolon, with the last phrase *ignemque subicere* not adding a new idea but elaborating on *ligna et sarmenta circumdare*. The lack of connectives in the first half enacts the rage of the attack, whereas the two connectives in the second half (*et* and -*que*, one linking nouns, the other verbs) matches well the more deliberate, step-by-step mode of operation required for setting the house afire.

cives Romani: note that Cicero here emphasizes the citizenship of the Roman 'businessmen' who intervene with sound advice; this is in pointed contrast to their colleagues who help Verres in executing the judicial murder of Philodamus and his son out of greed: Cicero calls them *togati creditores* (§ 73).

negotiabantur: a deponent, here used in the intransitive sense 'to do business'.

gravius … nomen legationis quam iniuria legati: Cicero ascribes the same argument to the Roman businessmen at Lampsacus in their reasoning with the enraged citizens that he will make throughout the oration, namely that one needs to distinguish between an office and its holder. The further distinction between *homo* and *legatus* at the end of the paragraph follows a similar logic (see below).

sese intellegere – levius peccatum fore: *sese* and *levius peccatum* are the subjective accusatives, *intellegere* and *fore* the verbs of an indirect statement; the main verb (something like *dicunt*) is implied.

si homini scelerato pepercissent quam si legato non pepercissent: the Roman citizens formulate a dilemma: the Lampsacenes can sin *either* by sparing the wicked human being *or* by not sparing a magistrate of the Roman people. They submit that the former transgression is lighter, under the circumstances – Verres, after all, failed to carry out the misdeed he had planned and would shortly depart from Lampsacus forever anyway. Killing a Roman magistrate, on the other hand, even if he had proved himself wicked and worthless, would inevitably entail drastic retaliation on the part of Rome's military machine – a thought that the Roman citizens who argue with the enraged Lampsacenes only hint at.

§ 70

Cicero here faces a tricky moment: he needs to justify the claim that Verres, who was, after all, a Roman official, would have deserved to be killed by a provincial mob. This is not a notion easily rendered plausible in front of Roman judges. Cicero adduces a precedent (Hadrianus); and then focuses on the fact that Verres himself never offered an adequate explanation of why the inhabitants of Lampsacus behaved the way they did – the implication being that the reasons he has just provided in his own version of events must be true. Cicero then proceeds to rule out systematically that the tumult had anything to do with any legitimate action that Verres undertook as a Roman official, to reinforce the impression that the uproar was caused entirely by his criminal lust. He concludes this line of reasoning with the counterfactual condition that even if Verres were to justify the events on the grounds that he executed his official business in, perhaps, too harsh a fashion, he would be responsible for what happened on account of his maltreatment of allies. The argument in this paragraph thus also sounds out – and tries to establish – parameters of what is to count as acceptable practice in provincial administration.

iste ... ille Hadrianus ... Ille ... hic...: the first half of the paragraph is taken up by a two-part comparison between Verres and Hadrianus. Cicero employs a **husteron proteron*: he first draws the conclusion, then details the respective facts on which it is based. Overall, the arrangement is **chiastic: Verres (*iste*, *hic*) comes first and last, Hadrianus (*ille – ille*), the foil, takes the less conspicuous position in the middle.

Hadrianus: C. Fabius Hadrianus was praetor or propraetor of the province Africa in the late 80s BC. In 84, he prevented Metellus Pius from taking charge of the province for Sulla; in 82, he was burned to death in his praetorium. As Mitchell (1986) 191 notes: 'Cicero naturally omits any reference to his political affiliations, almost certainly the reason his murder went unpunished.' Put differently, he spins the deplorable incident in such a way as to turn it into a suitable precedent for what happened at Lampsacus.

multo ... aliquanto: *multo* is an ablative of the measure of difference and together with the adverb *aliquanto* ('considerably') indicates the different degrees to which Verres was more criminal (*sceleratior*) and wicked (*nequior*) as well as luckier (*felicior*) than Hadrianus. Cicero points to an imbalance in justice, contained within the surprising phrase *aliquanto etiam felicior*: for to the extent that Verres outdoes Hadrianus in vice one would have expected him to be more wretched (*miserior*) rather than luckier if the universe were just; yet while Verres, the greater criminal, suffered some harm, he still came out of the affair better than his counterpart. Cicero, however, always clung to the belief in the overall justice of the universe (however rough and ready this might be), even in the face of massive evidence to the contrary. And in the following paragraph he counters the challenge to the notion that the universe is just, which he here implicitly issues: he makes it clear that Verres only *appeared* to outdo Hadrianus in luck by escaping; in fact, Fortuna had a providential hand in it since she wanted to ensure that Verres would receive his punishment at Rome, in this very law court. The argument elevates the judges into arbiters and agents of cosmic justice.

Uticae domi suae: two locatives.

Uticae ... suae vivus exustus: note the **homoioteleuta.

exustus ... ambustus: Cicero operates his comparison by way of two compounds of *uro*: *exuro* here signifies 'to burn completely' whereas *amburo* (*ambi* + *uro*) means 'to burn around', i.e. only on the surface.

animadversio: picking up *animadvertendum* from § 68.

ex illa flamma periculoque: a *hendiadys. The lexeme *periculum* recurs twice more in the paragraph (*ut in tantum periculum veniret; in tantum adductus periculum*) and is further developed in § 71 (*ex illo periculo*). Throughout the episode Cicero exploits the puzzling gaps between the peace-loving nature of the Lampsacenes and the danger in which Verres found himself.

Non enim potest dicere: what follows is a list of reasons that may provoke allies and provincials to resort to violence against Roman officials – Cicero categorically denies that Verres can adduce any of them to explain the attack of the Lampsacenes.

cum ... cum ... cum ... cum ... quod ... quod ... quod ... : Cicero splits the list into two halves, marked by a switch in his choice of causal conjunction; the *cum*-clauses specify official types of actions (summed up in the fourth), whereas the simpler *quod*-clauses indicate more personal failings, that is, ways in which Verres may have been lacking in 'emotional intelligence' in his dealings with the provincials.

seditionem sedare: an *alliterative *paronomasia.

stipendium: 'a cash payment levied from conquered states to defray the expenses of the occupying army': *OLD* s.v. 3.

Quae si diceret: *quae* is a connecting relative; *si* introduces a present counterfactual condition – apparently, the list of justification that Cicero just rehearsed are all hypothetical defences that Verres never actually brought into play, and even if he did he would still have to bear the blame for what happened.

nimis atrociter imperando: Cicero here realistically rephrases the (euphemistic) *quod acrius imperavi* that he had put into Verres' mouth.

Alternatively, we could read Verres' formulation as truthful and Cicero's rewriting as *hyperbolic.

adductus: supply *esse*.

§ 71

It is hardly a coincidence that only now, after establishing his version of what happened at Lampsacus and adducing Verres' silence in support of its veracity, Cicero brings his witnesses into play: however much he talks up P. Tettius and C. Varro, they rank lower in *dignitas* and possess less *auctoritas* than the Roman officials who handled the Lampsacus incident, notably C. Nero and Dolabella – a serious problem in a Roman court. Even more damningly for Cicero, a Roman magistrate and his *consilium* had condemned Philodamus and his son to death – a fact duly brought to the attention of the court by Hortensius; Cicero is unable to dispute this (and will spend several paragraphs explaining why this verdict constituted an outrageous miscarriage of justice). Here he belittles Hortensius' earlier intervention as a move of desperation: Verres' case is so weak that the famous orator took advantage of any opening, however small, to get a word in edgewise but was most of the time consigned to silence. Needless to say, this derogatory comment has nothing to do with the point at issue.

The paragraph consists of two long, complex periods. The first begins with a series of *cum*-clauses, before a brief main clause (*potestis dubitare*), and the concluding *quin*-clause. The second begins with a conditional clause (introduced by *nisi*), part of which is a relative clause (*quod*) that leads on to a further relative clause (introduced by *quo tempore*) and some further subordinate clauses (until ... *quod diceret*); only at this point does Cicero reach the main clause (*hoc tum dixit*) and the concluding indirect statement. The syntax is so contrived and so difficult to follow, especially if compared to his rather straightforward account of what transpired at Lampsacus, that it detracts from the audience's ability to take in what, precisely, Cicero is saying here: most likely a deliberate effect. For Cicero here finally names his sources of information and also confronts an obvious objection to his version of the events, which Hortensius, a member of Verres' defence team, had already voiced during the earlier proceeding.

Nunc cum ipse ... audeat ..., homo autem ... dixerit ... dicat, potestis dubitare quin ... iudicium reservare?: One long period that starts with a subordinate *cum*-clause, which falls into three segments, each with its own subjects: Verres (*audeat*), P. Tettius (*dixerit*), and C. Varro (*dicat*), followed by the main clause – *potestis dubitare*, with the judges as subjects – which in turn introduces a subordinate *quin*-clause, the subject of which is *fortuna*. *autem* introduces a contrast within the *cum*-clause, between Verres on the one hand and Tettius and Varro on the other.

homo autem ... audisse dicat: in this part of the sentence Cicero introduces his two witnesses for his version of what happened at Lampsacus, P. Tettius and C. Varro. It is, of course, vital that their stories coincide, and Cicero takes care to stress that both of his informants reported exactly the same things (*haec eadem*). The table below illustrates how style enacts theme: Cicero has opted for a virtually identical overall design, into which he has inserted elements of variation to obviate monotony and boredom. In addition, he subtly foregrounds Varro, who has the higher rank and claims to have his information from Philodamus himself, whereas Tettius relied on hearsay he picked up in Lampsacus. (Cicero suppresses the fact that he and Varro were related: see below.) The design can be tabulated as follows:

	Tettius	**Varro**
1. Subject	homo	vir
2. Predicative attribute in the superlative	autem ordinis sui frugalissimus,	omnibus rebus ornatissimus,
3. Relative Clause (Tettius)/ Name in Apposition (Varro)	qui tum accensus C. Neroni fuit,	C. Varro,
4. Name in Apposition (Tettius)/ Relative Clause (Varro)	P. Tettius,	qui tum in Asia militum tribunus fuit,
5. Indirect Statement	haec eadem se Lampsaci cognosse	haec eadem se ipso ex Philodamo audisse
6. Verb	dixerit.	dicat.

1. Subject: *homo* and *vir* here function as virtual synonyms. Cicero may have been motivated to designate *Varro vir* by the *alliterative assonance; but *vir* is also a more distinguished designation than *homo*, recalling such qualities as *virtus* and masculine prowess.

2. Predicative attribute in the superlative (*frugalissimus, ornatissimus*) with further specification in the partitive genitive (*ordinis sui*) or the ablative of respect (*omnibus rebus*): both of the specifications consist of a noun (a) and an attribute (b), though in chiastic order: (a) *ordinis* (b) *sui* ~ (b) *omnibus* (a) *rebus*. In each case, the specification is designed to underscore the integrity, esteem and overall trustworthiness of the witness. Yet in line with Cicero's policy of foregrounding Varro, in Tettius' case his superlative ranking is confined to his *ordo*, whereas Varro excels in more general fashion 'in all things'.

3/4. Relative Clause and Name in Apposition: Cicero again opts for a chiastic order: (a) relative clause + (b) name (for Tettius) ~ (b) name + (a) relative clause (for Varro) to eschew tedious uniformity while still keeping the overall design exactly identical. The same principle is on display in the relative clause: each of the two consists of exactly the same elements, i.e. relative pronoun (*qui*), temporal adverb (*tum*), indication of role or office held (*accensus, militum tribunus*), further specification (*C. Neroni, in Asia*), verb (*fuit*); yet the office and the further specifications are again arranged chiastically: (a) *accensus* (b) *C. Neroni* ~ (b) *in Asia* (a) *militum tribunus*. A further nuance consists in the fact that in Tettius' case the specification is a dative that indicates lines of command, whereas in Varro's case it is a prepositional phrase in the ablative indicating geographical location: Cicero thereby marks Tettius as more of a subordinate than Varro.

5. Indirect statement: the accusative object of the indirect statement, the decisive phrase *haec eadem* is exactly the same as is the overall structure; *haec eadem* is followed in each case by the subject accusative (*se*) and specification of the source (*Lampsaci, ipso ex Philodamo*) and the verb of the indirect statement (*cognosse, audisse*).[77]

---

77. There is a textual issue here. Instead of the *se ipso* printed here, our codices have *ipsa se*, which does not make a lot of sense: *haec eadem* needs no further qualification. Peterson, in his *Oxford Classical Text*, therefore prints *ipse* (a conjecture by Benecke) *se*. But this is not unproblematic either: 'he personally says' introduces an undesirable contrast between

6.   Verb: Cicero uses the same verb (*dicere*) that he already used in the opening segment on Verres, moving from the perfect (*dixerit*) to the present subjunctive (*dicat*). The difference in tense may be due to the fact that Tettius was called up as witness and gave his testimony during the first *actio*, whereas Varro seems not to have done so – yet, so Cicero now insists, he is saying exactly the same.

accensus: formed from the perfect participle of *accenseo*, but used as a noun: 'an attendant, orderly': *OLD* s.v. 2. The *accensus* was one category among the staff of a high magistrate or pro-magistrate, not dissimilar to the *lictor*, though limited in its function to warfare or more generally the sphere of *militiae*. In ancient times, they were selected from the century of the *accensi velati* – non-armed participants of military campaigns – but in the late republic, (pro-)magistrates tended to select them from among their own freedmen; their stipend was slightly higher than that of lictors. It was a position of considerable influence and Cicero, in a letter to his brother Quintus (*Q. fr.* 1.1.13), recommends the careful selection of a person suitable for the position. What *accensi* actually did is difficult to reconstruct: most likely they were involved in organizing and facilitating the day-to-day affairs of their superiors.[78]

C. Neroni: Gaius Claudius Nero: as pro-praetor of Asia, Lampsacus fell within his jurisdiction; Cicero first mentions him at 2.1.50, as the target of envoys from Samos, who complained about Verres' attack on the temple of Juno. His reply was that for this sort of thing, which involved a legate of the Roman people and his alleged misbehaviour, they should not come to him, but go to Rome. In the following paragraphs, he emerges as the feeble colleague of Dolabella (Verres' direct superior), who was pro-praetor of Cilicia.

P. Tettius ... dixerit – C. Varro ... dicat: nothing further is known of Publius Tettius; Gaius Visellius Varro was Cicero's *consobrinus* or

---

homo (sc. *Tettius*) *dixerit* and *vir* (sc. *Varro*) *ipse dicat*. More promising is the correction, according to Peterson's apparatus proposed by both Haase and Kays, of *ipsa* into *ipso*. The phrase *ipso ex Philodamo* would stress the fact that Varro got his version of events from Philodamus *himself* – in contrast to Tettius, who has to rely on what he found out from hearsay in the city. Cicero's strictly parallel construction of Tettius and Varro perhaps offers some grounds for taking the further step of inverting *ipso se* to *se ipso*.

78. The information on *accensi* derives from Kunkel, W. (1995), *Staatsordnung und Staatspraxis der römischen Republik, Zweiter Abschnitt: Die Magistratur*, Munich, 126–28 ('Das Hilfspersonal der Magistrate: f) Der Accensus').

'cousin-german' (Varro's mother, Helvia, was Cicero's aunt); he was Cicero's near-contemporary (c. 104 - 58 BC); like Cicero he came from Arpinum, though went to Rome early on for his training and education.[79] The distinction between past (*dixerit*) and present (*dicat*) is curious. As the second half of the paragraph makes clear, Tettius was one of Cicero's witnesses in the *actio prima*; there is no indication, however, that Varro was as well. Perhaps Cicero kept him out of the proceedings deliberately to save time; or, since Tettius' was interrupted during his testimony by a cat-calling Hortensius, he now adds him on as a 'further voice' to back up Tettius' version of the events. Steel (2004) 236 n. 4 suggests that Cicero may have heard about the incident from Varro right after his return from the East and now, a decade later, puts it to good use in the trial. Conveniently, Varro got his version of the events – or so Cicero claims – straight from Philodamus; to what extent that proves anything must remain an open question.

potestis dubitare...?: a rhetorical question that demands a negative answer ('of course not!'); Cicero often uses this bullying device when he advances a feeble argument: of course his audience was at liberty to doubt his dubious assertion.

fortuna: the goddess of caprice or happenstance, who here acts as an agent of justice – Verres' escape from the conflagration was not due to luck (*fortuna*, in the sense of the Greek *tuche*, that is, an irrational force who distributes her favours indiscriminately without regard for merit), but foresight (*fortuna*, in the sense of a divine force who presides over a universe that exhibits patterns of rationality and justice): Verres was saved so that he could get his comeuppance in Rome during the present trial. The appeal to *fortuna* comes as a bit of a surprise, almost as a *dea ex machina* to help Cicero out of a tight spot in the argument, even though the inexorable workings of supernatural justice are a prevalent theme throughout the *Verrines*.[80]

dicet: Cicero imagines that Verres will repeat what Hortensius said by way of a (rude) interruption in the first proceeding, when Tettius gave his evidence.

---

79. Gundel, H. (1961), '3) C. Visellius Varro', *Realencyclopädie* 9 A 1, 355–58.
80. On the different semantics of Fortuna see Gildenhard (2011) 40–49.

Hortensius: Quintus Hortensius Hortalus (114 – 50 BC; cos. 69) was Cicero's formidable rival and – until Cicero dethroned him by winning his case against Verres to take his place – 'king' of the Roman courts. In the early part of his career (up to and including the *Verrines*), Cicero attacks him as a representative of the established ruling elite who abuses his influence in helping his clients; but in his late *philosophica*, he appreciates and honours his rival as an outstanding representive of free speech and the senatorial tradition of republican government, notably at the end of the *de Oratore*, the opening of the *Brutus*, and in the *Hortensius* (a dialogue that has only survived in meagre fragments).[81]

quo tempore ... diceret: before Cicero deigns to share what it was that Hortensius brought into play he takes a detour to ridicule his opponent and proleptically discredit his objection. He portrays his adversary as so hard put to say anything at all in the face of the evidence that he grasped at every tenuous opportunity to say *something* – and *still* was forced to remain silent most of the time. Cicero thereby intimates that whatever he did say on those few occasions where he spoke up was by definition insignificant – an act of despair or a token gesture, rather than a substantial contribution to the issue at hand. In the second *actio*, Cicero refers frequently to Hortensius' failure to turn the cross-examination of witnesses during the first *actio* to his advantage: see *Ver.* 2.1.151, 2.2.156, and 2.5.155.

signi satis: *signi* is a partitive genitive depending on *satis*.

si quid: after *si*, the *ali-* of *aliquid* disappears. See above § 64.

ut ... scire omnes possemus nihil habuisse quod diceret: *omnes* is the subject of the consecutive *ut*-clause ('we all'); the complementary infinitive *scire* introduces an indirect statement (*nihil habuisse*), in which the subject accusative (*se*, i.e. Hortensius) needs to be supplied. The *ellipsis hardly registers, given that it comes in the immediate wake of the earlier (complete) indirect statement *se tacere non posse*.

hoc tum dixit, Philodamum et filium eius a C. Nerone esse damnatos: only after Cicero has thoroughly discredited Hortensius' point does he

---

81. For their complex relationship and its evolution over time, see Dyck, A. R. (2008), 'Rivals into partners: Hortensius and Cicero', *Historia* 52, 142–73.

share what it was: it turns out that C. Nero, the superior of one of Cicero's principal witnesses, had actually condemned Philodamus and his son to death. This, of course, would seem to vindicate Verres and his version of what happened – and Cicero has a problem at his hand. He needs to explain the verdict and why it was wrong.

§ 72

This paragraph picks up the rather vital piece of information that Cicero shared almost *en passant* as a seemingly unimportant interjection of Hortensius at the end of the previous paragraph: that the pro-magistrate in charge of Asia at the time, C. Nero, condemned Philodamus and his son to death after consideration of the case. In this and the following paragraphs, Cicero takes a closer look at how this verdict came into being, in effect launching a subtle campaign of besmearing first C. Nero's and then Dolabella's handling of provincial jurisdiction to show that the condemnation and eventual execution of the two Lampsacenes constituted an outrageous miscarriage of (Roman) justice and a human tragedy of the first order. To underscore his – often feeble – argument, Cicero digs deep into his rhetorical trick-box (not least in redefining Rome's constitutional realities as he sees fit: see below on *istius ille verbo lictor, re vera minister improbissimae cupiditatis*) and drumming up pathos (see below on *Audite ... et ... aliquando miseremini ... et ostendite*).

Cicero switches his attention between Dolabella and Nero. We begin with a paragraph featuring only Nero (71), as the one in charge of jurisdiction. Two paragraphs follow in which both are mentioned by name (72, 73); then Nero momentarily disappears: Dolabella dominates the paragraph in which Cicero recounts the final verdict (74), both feature in 75, but the paragraph on the execution only mentions Nero – in tears (76). Subsequently, Cicero turns to Dolabella only, in direct address for a final reckoning (77).

De quo ne multa disseram: an announcement by Cicero to limit himself to the essentials should alert the attentive reader that the argument has reached a tight spot, which Cicero wishes to dispatch quickly; of course, he often lingers nevertheless (as here).

consilium: the *consilium* is a typically Roman institution: it was in effect a group of esteemed and experienced persons who acted in an advisory capacity; any Roman in a position of power, whether in his role as *pater* *familias* or as a magistrate or pro-magistrate of the Roman people, was expected to consult his *consilium* before making an important or difficult decision. He alone was responsible for it, but if anything went wrong, disastrous decisions made after consultation of the *consilium* were more easily forgiven than those taken without consultation of the *consilium* (often seen as an act of unacceptable arrogance). Generally speaking, the *consilium* was therefore one means by which office-holders could diffuse the risk of making decisions by integrating others into the decision-making process; while the *consilium* operated in a largely informal capacity, the institution still significantly circumscribed the power of the (pro-)magistrate to act as he wished.[82] In the administration of criminal justice in the provinces, the *consilium* played the role of jury that voted on the innocence or guilt of the defendant. Only after the *consilium* had decided on a verdict of guilty (*condemnatio*) was the (pro-) magistrate able to set in motion the execution.[83] Nero, then, followed standard operating procedure and the fact that his *consilium*, at least eventually, opted to declare Philodamus and his son as guilty represents a significant rhetorical challenge for Cicero: he needed to discredit both Nero and his group of advisors – and this is the task he tackles in this and the subsequent paragraphs.

quod Cornelium lictorem occisum esse constaret, putasse non oportere esse cuiquam ne in ulciscenda quidem iniuria hominis occidendi potestatem: Cicero here obliquely ridicules Nero's handling of the case. Proper proceedings would have involved (a) ascertaining the facts and the wider circumstances, especially the motivation of the perpetrator; (b) reference to a code of law; (c) deliberation of guilt or innocence; (d) the passing and justification of the verdict. Nero and his *consilium*, however, at least in Cicero's account, do not enquire into the case beyond recognizing the obvious fact of homicide; and they judge the matter on the basis of the personal opinion (see *putasse*) that the desire for revenge does not justify homicide. The way Cicero presents this chain of reasoning is designed to throw doubt on the judgment of Nero and his advisors: there is no compelling logical connection between the indisputable fact that a homicide occurred and their belief that no one

82. Kunkel, W. (1995), *Staatsordnung und Staatspraxis der römischen Republik, Zweiter Abschnitt: Die Magistratur*, Munich, 135–41 ('Das magistratische Konsilium').
83. Kunkel, 138–39.

has the right to kill someone even to avenge an injustice. For Roman law recognized that in certain circumstances (such as self-defence) homicide was justified and did not entail any punitive sanctions. What mattered was the motivation of the killer, and this motivation had to be inferred from careful consideration on a case-by-case basis. Nero and his advisors are shown up doubly: the prohibition to kill to avenge an injustice is not a matter of belief, but of law; but in this case, this law is irrelevant since revenge was not the motivation behind the killing. Cicero puts matters so as to suggest a shocking degree of incompetence on the part of those who presided over the verdict.

putasse non oportere esse cuiquam ... hominis occidendi potestatem: a complicated bit of syntax that can be sorted into three different levels: (i) *putasse* is the main verb of an indirect statement dependent on *dico*, with Nero and his *consilium* being the implied subject accusative ('they believed that...'); (ii) *putasse* introduces an indirect statement of its own, consisting of the impersonal verb (*non*) *oportere*; (iii) *oportere* is complemented by the infinitive phrase *esse cuiquam hominis occidendi potestatem* (*cuiquam* being a dative of possession with *esse*).

in quo video ... caedis: Cicero points out that the legal principle that Nero and his *consilium* applied to establish the guilt of the defendant does not absolve Verres from crime: the homicide may have been punishable by death, but that does not do away with the *iniuria* which provoked it.

ne in ulciscenda quidem iniuria: apparently, Nero and his advisors did not view the incident as a case of 'self-defence', but considered the killing the result of an escalation of violence motivated by the desire for avenging an injury suffered. This throws an interesting, retrospective light on Cicero's partial account of what happened – the way he spun his tale the death of Cornelius was an unfortunate accident in a general brawl in which Verres and his men were the aggressors and Philodamus and his household the victims.

Audite ... et ... aliquando miseremini ... et ostendite: a highly emotional *tricolon of imperatives addressed to the judges. *aliquando* ('at long last') underscores the enormous deficit in humane feelings towards those who suffer from Roman exploitation and maladministration among members of the Roman elite.

quaeso, iudices: Cicero is pleading.

aliquid ... praesidi: *praesidi* is a partitive genitive depending on *aliquid*. The *hyperbaton stresses that Cicero is only asking for a minimal degree of protection.

aliquid iis in vestra fide praesidi esse oportere: the construction with *oportere* as the impersonal verb of an indirect statement mockingly recalls the wayward application of legal principles that Nero and his advisors believed in. It is as if Cicero shows that he alone knows how to argue logically and coherently.

Quod toti Asiae iure occisus ... iudicio liberatur: there is an apparent inconcinnity in Cicero's argument; up to this point, it appeared as if Nero and his *consilium* had condemned Philodamus and his son to death. Now, however, it becomes clear that this verdict was only reached after considerable complications. Initially, it seems to have looked as if the defendants might walk free, not least on account of an apparent upswell of public opinion and outrage throughout the entire province of Asia. At this point – apparently before the official part of the trial got underway and certainly long before the final verdict – Verres started to fear that matters might not take the course he was hoping for and solicited the help of his immediate superior, Dolabella. Cicero hardly ever tells it straight, but fits and bits and pieces of information around an overriding rhetorical agenda.

toti Asiae: another 'totalizing' expression. See Mitchell (1986) 192: 'Cicero commonly cites the *sermo vulgi* or the reactions of certain people and communities to reinforce the particular impression he is seeking to create.'

istius ille verbo lictor, re vera minister improbissimae cupiditatis: *verbo* ~ *re vera* marks a dichotomy between 'signifier' and 'signified', appearance and reality: Cornelius is Verres' *lictor* in name, but in name only: in fact (*re vera*) he is a servant of Verres' lust. There are two ways of looking at this: from Cicero's perspective, Verres perverts Roman constitutional realities – under his influence a lictor ceases to be what he officially was and turns into something else; from Verres' point of view, Cicero is illicitly challenging constitutional facts and Roman authority: a lictor is an appointed official and demands respect. Redefining constitutional realities according to his own criteria is a constant of Cicero's oratory, and he became more radical in applying this technique over time: Gildenhard (2011) 141–67.

ut de sua provincia decedat: the affairs at Lampsacus fell into the jurisdiction of the governor of the province of Asia, i.e. Nero; Verres, however, feared that Philodamus might walk free and therefore urged Dolabella to leave his province of Cilicia to join the judicial proceedings.

incolumem: Verres' concern for his personal safety is of course highly ironic.

§ 73

Cicero uses this paragraph to discredit thoroughly the group of advisors that helped Nero decide the case: Dolabella's arrival and intervention are uncalled-for and irresponsible; his crowding of Nero's *consilium* with his own men clearly prejudices the outcome; the presence of Verres among those deciding upon the case constitutes an injustice of the first order; and the inclusion of notoriously unscrupulous creditors, who have everything to gain from supporting Verres, adds insult to injury.

id ... ut ... relinqueret: a so-called epexegetical *ut*-clause, in apposition to *id*, which it explains further.

ut exercitum, provinciam, bellum relinqueret: an *asyndetic *tricolon, designed to emphasize the irresponsible haste with which Dolabella let drop all of his official responsibilities to help out his rogue legate. *Ver.* 2.1.154 suggests that Dolabella was at the moment involved in warfare against the pirates who had strongholds at the costal border of Cilicia.

hominis nequissimi ... aequissimus iudex ... improbissimi cuiusque legati: three superlatives, paired, respectively, with the generic *homo*, followed by two nouns ('judge' and 'legate') that designate official roles, which require a high level of ethics and sense of responsibility. *Nequissimus* and *improbissimus* heighten the bitter sarcasm of *aequissimus*. The fourth superlative in the paragraph, *plurimum*, integrates the Roman creditors into the corrupt economy of services that Roman magistrates and businessmen maintained for the exploitation of provincials.

causam cognosceret: *cognoscere* is a technical term of Roman criminal procedure and, when used of magistrates, refers generally speaking to those cases in which the magistrate personally oversees the taking of evidence of the case and the passing of a verdict.[84] Elsewhere in the *Verrines*, Cicero portrays how Verres, when presiding over a case, makes a mockery of proper procedure, including *cognitio* (2.2.75): *Tum iste aliquando 'Age dic!' inquit. Reus orare atque obsecrare ut cum consilio cognosceret. Tum repente iste testis citari iubet; dicit unus et alter breviter; nihil interrogatur; praeco dixisse pronuntiat. Iste, quasi metueret ne Petilius ... cum ceteris in consilium reverteretur, ita properans de sella exsilit, hominem innocentem a C. Sacerdote absolutum indicta causa de sententia scribae medici haruspicisque condemnat.* (Then this man here finally said: 'Go on, speak!' The accused begged and beseeched him to investigate the matter in the presence of his advisory council. Then this man here suddenly orders the witnesses to be called in; one or the other speaks briefly; there is no cross-examination; the herald announces that each party has spoken. This man here jumped up from his seat with such haste, as if he feared that Petilius ... could come back with the others into the advisory council, and, without the case having been properly pleaded,[85] sentences the innocent man, who had been freed by C. Sacerdos, on the basis of the opinion of his scribe, his doctor, and his soothsayer.)

Venerat ipse qui esset in consilio et primus sententiam diceret: a relative clause of purpose (hence the subjunctive).

praefectos et tribunos militaris suos: *praefecti* were officers in the Roman army in charge of a military unit; military tribunes were partly elected by the Roman people, partly appointed by the commanding officer, and were in charge of important military business. Put differently, Cicero suggests that Dolabella ridiculously overreacted in bringing along half of his staff of command (and leaving his own province exposed in the process) just to do Verres' bidding.

---

84. Kunkel, W. (1995), *Staatsordnung und Staatspraxis der römischen Republik, Zweiter Abschnitt: Die Magistratur*, Munich, 145.

85. *indicta causa* = the hasty processing of *cognitio* so as to obviate the possibility of a considered defence and the proper consultation of witnesses: Kunkel (1995) 145; *OLD* s.v. *indictus* 1b.

quos Nero omnis in consilium vocavit: a reminder that Nero stayed nominally in charge of proceedings.

togati creditores: creditors 'clad in the toga', i.e. Roman.[86] Pseudo-Asconius spots the euphemism: *noluit dicere equites Romanos* ('he [sc. Cicero] did not want to say "Roman knights"'). These moneylenders played a key role in the Roman system of provincial exploitation. Routinely charging outrageous interest rates, they often relied on the help of magistrates to enforce repayment. At the time, many were active in Asia, 'aiding' communities to meet indemnity obligations imposed upon them by Sulla, in the wake of the first war against Mithradates. As Steel (2004) 249 points out, 'given the extent to which the cities were in debt in this period, it would probably have been difficult for Nero to find any Romans of suitable standing who were *not* creditors of the Greeks.' See Plutarch, *Lucullus* 7.6 and 20 and Appian, *Roman History* 12, 62–63, two sources that describe the unholy alliance between Roman tax farmers (*publicani*) and Roman money-lenders (*creditores*) and the misery that Sulla's punitive sanctions brought to the cities of Asia.

improbissimi cuiusque legati plurimum prodest gratia: Cicero presents legates as more or less useful to creditors in direct proportion to the degree of their wickedness. Verres tops this scale: he is the most (*plurimum*) useful since he is the most wicked (*improbissimus*).

§ 74

Cicero here continues his description of how Verres and his supporters manipulated the proceedings against Philodamus, but adds a new twist: the basic theme of the paragraph consists of the contrast between the power and the resources at the disposal of Verres and the prosecution on the one hand, and the utter helplessness of the defendant on the other. The point of the contrast is that in spite of the fact that everything was stacked against Philodamus, the group judging the case was still not able to reach a verdict during the first hearing.

---

86. The *toga* was the distinctive, and distinctively cumbersome, Roman dress that turned those who wore it into moving statues; before the advent of toga-parties, the garment was immortalized by Virgil, *Aeneid* 1.282 (Jupiter speaking): *Romanos, rerum dominos gentemque togatam* ('The Romans, lords of the world, the people clad in the toga'). Augustus is said to have recited this line in disgust upon encountering a shoddily dressed crowd (Suetonius, *Divus Augustus* 40.5). See further Vout, C. (1996), 'The Myth of the Toga: Understanding the History of Roman Dress', *Greece and Rome* 43.2, 204-20.

quis enim esset ... qui ... ?: a rhetorical question; the imperfect subjunctive conveys the sense that the possibility of anyone, be it Roman, be it Greek, standing up for Philodamus was entirely counterfactual. The Romans kept quiet out of self-interest since they did not wish to court controversy with someone as influential as Dolabella; the Greeks since they were intimidated by Dolabella's official power and imperial command (*vi et imperio*).

togatus – Graecus: Cicero again uses the generic adjective *togatus* to specify persons in possession of Roman citizenship. On the *toga* as the distinctive Roman dress see above § 73.

gratia: here 'influence': *OLD* s.v. 5c.

adponitur – qui si dixisset ... posset exigere: the passive construction obfuscates who was behind the appointment, though Cicero later on in the paragraph specifies that it was Verres (*idem accusatorem parasset*). The syntax of the sentence *qui si dixisset ... exigere* produces a similar effect: it remains unclear who is responsible for briefing the prosecutor that getting Philodamus sentenced to death would be to his own advantage, though, as the clause *quod iste iussisset* suggests, it does not seem to have been Verres.

qui si dixisset ... posset exigere: an indirect statement depending on an imagined 'he was told that'; *qui* is a connecting relative pronoun.

Cum haec ... parasset: One long series of concessive *cum*-clauses; Cicero sums up the machinations on the part of Dolabella and Verres with *haec cum omnia fierent* and then adds the fact that someone had been killed before continuing with the corresponding *tamen*.

tanta contentione, tantis copiis – multi accusarent, nemo defenderet: two ablatives of instrument, enumerated *asyndetically but linked by an *anaphoric *polyptoton (*tanta* ~ *tantis*) and *alliteration; the (stylistic) coordination of effort and resources in the first *cum*-clause contrasts with the antithetical design in the subsequent *cum*-clause (*multi* ~ *nemo*; *accusarent* ~ *defenderet*).

cumque: by means of the *-que* Cicero distinguishes the *cum*-clauses that indicate the general set-up of the trial from those *cum*-clauses that detail the specific actions undertaken by the two main culprits, i.e. Dolabella and Verres, who are both subsumed under one *cum*.

cumque Dolabella cum suis praefectis pugnaret in consilio: *pugnare* is frequently used in the sense of 'to contend in word or action, e.g. in a law-court': *OLD* s.v. 4b. Nevertheless, Cicero's choice of idiom gives the impression that Dolabella overdoes his efforts considerably; there is an arch touch to the finishing flourish *in consilio*, which is designed to surprise: an advisory group is hardly the context to manoeuvre forcefully with one's military officers.

Verres fortunas agi suas diceret, idem testimonium diceret, idem esset in consilio, idem accusatorem parasset: four *asyndetic clauses that specify Verres' role in all this; the rhetorical design helps to produce a most damning effect: the triple *anaphora of *idem* that follows upon *Verres* reinforces Cicero's point that Verres dominated the trial as (self-styled) victim, witness, judge, and prosecutor all in one.

amplius pronuntiatur: for *amplius* in the technical juridical sense of 'judgement reserved' see *OLD* s.v. 1c. A Roman trial (*actio*) consisted of speeches by the prosecution and the defence, followed by a hearing (and cross-examination) of witnesses. If the jury was unable to decide after the first hearing, it could vote *amplius* or *non liquet* (a procedure known as *ampliatio*), necessitating a further hearing or hearings.[87] Despite the fact that everything was stacked against Philodamus, those sitting in judgement could not agree on a verdict in the first meeting and had to postpone the decision. That may indeed have been the case, but we are forced to take Cicero at his word as regards the reasons. Upon consideration, the notion that the group assembled by Nero and Dolabella was swayed to reconvene by its knowledge of Verres' immorality sounds rather implausible.

§ 75

Cicero now shifts the blame for the corrupt proceedings squarely onto Dolabella. Nero, in turn, emerges as a spineless coward who helplessly presides over a terrible miscarriage of justice that will result in two executions, which will move even him to tears (see § 76).

Quid ... quid ... quid?: an *anaphoric *tricolon of rhetorical questions that also functions as *praeteritio* – Cicero hints at the possibility of filling volumes

---

87. See Powell, J. G. F. (2010), 'Court Procedure and Rhetorical Strategy in Cicero', in D. H. Berry and A. Erskine (eds.), *Form and Function in Roman Oratory*, Cambridge, 21-36 (26-7).

on how the three protagonists behaved during the second hearing, without pursuing it. He thus generates a very effective tension between his own compressed account and the tremendous energy and effort expended by the 'triumvirate of evil' in charge of the proceedings to secure the desired outcome.

spiritus: the first of three accusative objects, each one referring to the mindset or conduct of one of the three Roman protagonists: Dolabella, Verres, Nero. Cicero links Dolabella and Nero in various ways: they are named, Verres is designated by a demonstrative pronoun (*huius*); *spiritus* and *animus* are virtual synonyms and refer to their respective frame of mind, in contrast to the theatrics of Verres; and Cicero uses one noun each for these two, but two nouns for Verres, so there is a gradual increase in quantity in the course of the *tricolon: one noun, two nouns, one noun + two attributes.

viri optimi atque innocentissimi, non nullis in rebus animum nimium timidum atque demissum: the two superlatives modifying *vir, optimus* and *innocentissimus*, are mockingly cancelled out by the two attributes of *animus*, kept laconically in the positive, though reinforced by an adverbial phrase and an adverb, indicating frequency (*non nullis in rebus*: Cicero uses a delicious *litotes) and excess (*nimium*). (The repetition of the connective *atque* reinforces the negative correlation.) Whatever his personal qualities, they are not worth much under pressure, and C. Nero, despite his high principles, stands revealed as a servile (*demissum*) coward (*timidum*) in practice.

quid facere potuerit non habebat: Peterson, W. (1903), 'Emendations of Cicero's Verrines', *Classical Review* 17, 198–202 (202) proposes to emend the *potuerit* of the manuscripts to *oporteret*, but the text may not need correction. We need to imagine Cicero saying, mockingly, 'There was absolutely nothing he could have done – except, of course, the obvious!'

nisi forte: see *OLD* s.v. *forte* 3b: '(*with nisi*) especially used to introduce an unlikely or absurd suggestion' – Cicero is being highly ironic: after first intimating that there was nothing Nero could have done differently, he introduces the utterly obvious possibility (but presented as outlandish or even absurd by means of the sly use of *forte*) of considering the case without having Dolabella or Verres present. Cicero, though, saps his own irony by adding *id quod omnes tum desiderabant*. But he accepts the loss of rhetorical force in return for leaving no doubt that Nero meekly bowed to power against the wishes of any impartial observer (see *omnes* with the following note).

Quicquid esset sine his actum, omnes probarent: a rather brilliant touch – Cicero suggests that 'everyone' (*omnes*) would have accepted any outcome of the hearing as long as it had taken place without Verres and Dolabella present. The implication of this counterfactual scenario is that without the machinations of Verres and the imperious interference of Dolabella on his behalf, Philodamus would have been judged innocent. Who are *omnes*? Cicero imagines a general audience of impartial observers.

non per Neronem iudicatum, sed per Dolabellam ereptum: Cicero reinforces his basic point that Nero was a mere puppet of Dolabella in this matter. There was never a proper verdict (cf. *iudicatum*), only a pronouncement of what Dolabella coerced Nero to say (cf. *ereptum*).

perpaucis sententiis: *per-* serves as intensifier of *paucis* – despite the fact that the hearing was skewed, when the final vote was taken, Philodamus, so Cicero claims, was only condemned by the narrowest of margins.

Condemnatur ... Adest, instat, urget: Cicero switches into the historical present for greater immediacy; the last three verbs form an *asyndetic *tricolon that enacts the hectic urgency of Dolabella to get on with the execution. The lack of connectives here contrasts with Cicero's drawn-out description of what happened at the execution in the subsequent paragraph, which he calls a *spectaculum acerbum et miserum et grave toti Asiae provinciae*.

securi feriantur: the subjects are Philodamus and his son, the mode of execution beheading.

quam minime multi: the combination of *minime* and *multi* generates an *oxymoron, which is reinforced by the *alliteration. Cicero here ridicules the futile attempt by Dolabella to suppress the truth, which many, so Cicero implies, did get to know nevertheless.

ex illis: Philodamus and his son.

§ 76

After his portrayal of the corrupt and hasty trial, Cicero now lingers on the scene of execution, which reduced everyone with even a bit of human decency to tears. This is pathos on a grand scale: father and son, both innocent victims, emerge as heroic protagonists in a tragedy, each more concerned for the welfare and the life of the other than their own. Cicero first focuses on each individually (*parens – filius; ille – hic*); then portrays them jointly as weeping (*flebat uterque*), before specifying that each weeps for the death of the other (*pater de fili morte, de patris filius*); the design re-enacts their common destiny, their courage, and their mutual *pietas*. Such bravery and sympathy in the face of death brought the entire Roman province to its knees with weeping, including the presiding Roman magistrate, Nero. Quintilian (*Institutio Oratoria* 4.2.111–15) cites this paragraph in support of his point that appeal to the emotions ought not to be reserved until the final part of the speech (*peroratio*); rather, it should be mustered in aid of rational argumentation (*probatio*) whenever apposite.

Laodiceae: a city on the river Lycus in Caria; 'it was the judicial centre closest to Dolabella's province of Cilicia, and was far removed from Lampsacum': Mitchell (1986) 193.

toti Asiae provinciae: *Asiae* is genitive depending on *provinciae* (which is in the dative).

grandis natu parens: *natu* is an ablative of respect depending on *grandis*.

ille quod pudicitiam liberorum, hic quod vitam patris famamque sororis defenderat: Cicero's phrasing enacts the tight-knit loyalty within the family of Philodamus; the three accusative objects (each with a genitive attribute) *pudicitiam liberorum, vitam patris*, and *famam sororis* correspond to the three family members involved in the affair, though of course only father and son face execution – hence the bipartite arrangement *ille – hic*. And whereas the concern of the father embraces both of his children, which results in the slightly inaccurate formulation *pudicitiam liberorum* insofar as only the chastity of his daughter had been at stake, the son had jumped to the defence of both father and sister. In short, the family forms a triangle, with the father caring for both of his children and the son for his father and his sibling – an inverse mirror-image, as it were, of the triumvirate of evil Dolabella, Nero, Verres.

pater de fili morte, de patris filius: Cicero uses *chiasmus (a) *pater* (b) *de fili morte* (b) *de patris* [sc. morte] (b) *filius* to underscore the distinct, yet interlinked perspectives of father and son; in addition, the *ellipsis of *morte* in the second half of the *chiasmus results in an emphasis on their joint destiny: death. The key term is placed right in the middle of the *chiasmus and points both backwards to *pater* and forward to *filius*. The pathos of the phrasing is profoundly tragic, and dimly recalls such scenes of the tragic theatre as the one in Euripides' *Iphigenia at Tauris*, when Pylades and Orestes are both willing to sacrifice their life on behalf of their friend. In the Latin version of Ennius, the scene, in which the two friends vie with one another for the privilege to be sacrificed, became a hit at Rome: see Cicero, *de Amicitia* 24 and *de Finibus* 2.79 and 5.63.

Quid lacrimarum ipsum Neronem putatis profudisse? quem fletum totius Asiae fuisse, quem luctum et gemitum Lampsacenorum?: the two indirect statements depend on *putatis*; *quid* has a double function as interrogative pronoun/ accusative object of the main clause and accusative object of the indirect statement.

putatis: Cicero here challenges his audience to picture the scene of the execution in his mind – a technique to generate empathy and pity for the victims.[88]

esse percussos: this indirect statement depends on the verbal force of *luctum* and *gemitum* in the previous sentence: it explicates the reason why there was such widespread weeping.

homines innocentis nobilis ... hominis flagitiosissimi: the repetition of *homo* to designate both the two innocent victims and the vicious perpetrator marks out a spectrum of what human beings are capable of, in good and in evil. As noted before, Cicero is fond of operating at an anthropological level, insofar as he assesses the worth of his characters as human beings, quite irrespective of whatever social role or status they may have. (Cf. above § 63.)

propter hominis flagitiosissimi singularem nequitiam atque improbissimam cupiditatem!: a weighty, remorseless ending to the account of how Verres' disgraceful conduct resulted in the death of two innocent human beings, friends and allies of the Roman people, no

---

88. For Cicero's 'vivid descriptions' see Innocenti, B. (1994), 'Towards a Theory of Vivid Description as Practiced in Cicero's Verrine *Orations*', *Rhetorica* 12, 355–81. Our passage is discussed on p. 376.

less. Cicero places the genitive (noun:attribute) in *chiastic position to the two phrases it modifies (attribute:noun, attribute:noun). If in the genitive phrase the number of syllables in noun (3) and attribute (7) are unequal, *singularem* (4) *nequitiam* (4) and *improbissimam* (5) *cupiditatem* (5) are perfectly and climactically balanced. Cicero again speaks in the superlative mode, with the 'thematic superlative' *singularis* providing some variation to the grammatical superlatives *flagitiosissimi* and *improbissimam*.

§ 77

After his account of the execution, Cicero turns to the perpetrators, first Dolabella (§ 77), then Verres (§ 78). By direct address and a string of rhetorical questions he explores possible motivations for Dolabella's conduct and offers a further evaluation of it. As a result, Dolabella emerges as both cruel and stupid, insofar as he employed excessive force to ensure the friendship and goodwill of an utterly worthless, indeed treacherous creature who already had a distinguished track-record of back-stabbing his benefactors when it suited him. Put differently, Dolabella could have known that supporting Verres would not yield dividends in terms of future loyalty, which he, according to Cicero, was after. Verres is so abominably wicked that he operates without regard to the principle of *manus manum lavat* (i.e. 'corrupt reciprocity').

Cicero enhances his attack on Dolabella through systematic use of the second person singular personal pronoun and the possive adjective: *tui, tuorum, tu, tibi* (in the mocking *alliteration *Verresne t̲ibi t̲anti fuit...?*), *tua, tibi, tibi, in te, te*.

Iam iam: see *OLD* s.v. 6: 'Now (after what has happened)'.

Dolabella: For Dolabella see page 101 above. The direct address here is curious: it implies that Dolabella was physically present during the (imagined) proceedings, even though he was condemned to exile after his return from Cilicia. We are, then, dealing with a moment of creative licence on the part of Cicero who addresses Dolabella *in absentia*. While Dolabella's fate of exile and the subsequent impoverishment of his children would in principle be pitiable, Cicero insists that any feelings of sympathy are misplaced: Dolabella's crimes on behalf of Verres were such that all of his sufferings (and the sufferings of his children) are well and fully deserved.

me tui neque tuorum liberorum ... misereri potest: *me miseret* is an impersonal expression that has its objects in the genitive.

tanti: genitive of worth, to be construed with *fuit*.

lui: a striking choice of verb – *luo* means 'to atone or make amends for, expiate' (*OLD* s.v. 2) and has religious connotations. Cicero here evokes the repulsive and perverse scenario that Dolabella wanted to commit sacrificial slaughter (see *sanguine*) 'to wash away' the sins of Verres' abominable lust with the blood of innocents.

Idcircone: *idcirco* + *ne* (an enclitic used to introduce a question).

exercitum atque hostem relinquebas: this harks back to § 73, where Cicero recounted that Dolabella left behind his official responsibilities as governor of Cilicia to come to Verres' aid (*fecit [sc. Dolabella] id quod multi reprehenderunt, ut exercitum, provinciam, bellum relinqueret*). Here Cicero employs a rhetorical question to wonder about Dolabella's motivation.

tua vi et crudelitate: the phrase recalls earlier expressions involving *vis* (see § 54: *vi cum exercitu imperioque* and § 55: *vi ac virtute*). It could not be more damning. The charge of *crudelitas* or 'bestial cruelty' (one of the antonyms of *humanitas* or 'humanity') is one of the strongest possible accusations in Cicero's register: it is the exact opposite of everything that makes up and stands for human civilization in general and, specifically, Rome's civic values. Cicero used it throughout his career as orator to stigmatize his opponents: Gildenhard (2011) 208–13.

tibi ... constitueras: *tibi* is an ethical dative.

quaestoris in loco: Verres was initially a legate in Dolabella's entourage, but was promoted to the status of a pro-quaestor (or 'acting quaestor') after the quaestor C. (Publicius) Malleolus was murdered. Cicero provides the requisite information at 2.1.41: *itaque idem iste* [sc. Verres], *quem Cn. Dolabella postea, C. Malleolo occiso, pro quaestore habuit*. Verres also took on the legal guardianship of Malleolus' under-age son and seems to have abused this position by embezzling the entire patrimony (some 2.5 million sesterces) for himself. Cicero provides lurid details of the affair at *Verr.* 2.1.90–94.

putasti? nesciebas?: by both ending one clause and beginning the next with the verb, Cicero achieves an effective juxtaposition that reinforces his mocking incredulity at the degree of Dolabella's naiveté: 'did you *actually* believe, Dolabella, that...? Can it *really* be that you did not know that...?'

Cn. Carbonem consulem: Gnaeus Papirius Carbo (c. 132 – 82 BC; *cos.* 85, 84, 82) was one of the main supporters of Marius and executed in the wake of Sulla's victory. Verres was his quaestor in 83, and as such in control of over two million sesterces meant for the consular army that stood in Gallia Cisalpina when Sulla returned to Italy after his victory of Mithradates. Verres violated the trust invested in him by Carbo, took the remaining money (c. 600,000 sesterces) and went over to Sulla – not because of any specific party loyalty, according to Cicero, but because he wanted to obfuscate his embezzlement of public funds. Cicero considers this affair, which he calls Verres' entry into the *cursus honorum*, at length at 2.1.34–42. Cicero is our main source.

Expertus ... es: *experior* here means 'to learn from personal experience' and stands in contrast to *nesciebas*: since Dolabella apparently did not know of (or refused to learn from) Verres' betrayal of Carbo, whose quaestor he had been just a few years earlier, he had to find out from personal experience that Verres, who was a prime witness in his trial for extortion, not least to cover up his own crimes, was not to be trusted.

perfidiam: *perfidia* – faithlessness, treachery – is the opposite of *fides*, the value, grounded in the principle of (asymmetric) reciprocity, that ideally underwrote all socio-political relations in ancient Rome.[89]

tum cum ... contulit, cum ... dixit, cum ... noluit: a *tricolon of *cum*-clauses that remorselessly recall how Verres betrayed Dolabella to save his own hide. Each *cum*-clause contains an attribute or pronoun referring to Dolabella (*ad inimicos tuos – in te – nisi damnato te*).

---

89. See Hölkeskamp, K.-J. (2000), '*Fides – deditio in fidem – dextra data et accepta*: Recht, Religion und Ritual in Rom', in C. Bruun (ed.), *The Roman Middle Republic: Politics, Religion, and Historiography c. 400–133 B.C.*, Rome, 223–50.

cum ipse se ad inimicos tuos contulit: *inimicus* means 'personal enemy' (in contrast to *hostis*, which designates a 'foreign enemy'); Cicero here refers to those (notably M. Aemilius Scaurus) who charged Dolabella with extortion upon his return to Rome and achieved his conviction and exile.

nisi damnato te: Verres wanted to wait until Dolabella had been exiled since then Dolabella had no means of objecting to the accounts given; *damnato te* is an ablative absolute, substituting for a conditional clause.

§ 78

Cicero here turns his attention again to Verres. As with Dolabella in the previous paragraph, he employs direct address. From here on until the end of the episode (the beginning of § 86), Cicero revisits the incident at Lampsacus, challenging Verres, mainly in the form of rhetorical questions, to explain this or that aspect in a way different from his own interpretation. In a sense, then, he puts his version of the events on trial to show that any alternative explanation that Verres may come up with does not stand up to scrutiny: the full scale of the disaster – a lictor dead, friends and allies of the Roman people in uproar, two innocent people executed – was ultimately caused by Verres' criminal passion. To leave no doubt about where he locates the driving force behind the events at Lampsacus, Cicero begins the paragraph with two magnificent rhetorical questions, which, by means of *hyperbole, try to measure out the enormity of Verres' lust, before settling down to a more fact-focused cross-examination in the second half of the paragraph.

Tantaene tuae ... ? Tune ... ?: the *alliterative drum of the opening words links the two rhetorical questions on the level of style as well as theme (with the second question explicating the first).

erunt: 'the future indicative is not uncommon in indignant rhetorical questions of this sort where the deliberative subjunctive might be expected': Mitchell (1986) 194. Cicero sticks to the future also in the following sentence (*immittentur, expugnabuntur, confugient*).

ut eas capere ac sustinere non provinciae populi Romani, non nationes exterae possint: the word order in this consecutive *ut*-clause (accusative object, complementary infinitives, subject, verb) reinforces the theme: Verres' passions (*eas*) stand prominently at the beginning, and try as they might (an idea hinted at by Cicero's advanced placement of the two infinitives) the territories exposed to them are unable to contain them. (The notion that the affected regions actively attempted to impose boundaries upon Verres' passion is of course slightly absurd.) The phrasing following on from *eas* is well-balanced: two infinitives linked by *ac* and the *asyndetic juxtaposition of the two subjects, further coordinated by reiteration of the negation (*non*).

non provinciae populi Romani, non nationes exterae: put differently, the entire known world – a clear instance of dramatic *hyperbole. Cicero distinguishes between territories under direct control of the Roman people (*provinciae*) and nations outside Roman jurisdiction (*nationes exterae*). In the second rhetorical question Cicero uses slightly different phrasing (*civitates pacatae; civitates sociorum atque amicorum*) and narrows the focus on to civic communities within Roman provinces.

Tune quod videris ... propulsare possint: this extraordinary rhetorical question consists of a conditional sequence (*nisi ... fuerit, nisi ... paruerit*), the main clause (a tricolon: *immittentur, expugnabuntur, confugient*), and a concluding *ut*-clause. The antecedent of the four initial relative clauses introduced by *quod* is the *id* after the first *nisi*; in effect, then, Cicero places the relative clauses before the *nisi*-clause into which they belong and additionally extrapolates the subject of the relative clauses (Verres) in the form of the personal pronoun *tu*, which he places at the beginning of the sentence. This arrangement corresponds to, and reinforces, the main theme of the sentence: the egomania of the sociopath Verres.

videris ... audieris ... concupieris ... cogitaris: future perfects (as are *fuerit* and *paruerit*); *concupieris* is the syncopated form of *concupiveris* and *cogitaris* of *cogitaveris*. Note the *homoioteleuton.

(a) immittentur (b) homines, (a) expugnabuntur (b) domus, (b) civitates ... (a) confugient: Cicero constructs a *tricolon with a twist: the first two cola feature passive verbs and Cicero clearly implies that the people and the houses that come under threat are the victims of Verres' libidinous aggression. In the third colon, however, we get a *chiastic inversion: Cicero starts with the subject (*civitates*) and the dynamic of the sentence suggests that they, too, are the passive victims of violence. In the course of the sentence, however, it becomes clear that they are in fact opting for violent resistance. This twist invites a re-evaluation of the first part of the sentence: those who issued threats and stormed a house in the Philodamus-incident were after all the inhabitants of Lampsacus, not Verres or his men. The studied ambiguity seems deliberate: it portrays Verres as someone who both uses and incites violence.

civitates non modo pacatae, verum etiam sociorum atque amicorum ad vim atque ad arma confugient, ut ab se atque a liberis suis legati populi Romani scelus ac libidinem propulsare possint?: after Cicero uses *asyndeton in the first part of the sentence (the four *quod*-clauses, the two *nisi*-clauses, and the three pairs of subjects and main verbs are all unlinked by any connectives), he switches to a more deliberate exposition in the second half, with a sequence of noun phrases paired by *atque* or *ac*. Cicero thereby highlights, if in different ways, both Verres' aggression and the comprehensive nature of the response.

ab se atque a liberis suis – scelus ac libidinem: *alliteration links *se* with *scelus* and *liberis* with *libidinem*; *scelus ac libidinem* may be understood as a *hendiadys ('crime of passion').

propulsare possint: note the *alliteration. The two rhetorical questions end with the same word (*possint*).

Nam quaero abs te ... Lampsaceni?: Cicero here revisits elements of his narration (see § 69) as if he were cross-examining Verres; the posture presupposes the hypothetical scenario that the defendant somehow wishes or tries to deny that the recounted events actually took place. If Verres was out of control in the first half of the paragraph, Cicero is in control in the second half, and he foregrounds this by placing the verbs up front: *quaero* is followed by *habeo* (twice).

deversabare: an alternative form of *deversabaris*, i.e. second person singular imperfect passive of the deponent *deversari*. Cicero also uses the verb at the end of § 64.

testimonium tuum – quas ... litteras: somehow Cicero managed to procure pieces of the correspondence between Verres and Nero, in which Verres informed the governor of the province of what had happened at Lampsacus.

Recita: an order to the court official to read from the documents. See above § 57.

Testimonium C. Verris in Artemidorum. non multo post in domum: apparently, Verres singled out one Artemidorus as being a ringleader in the attack on his house. The incomplete sentence *non multo post in domum* introduces the passage that Cicero wanted to have read out.

§ 79

In this paragraph, Cicero rehearses and excludes alternative explanations for the conduct of the Lampsacenes. He dismisses the possibility that the uproar was an uprising and that the Lampsacenes wanted to revolt against Roman rule: in that case, surely, heavy sanctioned would have been imposed upon the entire community or war would have been declared.

conabatur? ... volebat?: two rhetorical questions, to which the obvious answer is 'no'.

ab imperio ac nomine nostro: in the phrase *nomen nostrum* (sc. *Romanum*) Cicero evokes both Roman rule and power grounded in military superiority (*imperium*) and an ethnic concept of Roman identity. The passage is listed by the *OLD* s.v. *nomen* 19, but this particular sense, though favoured by Cicero, is not all that common; in Roman political discourse, ethnic use of the *nomen* (*gentile*) was first and foremost a marker of what family-network (*gens*) an individual member of Rome's ruling elite belonged to. See further Gildenhard (2011) 52.

ex iis quae legi et audivi intellego: Cicero specifies two sources of information about past practice: written records and oral sources. But he remains vague as to the genre – is he thinking of official records or literary texts, mere hearsay or public proceedings? The entire posture is at any rate mildly ironic: there is hardly any need for 'fact finding' to realize that the actions detailed would, under normal circumstances, have resulted in a declaration of war.

in qua civitate ... ei civitati: *civitati* is the antecedent of *qua*; here it is attracted into the relative clause and repeated afterwards, both for emphasis and clarity.

legatus populi Romani: the paragraph advances Cicero's strategy of questioning Verres' official status as a legate of the Roman people, by splitting the man from the norms and expectations of the office. The following syllogism underlies the argument:

(a) Any attack on a Roman legate entails a demand for reparation or a declaration of war.
(b) Verres has been violently attacked.
(c) No reparation was demanded, no war was declared.
(d) *Ergo*: Verres could not have been a proper Roman legate.

non modo legatus populi Romani circumsessus, non modo igni, ferro, manu, copiis oppugnatus, sed aliqua ex parte violatus sit: the three verbs *circumsessus, oppugnatus*, and *violatus* are arranged climactically, whereas the degree of violence implied by *igni, ferro, manu, copiis* (note the *asyndetic enumeration) and *aliqua ex parte violatus* anticlimactically decreases. The careful balance reinforces Cicero's point that what happened to Verres at Lampsacus ought to have resulted in a demand for reparation or even military retaliation, if not outright war. That nothing happened Cicero takes as clear evidence that everyone condoned the actions that the Lampsacenes took against Verres, *in spite of the fact* that Verres was a Roman legate.

aliqua ex parte: 'to any degree' – however small the amount of physical harm suffered by an official representative of the Roman people, when any occurred – so Cicero claims – it was usually a sufficient cause for war unless satisfactory reparation was made.

publice: 'at public expense', 'as a community' – the adverb stresses the fact that the entire community was liable for acts of transgression against a Roman official.

§ 80

After Cicero has established once more *what* has happened, he proceeds to explore once again *why* the Lampsacenes acted as they did. The key term of the paragraph, then, is *causa*, which Cicero uses five times. Verres is unable to give any reason for the uproar; Cicero raises and dismisses the possibility that Rubrius alone is to blame; and his witnesses blame Verres: all this Cicero takes to confirm Verres' guilt in the matter. The paragraph thus continues the theme that Cicero first introduced in § 70: that Verres has never been able to offer a satisfactory explanation for why the people of Lampsacus attacked his house during his visit (... *neque adhuc causam ullam excogitare potuit quam ob rem commiserit, aut quid evenerit, ut in tantum periculum veniret*).

Quae fuit igitur causa ... ? ... causam tanti tumultus ostendis ullam: the *ullam* ('not any') is placed emphatically and *climactically at the end of the sentence, an effect further reinforced by the *hyperbaton *causam – ullam*.

causa cur cuncta civitas Lampsacenorum de contione: note the *alliteration.

tute: an emphatic form of *tu*; in prose, *tûte* is indistinguishable from *tûtê*, the adverb of *tutus* ('safely', 'securely').

scribis – mittis – ostendis – dicis – dicis – negas – occultas: Cicero uses the present tense throughout to enhance the immediacy and vividness of his direct attack on Verres.

Obsessum te dicis, ignem adlatum, sarmenta circumdata, lictorem tuum occisum esse dicis, prodeundi tibi in publicum potestatem factam negas: if in the previous sentence Cicero reports what he himself has gleaned from Verres' documents and testimony, he now reports what Verres is saying: his syntax generates the impression of disorder and confusion. To begin with, we get the events out of any coherent narrative order: Verres, egomaniac that he is, begins by saying 'I was beset'; then he gives two details (fire and brushwood) in inverted chronological order, before concluding, almost as an afterthought, with the most significant detail of all, the killing of his lictor, which preceded any of his own perils. The following sentence – Verres' inability to appear in public – comes as a bathetic anti-*climax.

Nam ... venirent: Cicero now considers the possibility that Rubrius acted on his own accord, rather than following the instructions of Verres; he argues that in that case, the Lampsacenes would have congregated in front of Verres' house to issue a complaint, rather than to resort to violence. But here

Cicero may be splitting hairs and he is at any rate operating on the arguably unwarranted assumption that the Lampsacenes carefully differentiated between Verres and members of his entourage. Cicero never explains how the Lampsacenes would have been able to determine that Rubrius acted on Verres' orders. Also, Cicero never acknowledges three other possibilities that are at least as plausible as the scenario he tries to establish as the true one (a) that Rubrius caused the uproar and the Lampsacenes *wrongly* assumed that Verres was to blame; (b) that the events at the dinner party or the Roman businessmen who intervened enraged the inhabitants to such a degree that they wanted to vent their anger against the principal representative of Roman rule rather than an insignificant underling; (c) that they were after Rubrius, who was hiding in Verres' house.

si quam ... iniuriam: *quam* = *(ali)quam*, modifying *iniuriam*.

(a) **impulsu** (b) **tuo et** (b) **tua** (a) **cupiditate**: a *chiasmus, designed to outweigh the alternative *suo nomine*.

questum – oppugnatum: two supines expressing purpose.

testes a nobis producti: in legal contexts, *producere* means 'to bring (witnesses etc.) into court': *OLD* s.v. 2b.

cum illorum testimonia tum istius taciturnitas perpetua: *cum ~ tum* correlates two circumstances but puts special emphasis on the second one, an effect that Cicero reinforces by endowing *taciturnitas* with the attribute *perpetua*, which is highly emphatic not least because it breaks the otherwise perfectly parallel construction: *cum ~ tum, illorum ~ istius* (linked by *alliteration), *testimonia ~ taciturnitas* (also linked by *alliteration). Cicero thereby foregrounds Verres' self-indictment: his persistent silence and inability to specify a plausible cause for the behaviour of the Lampsacenes is more important than the testimony of the witnesses that confirm his version of the events.

celarit: syncopated form of *celaverit*.

§ 81

Cicero begins this and the following paragraph with a direct appeal to the judges, to alleviate the monotony of his remorseless cross-examination of

Verres. From here onwards, his principal focus remains Verres' claim that he was the target of an attack by the Lampsacenes. Throughout, Cicero bases his argument on elements that were previously introduced in the narration as facts, revisiting his ethnographic appraisal of the Lampsacenes at the outset of the episode (§ 63) to argue that it took someone like Verres and his singular lust to stir such a peace-loving community into violent action, irrespective of their ingrained respect for the Romans or the consequences for themselves. Another technique Cicero employs is the reiteration in his own voice of things that were allegedly said during the public meeting of the Lampsacenes on the morning after the dinner party (compare, for instance, § 68: ... *quidvis esse* <u>*perpeti satius quam*</u> *in* <u>*tanta vi atque acerbitate*</u> *versari* with § 81: ... *ut perspicuum sit omnibus, nisi* <u>*tanta acerbitas iniuriae,*</u> <u>*tanta vis sceleris fuisset ut Lampsaceni moriendum sibi*</u> <u>*potius quam perpetiendum*</u> *putarent* or § 69: ... *ut* <u>*gravius*</u> *apud eos* <u>*nomen legationis quam iniuria legati*</u> *putaretur* with § 81: ... *ut* <u>*vehementius*</u> <u>*odio libidinis tuae quam legationis metu*</u> *moverentur*).

Huic homini parcetis, igitur, iudices ... : Cicero continues in his anthropological idiom, suggesting to the judges that they have to pass a verdict on a wicked human being, rather than a former magistrate or senatorial peer. The theme of 'sparing' has already occurred twice during the episode: the Roman citizens plead with the Lampsacenes to spare Verres in order to avoid punitive sanctions (§ 69) and Cicero suggests that Fortune has spared Verres for legal punishment in Rome (§ 70). Now, however, the time of leniency is over.

neque legitimum tempus exspectare ad ulciscendum neque vim tantam doloris in posterum differre: two parallel infinitive phrases depending on *potuerint*, with two *chiastic variations: (a) *legitimum* (b) *tempus* – (b) *vim* (a) *tantam*; (a) *exspectare* (b) *ad ulciscendum* – (b) *in posterum* (a) *differre*.

legitimum tempus: 'the normal and only lawful process would have involved taking the case to Rome and initiating a prosecution under the *lex de repetundis*': Mitchell (1986) 195. Roman magistrates enjoyed immunity from prosecution; the Lampsacenes would therefore have had to wait until the end of Verres' stint in office and his return to the status of a *privatus* (someone not holding a public office). That they did not wait but took justice into their own hands was of course an unacceptable breach of the peace, but Cicero manages to turn the fault into a feature by arguing that they were provoked into an act of retaliation commensurate with Verres' crimes.

Circumsessus es: after his address to the judges, Cicero again turns to Verres, for some mocking cross-examination.

A quibus [*circumsessus es*]? An ablative of agency; *circumsessus es* also has to be supplied after *A Lampsacenis*.

Barbaris hominibus, credo, aut iis qui populi Romani nomen contemnerent: *barbaris hominibus* stands in apposition to *A Lampsacenis*. *barbarus* is a loanword from the Greek (*barbaros*), which, from the Greek point of view, signified non-Greeks, including, of course, the Romans. (The playwright Plautus, for instance, liked to joke that he translated comic scripts from Greek into 'barbarian', that is, Latin.) Romans then came to use the term to differentiate roughly between the 'civilized cultures' of Greece and Rome and all the others, which they stigmatized, in Greek vein, as 'barbarians'.[90] The sentence is of course highly ironic – the Lampsacenes are civilized Greeks, i.e. anything but a barbarian horde; they are also very respectful of the Roman people, as Cicero stressed at the outset (§ 63: *homines autem ipsi Lampsaceni ... summe in omnis civis Romanos officiosi*). For the use of parenthetical *credo* to introduce irony see *OLD* s.v. 8c and Cicero's earlier use of the device at § 63: *At credo*.

Immo vero ab hominibus ... : the implied verb of this sentence is still *circumsessus es*: *ab hominibus* is ablative of agency.

et natura et consuetudine et disciplina: a *polysyndetic *tricolon, designed to underscore how gentle the Lampsacenes really are, from every point of view. *natura*, *consuetudine*, and *disciplina* are ablatives of respect, specifying natural endowment, habitual behaviour, and educational practices as the three main forces that shape character and identity. For Cicero's fondness of the category 'nature', either on its own or, as here, in combination with other, cultural factors, see Gildenhard (2011) 50–68.

---

90. For a monographic treatment of the topic, see Dauge, Y. A. (1981), *Le barbare: recherches sur la conception romaine de la barbarie et la civilisation*, Brussels.

populi Romani condicione sociis, fortuna servis, voluntate supplicibus: Cicero follows up his *polysyndetic *tricolon with an *asyndetic *tricolon; the genitive *populi Romani* modifies all items in the *alliterative sequence *sociis – servis – supplicibus* (all of which are still ablatives of agency, whereas *condicione, fortuna,* and *voluntate* are ablatives of respect). *Condicio* refers to the legal status of the Lampsacenes (*OLD* s.v. 7), which Cicero follows up with two quasi- or extra-legal conditions: whimsical fortune has turned them metaphorically into slaves, and they conceive of themselves (see *voluntate*) as suppliants, rather than allies, in that they plead for mercy with the all-powerful Roman people instead of insisting on the legal terms of the treaty. Overall, Cicero continues his policy of reducing the Lampsacenes to harmless and peace-loving non-entities, utterly beholden to Roman interest and at the whim and will of the Roman people and their representatives, to argue that only the most outrageous conduct on the part of Verres could have moved such people to violent action.

ut perspicuum sit omnibus, nisi tanta acerbitas iniuriae, tanta vis sceleris fuisset ut Lampsaceni moriendum sibi potius quam perpetiendum putarent, numquam illos in eum locum progressuros fuisse ut vehementius odio libidinis tuae quam legationis metu moverentur: Cicero here continues his elliptical and associative train of thought (the last main verb he used remains *circumsessus es*). There is no main clause (supplied from what precedes, it would run something like 'you were beset by the peace-loving and overall utterly innocuous people of Lampsacus'), as Cicero launches straight into a consecutive *ut*-clause (*ut perspicuum sit omnibus*), which introduces the conditional sentence in indirect statement: *nisi ... fuisset* (followed by a consecutive *ut*-clause: *ut ... putarent*) (protasis); *numquam illos in eum locum progressuros fuisse* (also followed by a consecutive *ut*-clause: *ut ... moverentur*) (apodosis).

nisi (a) tanta (b) acerbitas (c) iniuriae, (a) tanta (b) vis (c) sceleris fuisset: a powerful and measured parallel construction, reinforced by the reiteration of *tanta*, and contrasting with the *chiastic design in the second half of the sentence (see below).

moriendum sibi potius quam perpetiendum: *sibi* is dative of agency with the gerundives. Cicero here spells out what he let the Lampsacenes leave vague in § 68, where they are said to prefer to suffer 'anything' rather than remain the victims of such bitter violence (*quidvis esse perpeti satius quam in tanta vi atque acerbitate versari*): the ultimate of *quidvis* is of course death.

odio libidinis tuae quam legationis metu: *chiastic arrangement (a) *odio* (b) *libidinis tuae* – (b) *legationis* (a) *metu*; the *alliteration *libidinis ~ legationis* underscores the contrastive correlation of the two conflicting aspects of Verres' identity: his lust and his lieutenancy.

§ 82

In his narration (§ 69) Cicero made it appear that the intervention of the Roman businessmen, who warned the Lampsacenes of the dire consequences of attacking a Roman official, defused the situation. Now he suggests that the reason why the Lampsacenes desisted from the use of violence was not self-interest, but their belief that Verres' would receive his comeuppance in a Roman court of law. The sudden trust on the part of the provincials in due process and the Roman legal system comes out of nowhere: it is a ploy designed to put pressure on the judges, a variant of Cicero's equally far-fetched suggestion in § 71 that Verres' escape owed itself to the intervention of Fortune so that he could stand trial in Rome (*potestis dubitare quin istum fortuna non tam ex illo periculo eripere voluerit quam ad vestrum iudicium reservare?*).

Nolite: Cicero turns back to the judges with the challenge that it is up to them not to force non-Roman communities to resort to violent resistance out of desperation.

Nolite ... hoc uti perfugio, quo ... utentur necessario!: *uti* is complementary infinitive to *nolite* and takes *hoc perfugio* as ablative object, which is also the antecedent of *quo*. *quo*, in turn, is ablative object of *utentur* with *necessario* as predicative complement (in place of an adverb).

per deos immortalis: an emotive invocation of the gods; Cicero uses this device frequently in moments of special pathos or outrage. See further Gildenhard (2011) 246.

hoc ... perfugio: violent resistance to death.

perfugio – ad vim, ad manus, ad arma confugere – perfugium: the notion frames the paragraph, but in each case it is cancelled out – the Lampsacenes' refuge is violence and, perhaps, death; Verres' the Roman law courts.

nisi vos vindicatis: *vindicare* here has the meaning 'to protect': *OLD* s.v. 4 and thus continues the semantic field of *perfugium*. Note the emphatic use of *vos*.

Lampsacenos in istum numquam ulla res mitigasset nisi eum poenas Romae daturum credidissent: a past counterfactual condition, which introduces a new aspect into Cicero's portrayal of the inhabitants of Lampsacus, that is, their faith in the justice of the Roman legal system.

Tu mihi,

(i)   **cum circumsessus a tam inlustri civitate sis propter tuum scelus atque flagitium,**

(ii)   **cum coegeris homines miseros et calamitosos quasi desperatis nostris legibus et iudiciis ad vim, ad manus, ad arma confugere,**

(iii) **cum te in oppidis et civitatibus amicorum non legatum populi Romani, sed tyrannum libidinosum crudelemque praebueris,**

(iv)   **cum apud exteras nationes imperi nominisque nostri famam tuis probris flagitiisque violaris,**

(v)   **cum te ex ferro amicorum populi Romani eripueris atque ex flamma sociorum evolaris,**

hic tibi perfugium speras futurum:

A remarkable sentence, framed by the two datives *mihi* – *tibi*. The five *cum*-clauses are arranged symmetrically. (i) correlates with (v): *circumsessus sis* gets resolved by *te eripueris atque evolaris*. (ii) correlates with (iv): Verres' coercive actions (*coegeris*) entail his violation (*violaris*) of Rome's reputation abroad. And at the very centre (v), Cicero has placed the key idea: Verres has shown himself not an officer of the Roman people, but as a tyrant. A further pattern emerges if one looks at how Verres features in the *cum*-clauses: he starts out as the subject of a passive verb (i); in (ii) – (v) he is the subject of active verbs, with the accusative objects alternating between external targets (ii: *homines*; iv: *famam*) and himself (iii: *te*; v: *te*). The grammar also underscores the central position of (iii): apart from the prepositional phrase *in oppidis et civitatibus amicorum* the entire sentence is taken up by the direct object and its predicative extension *te ... non legatum populi Romani, sed tyrannum libidinosum crudelemque*. In the other *cum*-clauses, other constructions dominate.

In the *cum*-clauses, Cicero for the most part opts for weighty, pleonastic phrasing: *tuum scelus atque flagitium; homines miseros et calamitosos; nostris legibus et iudiciis; in oppidis et civitatibus; tyrannum libidinosum crudelemque; imperi nominisque nostri famam; tuis probris flagitiisque; eripueris atque evolaris.* (The pattern of connectives – *atque, et, et, et, -que, -que, -que, atque* – is hardly coincidental: it is a good example of the extreme care Cicero took over his writing, down to the last, loving detail.) The very deliberate style of exposition contrasts with the dramatic *asyndetic tricolon *ad vim, ad manus, ad arma confugere* and the simple punch line *hic tibi perfugium speras futurum?* Another rhetorical drama that plays itself out subliminally in the sentence is Cicero use of pronouns: *tu – mihi – proper tuum scelus atque flagitium – desperatis nostris legibus et iudiciis – te non legatum, sed tryannum praebueris – imperi nominisque nostri famam – tuis probris flagitiisque – te eripueris – tibi.* Put differently, Cicero uses the *cum*-clauses to invoke Rome's civic community, which is grounded in law and respected for this abroad and which Verres' criminal activity has irreparably damaged; this serves as apposite foil for the rhetorical question that Verres seeks safety in Rome, of all places.

quasi desperatis nostris legibus et iudiciis: ablative absolute.

tyrannum libidinosum crudelemque: *tyrannus* is a Greek loanword in Latin, which began to mesh with the indigenous anti-*regnum* discourse in the last few centuries of the Republic; it was used to describe the abuse of power. In Greece, the figure of the tyrant accrued certain attributes, among which an existence driven by passions and pleasure in cruelty. (Phalaris, for instance, the legenday tyrant of the Sicilian town of Acragas, is said to have roasted his enemies in an iron-bull, delighting in the roaring groans that issued from the contraption.) The *Verrines* are the earliest speeches in which Cicero systematically stigmatizes his adversary as a tyrant. See further Gildenhard (2011) 85–92, with a discussion of Verres on 90–1.

Erras: short and to the point, the sentence offers a powerful complement and conclusion to the elaborate rhetorical question that precedes it. (Note that Cicero imagines Verres to have answered the question in the affirmative, and his *erras* responds to Verres imagined reply.)

ut huc incideres, non ut hic conquiesceres, illi te vivum exire passi sunt: Cicero has it both ways: he motivates the initial violence by arguing that the inhabitants of Lampsacus despaired of attaining justice by means of legal procedure; and he explains the survival of Verres by suggesting that in the end they changed their mind and decided to put their hope into the Roman legal system, rather than taking justice into their own hands. This, of course, puts the judges trying Verres under pressure to prove worthy of the trust invested in them.

§ 83

In the final three paragraphs that Cicero devotes to the Lampsacus episode, he explores another line of defence that, he claims, Verres adopted: that the guilty verdicts passed on Philodamus and his son proved that the inhabitants of Lampsacus were wrong in besieging his house. Cicero counters this claim with a piece of evidence provided by Verres himself: in the letter to Nero that provided details of the uproar, he singled out two ringleaders by name, Themistagoras and Thessalus, yet in the end he never pressed formal charges against them. For Cicero, this is not only an egregious dereliction of duty, insofar as Verres strikingly failed to uphold the dignity of his office as legate. It is also prime evidence that he tried to cover up his crimes by pursuing a private course of vengeance against the Philodamus family.

Et ais iudicium esse factum te iniuria circumsessum esse Lampsaci: *ais* introduces the indirect statement *iudicium esse factum*, which in turn introduces the indirect statement *te ... circumsessum esse*. *Lampsaci* is in the locative: 'in Lampsacus'.

Quid, si doceo ... idoneo: an *anacoluthon, i.e. a sentence that breaks off in a state of incompletion. In this case, the *si*-clause does not have an apodosis, as Cicero changes tack by specifying who that depraved human being is whom he will use as witness, namely Verres himself.

si doceo, si planum facio: Cicero uses synonymous expressions in *asyndetic sequence for emphasis.

teste homine nequam ... idoneo: *teste homine* is a nominal ablative absolute (i.e. an ablative absolute consisting of two nouns, with no verb):

'through a human being as witness'; *homine* has two attributes (*nequam*, an indeclinable adjective, meaning 'morally worthless, depraved' and *idoneo*) which together form an *oxymoron (how can a worthless human being be an appropriate witness?), which Cicero resolves in what follows: the witness is Verres, who indicts himself.

huius circumsessionis tuae: the two attributes *huius* and *tuae* that frame *circumsessionis* give the phrase a mocking undertone.

in alios ... in eos: *in alios* (to be construed with *transtulisse*) refers to Philodamus and his son (innocent people who were executed); *in eos* (to be construed with *esse animadversum*) refers to Themistagoras and Thessalus, whom Verres named in his letter to Nero (the allegedly guilty men whom Verres allowed to walk free).

neque in eos ... esse animadversum: for the idiom *animadvertere* + *in* see above § 68 on *in eam civitatem animadvertendum*.

insimularas: syncopated pluperfect form of *insimulaveras*.

Recita quas ad Neronem litteras misit: *litteras*, the antecedent of *quas*, has been attracted into the relative clause.

Quem populum?: The verb is missing – 'which people [do you mean]?'

Qui te circumsedit, qui te vivum comburere conatus est: the antecedent of each *qui* is *populus* – 'the people, who...'

Ubi hos persequeris, ubi accusas, ubi defendis ius nomenque legati?: *hos* are Themistagoras and Thessalus. The demonstrative pronoun is the accusative object of both *persequeris* and *accusas*. Cicero uses an *asyndetic *tricolon reinforced by *anaphora (*ubi*). The *climactic third clause sums up the point of the first two clauses, which are by and large synonymous: Cicero argues that Verres should have taken legal action against the ringleaders he named in his letter to Nero in order to protect the institution and office of the Roman legate.

in Philodami iudicio dices id actum?: Cicero imagines Verres as responding to this rhetorical question (*dices* – in the future) that the matter was dealt with in the trial of Philodamus.

§ 84

Cicero devotes the entire paragraph to incriminating Verres' failure to press charges against the Lampsacene troublemakers named in his letter to Nero. His method of choice is a 'philological' examination of Verres' testimony at the trial of Philodamus, in particular his statement that he would pursue this other matter at some other time. By not having done so, Cicero submits, Verres has done significant harm to the Roman people and weakened the institution of legate.

cedo: an imperative, consisting of *ce* + *do*: see *OLD* s.v. *cedo*² 1c: 'produce, show us (esp. as evidence or exhibits in a trial)'.

videamus: hortative subjunctive: 'let us see!'

iuratus: under oath.

AB ACCUSATORE ROGATUS: the *accusator* in question is the one who pressed the charges against Philodamus and his son.

NON PERSEQUI ... PERSEQUI: here and later in the paragraph, Cicero elides the accusative object (*hos*).

(a) **Legatus cum** (b1) **esses** (b2) **circumsessus, cumque ...** (b2) **facta** (b1) **esset** (a) **insignis iniuria**: adversative *cum*-clauses, with a *chiastic arrangement of subjects and verbs; the effect is a special emphasis on *insignis iniuria* – despite the fact that Verres himself labelled the events an egregious injury and a dangerous precedent, he took no action.

tute: an emphatic form of *tu*: 'as you *yourself* wrote to Nero.'

dicis tibi in animo esse alio tempore persequi. Quod fuit id tempus? quando es persecutus?: Cicero here uses one of his favourite techniques, that is, quoting back at an opponent his own words, only to take them apart. ('Now let us see, you say that...') The delivery of *tibi in animo esse* is best imagined as highly mocking in tone, to prepare for Cicero's quizzing of the key phrase *alio tempore* ('some other time'), which never came.

cur ... cur ... cur ... ? non ... non ... non ... ?: a string of rhetorical questions in *asyndetic sequence, split into two *anaphoric *tricola.

(a) **imminuisti** (b) **ius legationis** – (b) **causam populi Romani** (a) **deseruisti ac prodidisti** – (b) **iniurias tuas** ... (a) **reliquisti?**: the second and the third cola of the first *tricolon stand in *chiastic order to the first.

iniurias tuas coniunctas cum publicis: sc. *iniuriis*.

causam deferre: in the technical legal sense, 'to bring a case into court'; here to bring the case to the attention of the senate, as the public body responsible for dealing with matters of foreign policy, such as diplomatic incidents.

eos homines ... evocandos curare: after *deferre* and *conqueri*, *curare* ('to see to it') is the third complementary infinitive to go with *oportuit* and in turn introduces an indirect statement (*eos homines ... evocandos*). Cicero elides the *esse* that goes with *evocandos*. *evocare* in the technical legal sense means 'to summon to appear in court'; here it refers to a writ issued by the consuls, the highest magistrates of the Roman people, to appear before them for a hearing and a verdict. Cicero blames Verres for failing to take up the matter at the level that would have been appropriate for the seriousness of the charges.

concitarant: the syncopated pluperfect form of *concitaverant*.

consulum: genitive plural of *consul*, depending on *litteris*.

§ 85 and 86a

To support the claims advanced in the previous paragraph, Cicero now outlines an analogous incident in which the magistrate in charge acted as Verres ought to have done.

Nuper: an adverb of time that refers to the recent past. But the notion of 'recent' is of considerable elasticity: it can refer to a period of a couple of days or (as here) half a century (see next note).

M. Aurelio Scauro: Marcus Aurelius Scaurus was quaestor in 117 BC. Several aspects make this an opportune comparandum, both in terms of similarities and differences. The rank of the Roman officials involved was more or less similar (Scaurus was quaestor, Verres was a legate, but promoted to the rank of pro-quaestor) and the geographic region the same (Asia Minor). Conversely, the transgression that drew Scaurus' ire (a local aristocrat protecting the religious institution of asylum) was incomparably lighter than the rioting in Lampsacus that Verres' reported – and the Roman response was incomparably harsher. Likewise, Cicero emphasizes the high standing of the offending provincial in Scaurus' case (see below on *homo nobilissimus*), whereas the two men whom Verres fingered as the main culprits (Themistagoras and Thessalus) remain entirely faceless.

postulante: see *OLD* s.v. *postulo* 2, for the technical legal sense of 'making an application to the praetor or other magistrate'.

Ephesi: a locative ('in Ephesus').

quo minus: literally, the phrase means 'by which the less' and is used after verbs of hindering and preventing. It 'does not translate into idiomatic English': Morwood (1999) 131.

e fano Dianae: the temple of Artemis (Cicero uses the Roman name for the goddess) at Ephesus was one of the seven wonders of the ancient world.

asylum: a Greek technical term (here used as a loanword in Latin), designating a place that affords sanctuary for criminals or fugitives.[91] Augustan writers famously employ the term with reference to the 'asylum of Romulus': see Virgil, *Aeneid* 8. 342 and Livy 1.8.5.[92] The temple of Artemis at Ephesus was a distinguished place of refuge in the Greek world, though it is clear from Cicero's account that Roman magistrates saw no need to respect Greek asylum conventions.

homo nobilissimus: Cicero creates an implicit contrast between the renowned and high-ranking provincial who got summoned to Rome in

---

91. See further Rigsby, K. J. (1997), *Asylia: Territorial Inviolability in the Hellenistic World*, Berkeley.
92. See further Dench, E. (2005), *Romulus' Asylum: Roman Identities from the Age of Alexander to the Age of Hadrian*, Oxford.

this case, and the instigators whom Verres identified in his letter to Nero and who figure in Cicero's narrative without any marks of distinction. The force of the adjective is thus adversative: *even though* he was a man of the highest distinction locally, he was *nevertheless* summoned to Rome.

tu, si te legatum ita Lampsaci tractatum esse senatum docuisses ut tui comites vulnerarentur, lictor occideretur, ipse circumsessus paene incenderere, eius autem rei duces et auctores et principes fuisse, quos scribis, Themistagoram et Thessalum ... : a complicated *si*-clause. The verb is *docuisses* (pluperfect subjunctive to indicate a remote and unfulfilled condition), which takes *senatum* as accusative object and introduces an indirect statement that falls into two parts, linked by *autem*: *te ... tractatum esse* (followed by an *asyndetic *tricolon of consecutive *ut*-clauses: see next note) and *eius autem rei duces ... fuisse ... Thessalum*. The first part (*te ... ita ... tractatum esse*) introduces a consecutive *ut*-clause (*ut ... incenderere*).

ut tui comites vulnerarentur, lictor occideretur, ipse circumsessus paene incenderere: the *asyndetic *tricolon is arranged *climactically; the lack of connectives again underscores the drama of what happened and contrasts with the more expansive style Cicero uses of the perpetrators.

te legatum: the construction picks up and parallels *se quaestorem*. *legatum* is a predicative complement to *te*: 'you, as legate...'

Lampsaci: another locative, in parallel to *Ephesi*.

duces et auctores et principes: a *polysyndetic *tricolon, which emphasizes the leading role of Themistagoras and Thessalus in the civic unrest at Lampsacus.

incenderere: second person singular imperfect subjunctive passive; an alternative form of *incendereris*.

quis non commoveretur, quis non ex iniuria quae tibi esset facta sibi provideret, quis non in ea re causam tuam periculum commune agi arbitraretur?: The main clause (apodosis), too, is designed as a *climactic and *asyndetic *tricolon (reinforced by the anaphora of *quis non*) as well as a rhetorical question. Cicero gradually moves from an unspecific emotional response (*commoveretur*) to a self-reflective reaction (what happened to Verres could also happen to me – I'd better take precautions: *sibi provideret*) to the realization that, beyond issues of personal safety, Rome's public interest more generally is at stake (*periculum commune agi arbitraretur*). He thus gradually builds up to the point that the senate would have considered the incident as Lampsacus a dangerous precedent for Roman interests in the provinces more generally.

Magnum hoc Lampsacenum crimen est libidinis atque improbissimae cupiditatis: Cicero concludes his account of what happened at Lampsacus by reiterating the motivating impulse that set the dire sequence of events into motion: Verres' lust, *pleonastically invoked by the virtual synonyms *libido* and *cupiditas*. This is a final exclamation mark before Cicero moves on to another vice: greed (*avaritia*).

List of Abbreviations

cos. = consul

N.B. = *nota* (or *notate*) *bene*! ('Take note')

OLD = Oxford Latin Dictionary

s.v. = *sub voce* ('under the word'), i.e. in the dictionary entry of this word.

sc. = scilicet ('of course')

Abbreviated references to secondary literature:

Gildenhard (2011) = Gildenhard, I. (2011), *Creative Eloquence: The Construction of Reality in Cicero's Speeches*, Oxford.

Mitchell (1986) = Mitchell, T. N. (1986), *Cicero, Verrines II.1, with Translation and Commentary*, Warminster.

Morwood (1999) = Morwood, J. (1999), *A Latin Grammar*, Oxford.

Steel (2004) = Steel, C. (2004), 'Being Economical with the Truth: What Really Happened at Lampsacus?', in J. Powell and J. Paterson (eds.), *Cicero the Advocate*, Oxford, 233–51.

List of Rhetorical Terms

N.B.:

(i) The list contains only those terms actually used in the commentary. More complete lists are available in standard textbooks (e.g. Morwood (1999) 150–54: 'Some literary terms') or on the web (e.g. *Silva Rhetoricae: The Forest of Rhetoric*: http://rhetoric.byu.edu/).

(ii) Most of the terms derive from, or indeed are, either Greek or Latin; I have therefore provided an etymological explanation for each, not least to show that the terminological abracadabra makes perfectly good sense – even though it takes a smattering of ancient Greek and Latin to see this.

(iii) The English examples are from Shakespeare; unless otherwise indicated they come from the Pyramus-and-Thisbe episode in Act 5 of *A Midsummer Night's Dream*. The main reason for drawing on the *oeuvre* of an (early) modern author for illustration is to convey a sense of the continuity of classical and classicizing rhetoric in the western cultural tradition.

alliteration: the repeated use of the same sound, especially a consonant, at the beginning of words in close proximity.

Etymology: from (un-classical) Latin *alliterare*, 'to begin with the same letter'.

Examples: 'O dainty duck! O dear!' 'When lion rough in wildest rage doth roar.' 'Whereat, with blade, with bloody, blameful blade/ He bravely broach'd his boiling bloody breast.'

anacoluthon: a sudden break in a sentence, resulting in an incomplete grammatical or syntactical unit; a change in construction in mid-sentence.

Etymology: from Greek *anakolouthos*, 'inconsistent, anomalous, inconsequent'.

Example: 'No, you unnatural hags,/ I will have such revenges on you both,/ That all the world shall – I will do such things…' (*King Lear*, Act 2, Scene 4).

anaphora: the repetition of the same word or phrase at the beginning of several successive syntactic units.

Etymology: from Greek *anapherein*, 'to carry back, to repeat'

Example: 'O grim-look'd night! O night with hue so black! O night, which ever art when day is not! O night, O night, alack, alack, alack!'

antithesis: literally 'a placing against'; the (balanced) juxtaposition of contrasting ideas.

Etymology: from Greek *antitithenai*, 'to place (*tithenai*) against (*anti-*)'.

Example: ''Tide life, 'tide death, I come without delay.'

apo koinou: two constructions that have a word or phrase in common; or, put the other way around, a word or phrase shared by two different constructions.

Etymology: from the Greek phrase *apo koinou lambanein*, used by ancient grammarians of two clauses taking (*apo … lambanein*) a word in common (*koinou*, the genitive of *koinon* after the preposition *apo*).

Example: 'There was a man … dwelt by a churchyard' (*The Winter's Tale*, Act 2, Scene 1).

assonance: a type of alliteration (see above) in which the leading letter is a vowel.

Etymology: from Latin *adsonare*, 'to sound (*sonare*) to (*ad*)', via French *assonance*.

asyndeton: the absence or omission of conjunctions (see also below *polysyndeton*).

Etymology: from Greek *asyndetos*, 'not (*a*-privativum) bound (*detos*, from *dein*, to bind) together (*sun*)'.

Example: 'O Fates, come, come, cut thread and thrum; quail, crush, conclude, and quell!'

captatio benevolentiae: a Latin phrase that literally means 'the capture of goodwill', i.e. a rhetorical technique designed to render the audience kindly disposed towards the speaker.

> *(Botched) example*: 'If we offend, it is with our good will. That you should think, we come not to offend. But with good will.'[93]

chiasmus: the repetition of a grammatical pattern in inverse order: *a b – b a*.

> *Etymology*: from Greek *chiasmos*, 'a placing crosswise', from the letter X (pronounced *chi*) of the Greek alphabet. (Imagine the two *a* at either end of the first diagonal line of X, and at either end of the second diagonal line the two *b*; then read the top half first and afterwards the bottom half and you get *a b – b a*.)
>
> *Example*:   '(a) Sweet Moon, (b) I thank thee …, (b) I thank thee, (a) Moon…'

climax: a series or sequence of units that gradually increase in import or force.

> *Etymology*: from Greek *klimax*, 'ladder'.
> *Example*:   'Tongue, lose thy light;/ Moon take thy flight: Now die, die, die, die, die' (Pyramus before stabbing himself).

ellipsis: the omission of one or more words in a sentence necessary for a complete grammatical construction.

> *Etymology*: from Greek *elleipein*, 'to fall short, leave out'.
> *Example*:   'I neither know it nor can learn of him' (*Romeo and Juliet*, Act 1, Scene 1).[94]

figura etymologica: a Latin phrase referring to words of the same etymological derivation used in close proximity to one another.

> *Example*: 'So long <u>lives</u> this, and this gives <u>life</u> to thee' (*Sonnet* 18).

hendiadys: one idea expressed by two words joined by 'and', such as two nouns used in place of a noun and an adjective.

> *Etymology*: from Greek *hen-dia-duoin*, 'one thing (*hen*) by means of (*dia*) two (*duoin*)'.
> *Example*:   'The service and the loyalty I owe' (*Macbeth*, Act 1, Scene 4), for 'the loyal service'.

---

93. Note that Shakespeare's character here, hilariously, 'translates' the Latin *benevolentia* of the rhetorical figure, but, perversely, refers to the 'good will' of himself, the speaker, rather than that of the audience.
94. Filling in the items elided would results in something like 'I neither know it nor can I learn anything about it from him'.

homoioteleuton: similarity of ending in words in close proximity to one another.

Etymology: from Greek *homoios*, 'like', and *teleute*, 'ending'.

Example: 'My mother weep<u>ing</u>, my father wail<u>ing</u>, my sister cry<u>ing</u>, our maid howl<u>ing</u>, our cat wring<u>ing</u> her hands' (*The Two Gentlemen of Verona*, Act 2, Scene 3).[95]

hyperbaton: dislocation of the customary or logical word order, with the result that items that normally go together are separated.

Etymology: from Greek *huperbaino*, 'to step (*bainein*) over (*huper-*)'. (Imagine, for instance, that if an adjective is placed apart from the noun it modifies you have to 'step over' the intervening words to get from one to the other.)

Example: 'Some rise by sin, and some by virtue fall' (*Measure for Measure*, Act 2, Scene 1).[96]

hyperbole: the use of exaggeration.

Etymology: from Greek *huperballein*, 'to throw (*ballein*, from which derives *bole*, "a throwing") over or beyond (*huper*)'.

Example: 'Will all great Neptune's ocean wash this blood/ Clean from my hand? No, this my hand will rather/ The multitudinous seas incarnadine,/ Making the green one red' (*Macbeth*, Act 2, Scene 2).[97]

husteron proteron: A Greek phrase, meaning 'the latter (*husteron*) first (*proteron*)', producing chronological disorder.

Example: 'The Antoniad, the Egyptian admiral,/ With all their sixty, fly and turn the rudder' (*Antony and Cleopatra*, Act 3, Scene10).[98]

---

95. Note that the last item in the list (wring-ing) contains the -ing sound twice, a stylistic *climax that reinforces the *climax in content achieved through the anthropomorphism of the cat and the unexpected switch from sound (weeping etc.) to silence (wringing).
96. Natural word order would require 'some fall by virtue'. Note that the *hyperbaton also produces a *chiasmus – Some (a) rise (b) by sin, and some (b) by virtue (a) fall –, which is ideally suited to reinforce the elegant *antitheses of sin and virtue, rising and falling. One could further argue that the hyperbaton, which produces disorder on the level of grammar and syntax, is the perfect figure of speech for the basic idea of the utterance: *moral* disorder, which manifests itself in the reward of sin and the punishment of virtue and implies that our universe is devoid of justice, i.e. as chaotic as the hyperbatic word order.
97. 'To incarnadine' means 'to turn into the colour of flesh (Latin *caro/carnis, carnis*), dye red, redden'. A more familiar term with a similar etymology is 'incarnation'.
98. The logical sequence would require 'they turn the rudder and fly'. The example is a beautiful instance of enactment since the *husteron proteron* conveys a sense of how hastily ('head over heel') everyone is trying to get away.

litotes: a 'double negation', in which a statement, quality, or attribute is affirmed by the negation of its opposite; assertion by means of understatement, frequently for the purpose of intensification.

> *Etymology*: from Greek *litos*, 'simple, plain, petty, small'.
>
> *Example*: 'That I was <u>not ignoble</u> of descent' (*Henry VI*, Part 3, Act 4, Scene 1).[99]

onomatopoesis/ onomatopoeia: expressions where the sound suggests the sense.

> *Etymology*: from Greek *onoma* (genitive *onomatos*), 'word, name', and *poiein* (noun: *poesis*), 'to make'.
>
> *Example*: 'Sea-nymphs hourly ring his knell/ Hark! now I hear them, – Ding-dong, bell' (*The Tempest*, Act 1, Scene 2).

oxymoron: a 'pointedly foolish' expression, resulting from the juxtaposition or combination of two words of contradictory meaning.

> *Etymology*: from Greek *oxus*, 'sharp', and *môros*, 'stupid'.
>
> *Examples*: '"A tedious brief scene of young Pyramus/ And his love Thisbe; very tragical mirth." Merry and tragical! tedious and brief!/ That is, hot ice and wondrous strange snow./ How shall we find the concord of this discord?'

paronomasia: a play upon words that sound alike; a pun.

> *Etymology*: from Greek *paronomazo*, 'to call with a slight change of name (onoma)'. Cicero discusses the figure (with examples) at *de Oratore* 2.256.
>
> *Examples*: 'Our sport shall be to <u>take</u> what they mis<u>take</u>'; 'You, ladies, you, whose gentle hearts do fear/ the smallest <u>monstrous mouse</u> that creeps on floor...'

pleonasm: a 'fullness of expression', that is, the use of more words than is strictly speaking necessary to convey the desired meaning.

> *Etymology*: from Greek *pleonazein*, 'to be more than enough or superfluous'.
>
> *Example*: 'the most unkindest cut of all' (*Julius Caesar*, Act 3, Scene 2, about Brutus' stabbing of Caesar). [100]

---

99. Note that in modern literary criticism litotes is often used loosely to refer to simple negation (e.g. Shakespeare, *Sonnet* 130: 'My mistress' eyes are nothing like the sun...').
100. Shakespeare expresses the degree to which Brutus' unkindness outdid that of all the others pleonastically by using both the adverb 'most' and the superlative ending -est.

polyptoton: the repetition of the same word, variously inflected.

> *Etymology*: from Greek *poluptoton*, 'many (*polu*) cases (from *ptôsis*, i.e.
> fall, grammatical case)'.
>
> *Example*:   'Then know that I, one Snug the joiner, am/ A lion-fell, nor
> else no lion's dam.'

polysyndeton: the frequent use of conjunctions such as 'and' or 'or' even
when they are not required.

> *Etymology*: from Greek *polusyndetos*, 'many times (*polu*) bound (*detos*, from
> *dein*, to bind) together (*sun*)'.
>
> *Example*:   'Peering in maps for ports and piers and roads' (*The
> Merchant of Venice*, Act 1, Scene 1).

praeteritio: a Latin term that means 'passing over'; as a rhetorical figure it
refers to the practice of mentioning something by not meaning to mention it.

> *Example*:   'Soft you; a word or two before you go./ I have done the
> state some service, and they know't. / No more of that'
> (*Othello*, Act 5, Scene 2).

tautology: the repetition of the same idea in different ways.

> *Etymology*: from Greek *tauto*, 'the same', and *logos*, 'word, idea'.
>
> *Example*:   'The ... mouse ... may now perchance both quake and
> tremble here.'

tmesis: the 'cutting apart' of a compound word by the interposition of
others.

> *Etymology*: from Greek *temnein*, 'to cut'.
>
> *Example*:   'that man – how dearly ever parted' (*Troilus and Cressida*,
> Act 3, Scene 3).

tricolon: the use of three parallel grammatical units (words, phrases,
clauses).

> *Etymology*: from Greek *tri-*, 'three', and *kôlon*, 'limb, member, clause,
> unit'.
>
> *Example*:   'Tongue, not a word;/ Come, trusty sword;/ Come, blade,
> my breast imbue.'

Translation

[53]   Aspendos, as you know, is an old and famous town in Pamphylia, chockfull of the most precious statues. I am not going to say that this or that statue was taken away from there. I am saying *this*: that you, Verres, did not leave a single statue in Aspendos; all were loaded up and carried away from the shrines, from the public places, openly, with everybody looking on, on wagons. And even that lyre-player of Aspendos, about whom you have often heard what is a proverbial expression among the Greeks – they used to say that he played all of his music inside – he took away and put in the innermost part of his house so that he seems to have outdone even the lyre player at his art.

[54]   We know that there is a very ancient and sacred shrine of Diana in Perge. I say that it, too, was stripped bare and despoiled by you, that from the cult statue of Diana herself whatever gold it had was removed and carried away. What, on earth, is this outrageous impudence and insanity! For if you had entered into the cities of our allies and friends, which you visited with the right and the title of a legate, by force with an army and holding a military command, you nevertheless, I think, should not have carried away the statues and treasures that you lifted from these cities into your house or the country houses of your friends, but to Rome as public possession.

[55]   What should I say about M. Marcellus, who captured Syracuse, a city most richly adorned with works of art? What about L. Scipio, who waged war in Asia and vanquished Antiochus, a most powerful king? What about Flamininus, who subdued Philip and Macedonia? What about L. Paulus, who overcame king Perses by force and excellence? What about L. Mummius, who took the most beautiful and most richly adorned city, Corinth, chockfull of every kind of treasure, and brought many cities of Achaia and Boeotia under the power and dominion of the Roman people?

Their houses, even though they shone by virtue of public distinction and personal excellence, were empty of statues and paintings; yet we see the entire city, the temples of the gods, and all regions of Italy richly adorned with their gifts and monuments.

[56]   I fear that someone might consider these examples excessively ancient and by now obsolete; for back then all were uniformly of such a kind that this praise of outstanding excellence and integrity seems to belong not only to the men, but also those times. P. Servilius, a most illustrious man, having performed the greatest deeds, is present to give his verdict on you: he captured Olympus by means of force, troops, good counsel, and personal excellence – an ancient city amplified and adorned with every kind of ornament. I put forward a recent example of a most courageous man: for Servilius, a general of the Roman people, captured Olympus, a hostile town, *after* you, a legate of the rank of a quaestor in those same regions, saw to it that the pacified townships of allies and friends be plundered and devastated.

[57]   What *you* have carried off in crime and banditry from the most sacred shrines we are unable to see except in your house or the houses of your friends: the statues and works of art that *P. Servilius* took according to the law of war and the right of the general from a hostile town captured by military force and excellence, these he brought to the Roman people, paraded in his triumph, and took care to have entered into the public records for the treasury. Learn from the public records the meticulous attentiveness of the most eminent man! Read them out! THE REGISTERED ACCOUNTS OF P. SERVILIUS. You see that not just the number of the statues, but even the size, shape and condition of each and any are described with precision in the records. Surely the agreeable feeling of excellence and victory is greater than that pleasure derived from lustfulness and desire! I declare that Servilius had the spoils of the Roman people far more carefully itemized and entered in the records than you your thefts.

[58]   You will state that your statues and paintings, too, served to adorn the city and the forum of the Roman people. O yes, I remember! Together with the Roman people I saw the forum and the comitium decorated with adornment that was spectacular to behold, but bitter and distressing to feeling and thought. I saw how everything shone in the splendour of

your thefts, the plunder of the provinces, the spoils of allies and friends. Indeed on this occasion, judges, this man received the greatest possible encouragement to carry out future misdeeds in like manner; for he saw that those, who wished to be called masters of the courts, were in fact slaves to these desires.

[59]   But our allies and foreign nations at that time first gave up all hope of recovering their possessions and fortunes because by chance a great number of ambassadors from Asia and Achaia were at Rome at the time, who kept worshipping in our forum the images of the gods that had been taken from their shrines; and likewise, when they recognized other statues and precious objects, they tearfully kept looking at each wherever it stood. At the time, we kept hearing that all of them expressed the opinion that there was no longer any reason why anyone should doubt the final destruction of allies and friends, when they actually saw that in the forum of the Roman people – the very location where previously those who had inflicted injury on the allies used to be put on trial and sentenced – those items were on public display that had been criminally carried and snatched away from the allies.

[60]   In the circumstances just indicated, I do not think that he will deny having in his possession statues galore and too many paintings to count; yet I believe he is in the habit of declaring over and again that he bought the objects he plundered and stole – because, indeed, he was sent to Achaia, Asia, and Pamphylia on public expenses and with the title of a legate as buyer of statues and paintings. I have all the account books both of this man and of his father, and I have read and studied them with utmost care – of the father for as long as he lived, yours for as long as you say you kept them. For as concerns this man, judges, you will discover the following innovation. We have heard that someone never kept accounts; this is the common opinion about Antonius, a wrong one, for he kept them with utmost care; but may this count as one possible approach, though in no way to be approved. We have heard that someone else did not keep them from the start, but began to do so from a certain point in time; there is a certain rationale even to this approach. But that practice is assuredly new and absurd, which this man mentioned in his response to us when we demanded his accounts from him, namely that he kept them up to the consulship of M. Terentius and C. Cassius, but ceased to do so afterwards.

[61] We shall look elsewhere into what kind of practice this is; at the moment, it does not matter to me. For for the period I am now concerned with I have your accounts and those of your father. You cannot deny that you have brought to Rome a great number of outstandingly beautiful statues and a great number of superb paintings. If only you denied it! Show me one, in either your accounts or those of your father, that has been bought: you have won. Not even for those two outstandingly beautiful statues that now stand at the pool in your inner courtyard, which for many years stood in front of the doors of the temple of Samnian Juno you are in a position to show how you bought them – these two, I mean, which are the only ones left in your house at this point, waiting for a buyer, left abandoned by the other statues.

[62] I suppose, then, that in these matters only was he wont to act on his untamed and unbridled lusts: his other desires were contained within some means or measure. How many free-born persons, how many married mothers do you think this man violated during his disgraceful and foul stint as legate? Has he set foot in any town without leaving more (im)prints of his adulteries and sexual assaults than (foot)prints of his coming? But I shall omit to mention anything that can be denied. Even matters that are utterly undeniable and absolutely notorious I shall leave aside. One only of his wicked deeds I shall select so that thereby I can come quicker at last to Sicily, which has laid this burdensome business upon me.

[63] On the Hellespont, there is a town called Lampsacus, members of the jury, among the best of the provinces of Asia, famous and renowned; the inhabitants, on the other hand, the Lampsacenes themselves, are not just in the highest degree obliging to all Roman citizens, but are, moreover, also extremely calm and peace-loving, predisposed almost more than the others towards the supreme leisure of the Greeks instead of violence of any kind or hostile disorder. It so happened – after this man here had demanded of Gnaeus Dolabella that he send him on an embassy to King Nicomedes and King Sadalas and had imperiously insisted on an itinerary for himself better suited to his own gain than the interest of the commonwealth – that he came in the course of this journey to Lampsacus, to the great disaster and near destruction of its citizenry. This man here was escorted to a certain host named Ianitor, and his entourage were likewise lodged with other hosts. As was the habit of this man here, and as his criminal lusts urged him to do, he instantly issued his companions, human beings of the most worthless and disgraceful type, with the task of scouting around and

inquiring about any young girl or woman worth his while, for the sake of which he might prolong his stay in Lampsacus.

[64]   One of his followers was a certain Rubrius, a man tailor-made for the lusts of this man here, who was wont to track all of this down with remarkable skill wherever they went. This man reported to Verres the following matter, namely that there was a certain Philodamus, easily the leading man among the inhabitants of Lampsacus in terms of family, standing, wealth, and reputation; that he had a daughter who lived with her father since she had no husband – a woman of outstanding beauty; but that she was thought to be of the highest probity and chastity. When our man heard this, he was so on fire with passion for something which he had never seen himself or even heard about from someone who had seen it, that he declared he wished to move in with Philodamus at once. His host Ianitor, who suspected nothing but feared that something about himself was causing offence, began to keep our man back with all his might. This one here, since he was unable to find a reason to leave his host, began to build a road towards the consumption of his illicit desire by alternative means. He declares that his darling Rubrius, his helper and confidant in all matters of this sort, has lodgings of insufficient quality; he gives orders to have him transferred to Philodamus.

[65]   When this was conveyed to Philodamus, even though he was ignorant of how much evil was already at this point decided for himself and his children, he nevertheless came to see this man here; he made it clear that this was not an obligation of his; that, when it was his turn to host visitors, he was accustomed to house praetors and consuls, not the hanger-ons of legates. This man here, who was carried along by one exclusive passion, ignored his entire request and reasoning; he gave orders that Rubrius be transferred by force to Philodamus, who had no obligation to house him. At this point, Philodamus, after having failed to obtain what was his right, tried hard to preserve his usual human kindness. As a man, who had always been considered most welcoming and friendly towards our men, he did not want to make it seem that he received even someone like Rubrius into his house against his will. He has a dinner prepared in grand and lavish fashion, as he was especially wealthy among his countrymen. He asks Rubrius to invite anyone whom he pleases and, if he so wished, reserve just one place for himself alone. He even sends his son, an outstanding young man, away to dine with some relative of his.

[66]   Rubrius invites the followers of this man here; Verres makes sure that all know what was required of them. They arrive punctually; everyone takes his place at table. Conversation arises among the diners and the suggestion to drink in the Greek manner: the host encourages everyone, they issue challenges with greater cups, the dinner swings through the conversation and the good mood of all. After it seemed to Rubrius that the matter has been sufficiently fired up, he says: 'Tell me, Philodamus, why don't you issue orders to have your daughter called inside to us?' Philodamus, as a human being of the highest seriousness and of advanced age and as her father, was taken aback by the suggestion of this disgraceful man. Rubrius urges him on. In response, so as to say something, he declared that it wasn't customary among the Greeks to have women lay down at a dinner-party of men. At this point, people from all over start yelling: 'This is truly intolerable! Let the woman be called!' At the same time Rubrius orders his slaves to lock the door and assume guard at the entrance.

[67]   As soon as Philodamus realized that what was happening and what was being prepared was the rape of his daughter, he summons his slaves. He commands them to disregard him, to defend his daughter; gives orders that someone should run off to report to his son this utmost evil threatening the house. In the meantime, uproar arises all over the house; a fight breaks out between the slaves of Rubrius and his own; the outstanding and highly regarded man is being thrown around in his own house. Everyone is fighting for himself. Finally Philodamus is drenched in boiling water by none other than Rubrius. As soon as these matters have been conveyed to his son, he instantly and breathlessly rushes to the house to save the life of the father and the chastity of his sister. In the same spirit, all Lampsacenes, as soon as they heard of this, came together at the house at night, moved by both the rank of Philodamus and, especially, by the magnitude of the outrage. At this point, Cornelius, the lictor of this man here, who had been stationed together with the slaves of Verres by Rubrius as if on guard to abduct the woman, is killed; some of the slaves suffer wounds; Rubrius himself is injured in the melee. This man here, who saw how great an uproar he had incited through his lust, wishes to flee somehow if he could.

[68]   On the following day, the men come together early in a meeting; they explore what best to do; those who possessed the highest degree of authority spoke in turn to the people, each presenting his own view. No-one was found who did not think and speak as follows, namely that if

the Lampsacenes were to avenge the unspeakable crime of this man here with the force of violence, they should not fear that the senate and the people of Rome would think this citizenry as deserving of punishment; but if legates of the Roman people employed the legal principle against allies and external nations that they were not permitted to keep the chastity of their children safe from their lust, it would be more satisfactory to suffer anything else than be the victims of such bitter violence.

[69]   Since all felt this and since everyone spoke in this way on account of his feeling of grief, all set out for the house in which this man was lodging. They began to break down the door with stones, to attack with swords, to set around wood and brush and to lay fire. At that point Roman citizens, who were in Lampsacus for business, rush together. They plead with the Lampsacenes to consider the name of the office of legate a more serious matter than the injustice of a legate; they say that they understand that that human being is impure and wicked but since he had not brought to fruition what he had attempted to do and would not be in Lampsacus afterwards, their transgression would be lighter if they spared a wicked human being than if they failed to spare a legate.

[70]   And thus this man, by far more criminal and wicked than that Hadrianus, was still considerably luckier. That one, because the Roman citizens were unable to tolerate his greed, was burned alive in his house in Utica; and it was considered to have befallen him so deservedly that all were glad and no punitive measure was taken. This one, having been singed in a conflagration set ablaze by allies, nevertheless escaped from that perilous fire, and yet he has until now been unable to contrive any explanation why he did what he did or why it happened that he fell into such danger. For he is unable to say 'since I wanted to put down a rebellion, since I was issuing an order for provision, since I was enforcing a tribute, since, finally, I did something on behalf of the commonwealth, because I gave an order too harshly, because I took punitive action, because I issued a threat.' Even if he were saying these things, he still ought not to be pardoned if he seemed to have been brought into such danger by giving orders to allies in an excessively harsh way.

[71]   Now, since he dares neither to state the true cause of this uproar nor to fabricate a false one, yet one of the most honest men of his own order, who at the time was an attendant to C. Nero, P. Tettius, stated that he had found

out these same things in Lampsacus, and a man distinguished in every respect, C. Varro, who at the time was military tribune in Asia, states that he had heard these same things from Philodamus himself, can you doubt that fortune did not wish so much to snatch this man from that danger as to reserve him for your judgment? Unless indeed he will say what Hortensius interjected at the testimony of Tettius in the previous hearing – on that occasion he made it sufficiently clear that he is unable to remain silent if there is anything at all that he could say so that we all are able to understand that he had absolutely nothing to say when he remained silent with the other witnesses: at the time he said that Philodamus and his son were condemned by C. Nero.

[72]   So as not to lose too many words about this, let me say only this, that Nero and his advisers endorsed the position that, since it was a matter of fact that the lictor Cornelius had been killed, they deemed that no-one ought to have the power to kill a human being, not even to avenge an injustice. By this judgment of Nero I do not see you to have been absolved of your wickedness, but those men to have been convicted of murder. But of what kind was this condemnation? Please listen, judges, and finally take pity on your allies and demonstrate that your tutelage ought to afford them *some* protection. Because to all of Asia that man who was in name a lictor of this man here, but in fact a servant of his most wicked lust, seemed to have been justly killed, this man here feared that Philodamus would be acquitted by Nero's verdict. He urged and entreated Dolabella to leave his province and travel to Nero. He makes it clear that he could not be secure if Philodamus were allowed to live and at some future time come to Rome.

[73]   Dolabella was won over; he did what many have censured, namely that he left his army, his province, his war and marched into Asia, into the province of someone else because of an utterly worthless human being. After he had come to Nero, he demanded of him to look into the case of Philodamus. He had come himself in order to be part of the group of advisors and to give his vote first. He had even brought along his prefects and military tribunes, all of whom Nero called into his advisory council. Part of the council was also that fairest of judges, Verres himself. There were also some Roman creditors of the Greeks, for whom the gratitude of whoever was the most wicked legate was of greatest use for the collection of money.

[74]   That wretched man was unable to find anyone to argue his case; for what Roman was there who was unmoved by Dolabella's influence or what Greek who was unmoved by the power and imperial command of the same man? But as prosecutor a Roman citizen was appointed from among the creditors of the Lampsacenes; [he was told that] if he said what this man here ordered, he could extract his money from the people with the aid of the lictors of that very same man here. Even though all this was put into motion with such urgency and such expenditure of resources; even though many were accusing that wretched man, and no-one was defending him; and even though Dolabella was fighting together with his prefects in the advisory group for a conviction, Verres kept repeating that his existence was at issue, was also giving testimony, was also present in the advisory group, and had also informed the prosecutor – even though all of this happened and even though it was a matter of fact that a man had been killed, nevertheless the force of this injustice and the wickedness in this man here was deemed to be such that the decision on Philodamus was postponed.

[75]   Why should I now report on Cn. Dolabella's imperious demeanour during the second hearing, why on the tears and the constant pacing of this man, why on the mindset of C. Nero, an excellent and most upright man, which was frequently overly apprehensive and subdued? In this matter, he did not have anything in his power that he could have done, if not perhaps what everyone at the time kept wishing for, namely deal with this matter without Verres and without Dolabella. Whatever would have been the outcome in the absence of these two, all would have approved of; but the verdict that was then announced was deemed not to have been a judgement passed by Nero, but one exacted by Dolabella. By very few votes Philodamus and his son are condemned. Dolabella was at hand, he urged, he insisted that they should be executed with the axe as quickly as possible so that as few as possible would be able to hear from them about the wicked crime of this man.

[76]   In the marketplace of Laodicea a spectacle – bitter and wretched and depressing for the entire province of Asia – is put on display; the elderly father is brought forth to his execution, from another part his son, the former since he had defended the chastity of his children, the latter because he had defended the life of his father and the reputation of his sister. Each of the two was lamenting not his own punishment, but the father the death of his son, the son the death of his father. How many tears, do you think, Nero himself shed? What weeping there was through all of Asia? What grief and sorrow among the inhabitants of Lampsacus? Innocent and high-ranking humans, allies and friends of the Roman people were struck by the axe of the executioner because of the unique worthlessness and most wicked lust of this most disgraceful human being!

[77]   After all this, Dolabella, I am unable to pity either you or your children, whom you have left wretchedly in poverty and devoid of any friends. Was Verres so dear to you that you wished to wash away his lust with the blood of innocent humans? Were you therefore leaving behind the army and the enemy so that you could mitigate through your violence and cruelty the dangers faced by this utterly wicked man here? Did you think that just because you had appointed him in the place of your quaestor, he would therefore be your friend forever? Did you not know that the consul Cn. Carbo, whose real quaestor he had been, was not only abandoned by him, but also stripped of supplies and money, and was attacked and betrayed by him in shameful fashion? Hence you experienced his treachery only when he joined the side of your personal enemies, when that man, himself guilty, gave the harshest evidence against you, when he refused to give accounts to the treasury until and unless you had been condemned.

[78]   Will your passions, Verres, be so great that the provinces of the Roman people, that foreign nations cannot fulfill and endure them? What you see, what you hear, what you desire, what you conceive of, unless it will be present at a mere nod of yours, unless it obeys your passion and desire, will humans be sent out, will houses be stormed, will citizenries not only pacified, but of allies and friends, flee to violence and arms so that they are able to fend off from themselves and their children the crime and lust of a legate of the Roman people? I ask you: were you beleaguered at Lampsacus, did the multitude begin to set fire to the house in which you took up lodgings, did the inhabitants of Lampsacus wish to burn alive a legate of the Roman people? You are unable to deny this. I have your own testimony, which you made in front of Nero, I have the letter that you sent to the same person. Read out this very passage from the testimony. THE TESTIMONY OF C. VERRES AGAINST ARTEMIDORUS. NOT MUCH LATER AGAINST THE HOUSE.

[79]   Did the citizenry of Lampsacus try to wage war on the Roman people? Did it want to defect from our command and name? For I see

and understand from what I have read and heard that in whichever civic community a legate of the Roman people suffered any degree of physical harm, let alone was beset, let alone was attacked with fire, sword, by force, and with troops, against that citizenry war tends to be declared and brought unless a sufficient reparation has been made by the entire community.

[80]   What, then, was the reason that the entire citizenry of Lampsacus rushed from the assembly to your house, as you yourself write? For neither in the letter that you send to Nero nor in your testimony do you give any reason for such an uproar. You say that you were beset, you say that fire was brought, that brushwood was heaped up all around, that your lictor was killed, you say that you were denied the right to appear in public: the reason for this enormous threat you keep secret. For if Rubrius had committed some harm in his own name and not at your prompting and because of your desire, they would have come to you to complain about the harm caused by your companion rather than to attack you. Since, therefore, the witnesses that I produced said what the reason of that uproar was and he himself kept it secret, does not the testimony of those and in particular the lasting silence of this man here confirm that reason we put forward?

[81]   Will you spare this human, then, judges, whose transgressions are so great that those whom he has harmed were unable to wait the time appointed by law to get their revenge or to postpone the force of their grief to a point in the future? You were set upon? By whom? By the inhabitants of Lampsacus. By barbarian humans, I suppose, or those who hold the name of the Roman people in contempt. In fact by humans most gentle in nature, habit, and education, and further, in terms of their legal status, allies of the Roman people, in terms of their fortune, slaves, in terms of their free will, suppliants. Hence it is utterly obvious to everyone that, unless the bitterness of the harm suffered and the violence of the crime had not been so great that the Lampsacenes believed they ought to die rather than to endure, they would never have advanced to the point that they were moved more energetically by the hatred of your lust than fear of the legate's office.

[82]   By the immortal gods, do not force allies and foreign nations to use that refuge which they use out of necessity, unless you vindicate them. Nothing would have ever calmed the inhabitants of Lampsacus towards this man here if they had not believed that he would receive punishment

in Rome: even though they had suffered such harm, for which they could not gain proper satisfaction through any law, they still preferred to submit their grievances to our laws and law courts rather than to yield to their grief. Although you have been beset by such a renowned citizenry because of your crime and outrage, although you have forced wretched and miserable human beings, once they had all but despaired of our laws and law courts, to take refuge in violence, physical resistance and arms, although you have shown yourself in the town and citizenries of our friends not as a legate of the Roman people, but as a passionate and savage tyrant, although you have violated with your wicked and outrageous deeds the reputation of our imperial sway and name with foreign nations, although you have snatched yourself from the sword of friends of the Roman people and fled from the fire set by allies, you hope that this here will serve as a refuge for you? You are wrong: they suffered you to depart alive so that you might fall into our hands here, not that you might find peace here.

[83]   And you say that a verdict has been given that you were beset unlawfully in Lampsacus because Philodamus was condemned together with his son. What if I show, if I demonstrate with a worthless human being as witness, but nevertheless suited for this purpose – with you yourself as witness, I say, will I show that you transferred the reason and the responsibility for this mobbing of yours onto others and that against those, whom you had implicated, no punitive action has been taken. Then the judgement of Nero no longer helps you at all. Read out the letter he wrote to Nero. The letter of C. Verres to Nero. Themistagoras and Thessalus. You write that Themistagoras and Thessalus roused the people. Which people? Those who beset you, those who tried to burn you alive. Where do you prosecute these men, where do you accuse them, where do you defend the right and the name of the legate? Will you say that this was done in the proceedings against Philodamus?

[84]   Show me the testimony of Verres himself: let us see what this same man said under oath. Read. Cross-examined by the prosecutor, he replied that he did not press his claim in this trial; he had in mind to do so some other time. How, therefore, does the verdict of Nero help you, how the sentencing of Philodamus? Even though you had been beset as a legate, and even though, as you yourself have written to Nero, a signal harm had been done to the Roman people and the common cause of the legates, you did not press any charges. You say you have in mind to do so some other

time. What was that time? When did you press your charges? Why did you diminish the legal position of the office of legate, why have you abandoned and betrayed the cause of the Roman people, why have you let be harms both personal and public? Was there no need to bring the case before the senate, to complain about such dreadful injuries, to see to it that those humans who had roused the people be summoned by a letter of the consuls?

[85]   Recently, at the application of M. Aurelius Scaurus, because he said that as quaestor he had been prohibited by force in Ephesus from dragging out of Diana's shrine his slave, who had fled into this place of asylum, the Ephesian Pericles, a human of the highest renown, was summoned to Rome because he was charged with having been the instigator of this injustice. You, if you had shown to the senate that you as legate had been treated in Lampsacus so that your followers were wounded, your lictor killed, you yourself were beset and almost burnt alive, but that the leaders, instigators, and main perpetrators of this thing were, as you write, Themistagoras and Thessalus, who would not have been moved, who would not have been concerned for himself because of the injustice which you had suffered, who would not have believed that in this matter your case as well as a common danger was at issue? For the name of the office of the legate ought to be such that it remains inviolate not only under the legal arrangements of our allies but even among the missiles of the enemy.

[86]   This crime of passion and utterly wicked lust at Lampsacus is great; listen now to a crime of greed hardly less serious in its kind...

Appendix: Issues for Further Discussion

The Lampsacus episode is well suited as a point of departure for discussing broader issues in Ciceronian oratory, (ancient) rhetoric and Roman imperialism. Here are some topics that may be worth exploring further either individually or as part of a group exercise:

1. Facts and Fiction in Law-court Rhetoric

If one boils down Cicero's account of what happened at Lampsacus to indisputable facts, one is left with precious little: (i) a visit of Verres at Lampsacus during a diplomatic mission; (ii) the death of one of his lictors during a dinner party at which Verres was not present, housed by the local notable Philodamus; (iii) unrest among the inhabitants of the town, instigated by Themistagoras and Thessalus (named by Verres in a letter to Nero); (iv) the trial and execution of Philodamus and his son for the homicide of the lictor. Cicero embeds these hard facts within a tale of sexual desire and attempted rape, which, he claims, he has heard from two witnesses, Tettius and Varro, who served on the staff of Nero at the time. Imagine you are a member of Verres' defence team: how would you attack Cicero's version of the events in a Roman court of law? Can you break down the coherent plot that Cicero construes into a series of unfortunate coincidences? Is it possible to question the veracity of Cicero's witnesses or his handling of circumstantial evidence? Are there gaps in his account that could be filled with an alternative story? (For instance, is the son, who was executed for homicide, really as innocent as Cicero makes him out to be?)

2. Ancient and Modern

Compare and contrast Cicero's use of evidence and argumentation with contemporary legal practice: which pieces of evidence, and which lines of argument would be permitted in a court today and what would be ruled out as inadmissible?[101]

3. Humour – Sophistication – Self-promotion

Cicero's oratory is designed to induce the audience to adopt his point of view and his version of the truth. But there is a difference between listening to an oral performance and the perusal of a written version. However attentive and suspicious a listener one may be, one is bound to be drawn into, or even to become mesmerized, by a good oral delivery, especially if the speaker is also a top performer, who combines verbal wizardry with the theatrical use of voice and gesture. In *reading* a speech, it is much easier to avoid being swept away in the drama of delivery and to resist emotional appeals. One can re-read and reflect upon the argument: how is it constructed? Where does it break down? What problems are being dodged and how? After his successful speech for Cluentius, Cicero bragged that he pulled one over on the judges, but nevertheless published a written version of his defence (the *pro Cluentio*), seemingly wishing to invite everyone to appreciate and admire how he had done it. Is something similar going on in his account of what happened at Lampsacus? Are there deliberate touches of humour and hyperbole that give the game away? Does Cicero invite us to read against the grain? Where and to what extent does he parade his ability to spin a few facts into a compelling story centred around the spectacularly vile figure of Verres, who is, however, in large part Cicero's own creation? What does this tell us about the power of words and the imagination?

4. Ethics and Empire

Catherine Steel, who systematically (and, I believe, by and large successfully) exculpates Verres from any wrongdoing at Lampsacus, implicitly incriminates Cicero for implying that the only problem with Rome's

---

101. A good starting point to explore this issue is Laws, J. (2004), 'Epilogue: Cicero and the Modern Advocate', in J. Powell and J. Paterson (eds.), *Cicero the Advocate*, Oxford, 401–16. (Lord Justice Laws is a Judge of the Court of Appeal.)

imperial administration and exploitation was with individuals, rather than the system as such: 'One of the consequences of Cicero's ascribing what happened to Verres' viciousness is that the potentially much wider problems inherent within the system of administration are obscured.' Later, however, she also recognizes that 'Cicero pulls off the astonishing feat of presenting Roman provincial government as completely, and convincingly, corrupt and oppressive.'[102] These observations raise the question: to what extent is Cicero critical of, to what extent collusive in, the system of Roman imperial administration – above and beyond his attack on a particularly vile representative of Rome's ruling elite?

5. Cultural Property and the History of Plunder

The case of Verres can serve as a good point of departure for exploring the fate of art in the context of war, conquest, and imperial plunder across history. The topic has lost none of its relevance. A good place to start from to explore both its historical dimension and its contemporary remit is Miles, M. M. (2008), *Art as Plunder: The Ancient Origins of Debate about Cultural Property*, New York. Her second chapter is on Cicero's *Verrines*.

---

102. Steel (2004) 242 and 251.

Map of Italy and the Greek East

The map features regions or locations mentioned in the commentary.

This book does not end here...

At Open Book Publishers, we are changing the nature of the traditional academic book. The title you have just read will not be left on a library shelf, but will be accessed online by hundreds of readers each month across the globe. We make all our books free to read online so that students, researchers and members of the public who can't afford a printed edition can still have access to the same ideas as you.

Our digital publishing model also allows us to produce online supplementary material, including extra chapters, reviews, links and other digital resources. Find *Cicero, Against Verres, 2.1.53–86* on our website to access its online extras. Please check this page regularly for ongoing updates, and join the conversation by leaving your own comments:

http://www.openbookpublishers.com/product.php/96

If you enjoyed the book you have just read, and feel that research like this should be available to all readers, regardless of their income, please think about donating to us. Our company is run entirely by academics, and our publishing decisions are based on intellectual merit and public value rather than on commercial viability. We do not operate for profit and all donations, as with all other revenue we generate, will be used to finance new Open Access publications.

For further information about what we do, how to donate to OBP, additional digital material related to our titles or to order our books, please visit our website.

OpenBook Publishers

Knowledge is for sharing

Lightning Source UK Ltd.
Milton Keynes UK
UKOW051420191112

202418UK00001B/8/P